MW01620409

Art Education for a Sustainable Planet

Embracing Ecopedagogy in K–12 Classrooms

Joy G. Bertling

Foreword by Olivia Gude

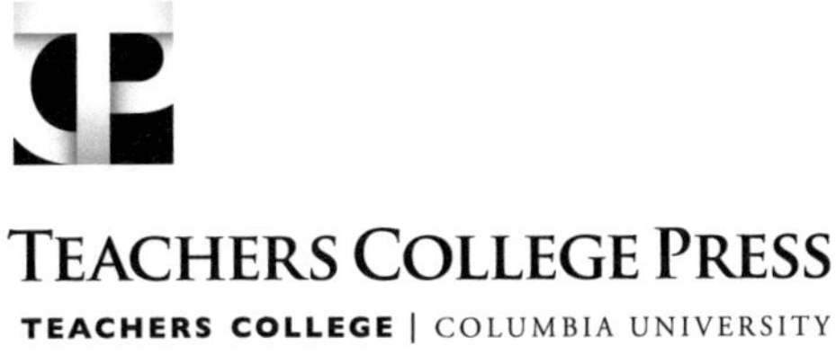

TEACHERS COLLEGE PRESS
TEACHERS COLLEGE | COLUMBIA UNIVERSITY
NEW YORK AND LONDON

Chapter 5 is an adaptation and extension of the author's article, "(Com)postmodernity: Artists Cultivating a Lust of Mortality," by J. G. Bertling, 2021, *Art Education*, 74(4), 51–57. https://doi.org/10.1080/00043125.2021.1905435. Reprinted by permission of Taylor & Francis Ltd. (http://www.tandfonline.com).

Published by Teachers College Press,® 1234 Amsterdam Avenue, New York, NY 10027

Cover art: Rogan Brown, *Ghost Coral Colour Variation*, 2020, laser-cut paper.

Library of Congress Cataloging-in-Publication Data is available at loc.gov

ISBN 978-0-8077-6770-2 (paper)
ISBN 978-0-8077-6771-9 (hardcover)
ISBN 978-0-8077-8140-1 (ebook)

Printed on acid-free paper
Manufactured in the United States of America

To my mother, Susan M. Gagliardi, and my father, Charles Gaulden, both ecopedagogues in their own ways

Contents

Foreword

In *Art Education for a Sustainable Planet: Embracing Ecopedagogy in K–12 Classrooms,* Dr. Joy Bertling calls for a curriculum that stimulates a sense of "agency and urgency." However, rather than pursuing this goal by inundating the reader (or students experiencing curriculum based on this book) with a plethora of disturbing facts, statistics, and images, Joy lures us into contemplative spaces in which we experience and cultivate empathic relationships, closely observe and accept recurring natural processes, and conceive of the possibility of being co-creators with other organisms. Though this book grows out of and shares critical awareness of a world of many rapidly deteriorating ecological systems, it is rooted in the pleasure of being embedded in natural environments and natural cycles of change, living as fellow creatures in complex systems. It advocates for a form of slow pedagogy, recognizing that without changing sensibilities, without opportunities to know, to care, and to value the more-than-human world, deep and substantive change in behaviors is unlikely to occur.

The influence of discipline-based art education (DBAE) is waning. While touting the importance of the arts in world culture, DBAE tended to devalue the relevance of art curriculum to 21st-century life in favor of focusing on the teaching and learning of traditional, mostly Western artworks, interpretations, and skills. In recent years art teachers have increasingly conceived of themselves as creative artist educators who, with their students, contribute to the unfolding of contemporary artistic and cultural knowledge. These changes in the conception of art teaching have opened up possibilities for the meaningful exploration of a wide range of content, including postmodern artistic and theoretical methods of constructing and deconstructing meaning, STEAM (science, technology, engineering, art, and math), design thinking, valuing Indigenous epistemologies, antiracist pedagogy, and community-based and collaborative artmaking. All of these approaches and many others can be found in *Art Education for a Sustainable Planet.* This is not because Joy sprinkles examples of various art education approaches and methods into a book about education and ecological concerns, but because her vision of art education ecopedagogy is authentically arts-based, diverse, and interdisciplinary.

All too often a teacher inspired to introduce new themes, content, and methods into their art curriculum will be overtaxed (if not overwhelmed) by the time-consuming process of identifying and researching new artists and art-making practices, articulating significant themes, developing key questions, and imagining relevant individual and collaborative art activities. Without being overly prescriptive, *Art Education for a Sustainable Planet* presents a powerful vision of a coherent-yet-flexible sequential curriculum, relevant to students of various ages.

The book is grounded in the rich complexity and diversity of many examples of contemporary ecological art. Just glancing at the names of some of the included artworks, projects, and groups (e.g., *The Night Is Filled with the Harmonics of Suburban Dreams*, Postcommodity, *Deconstructed Food Miles Smoothies, Earwax Necklace, Coastline Paradox, Brandalism, Death by Plastic,* and the Laboratory of Insurrectional Imagination) is a powerful stimulus to creative thinking and creative artmaking.

Art Education for a Sustainable Planet is overflowing with content and ideas, yet one does not feel uncomfortably inundated. Because of the book's careful organization, one feels buoyant and elated by so many possibilities. Each chapter in the Curriculum and Methods section is introduced by a compelling theme phrased as a necessary activity: cultivating, fostering, embracing, collecting, visualizing, confronting, envisioning, greening, restoring. Together these gerunds function as core principles of eco-art education. The introduction of each theme/activity is followed by a section on contemporary art and curriculum. These sections identify ways of engaging through a mix of traditional and contemporary artmaking strategies, including such things as attentiveness through observational drawing, walking, mapping, meditative practices, and researching to generate fresh perspectives by seeing through the eyes of others. Curricular Applications tables for each chapter align ecopedagogical goals, key concepts, discussion prompts, and possible artistic responses. Experienced as well as novice educators will be able to use these Curricular Applications tables and accompanying Questions for Educator Reflections to structure curriculum appropriate for various settings, sociopolitical contexts, audiences, and age-levels.

Art Education for a Sustainable Planet: Embracing Ecopedagogy in K–12 Classrooms presents a vision of a new sort of art education. It is grounded in the realities of contemporary art and culture, contemporary science, contemporary social life, and traditional knowledges from diverse cultures, as well as in the climate realities facing youth and communities. Some may call this a departure from a more conventional understanding of the role of art education. Yet the role of art education has always been about cultivating sensibilities—about enlarging capacities for sensation, feeling, consciousness, and responsiveness.

Some may think that it is creepy for youth to learn greater appreciation of the natural environment in tandem with learning about the multiple threats to its survival. However, isn't it even creepier to conduct hermetic aesthetic education as the destruction of our world creeps up on us? Together we must imagine a more subtle and engaging art education, incorporating concepts such as complexity, liminality, and uncertainty as well as vocabulary associated with Paulo Freire (and with all great spiritual practices)—a pedagogy of humility, compassion, and hope.

—Olivia Gude
Angela Gregory Paterakis Professor of Art Education
School of the Art Institute of Chicago

Acknowledgments

In keeping with the relational paradigms this book promotes, I would like to emphasize the webs of relation in which this text emerged. Numerous individuals from multiple spheres have come together or intersected to influence this project, and I am deeply grateful.

First, I would like to recognize two exceptional graduate student coauthors: Jonathan Purtill, who coauthored Chapter 8, and Lauren Farkas, who coauthored Chapter 9. It was a genuine pleasure collaborating with each of you over the course of one summer. A number of other graduate students have played important roles in the development of this book, compiling relevant literature and a long list of eco-artworks, upon which I drew for the appendix and, often, Chapters 4 through 9. Thank you, Meghan Bennett, Nicole Gentry, Samantha Hale, Lauren Farkas, Jidal Lockhart, Amanda McDonald, and Hannah Oakes for your exciting finds. I would also like to thank art education graduate student and talented designer Samantha Hale for collaborating with me to craft the Chapter 1 diagrams. Also, thank you to Amanda McDonald for corresponding with artists to secure image permissions over the course of so many months.

Few authors are able to credit their own mothers with contributing to their writing process, but I have had that special privilege throughout my life. I would like to thank my mother, retired English teacher Susan M. Gagliardi, for reviewing the proposal and book draft meticulously, with insightful feedback and encouragement along the way. Thank you for always being willing to review my writing.

My department has also been especially supportive. I would like to thank my mentor, Stewart Waters, for his feedback on the proposal, and my two department heads, Sherry Bell and Lynn Hodge, for actively allowing me the time to write.

As successive Teachers College Press editors, Sarah Biondello and Sarah Jubar have been instrumental to this book's development. Thank you, Sarah Biondello, for immediately championing the book, calling it "unique and necessary," and Sarah Jubar, for carrying it through to fruition. I especially enjoyed your feedback on the title and cover design. My appreciation also extends to the many artists who gave permission for their works to be included here, including Rogan Brown's exquisite work on the cover.

While they were not directly involved in the development of this book, I would like to thank my husband, David, and daughters, Charlotte and Eleanor, for being their joyous, loving selves, which always sustains such work.

Finally, I would like to thank the 742 U.S. K–12 art educators who participated in a research study Tara Moore and I conducted a few years ago (Bertling & Moore, 2021a, 2021b). Many of these educators expressed an interest in engaging in ecological/environmental art pedagogies but requested resources to support them in this process. As one participant stated, "I would like to do more, just don't know exactly how" (Bertling & Moore, 2021a, p. 393). Your striking feedback encouraged me to write this text a year earlier than I had intended. I hope this book will be the resource you said you needed.

Introduction

Utopia. Maybe not the first word that comes to mind when one is introduced to *ecopedagogy*, or cultivating students' ecological sensibilities toward taking ethical environmental action. When I first heard ecopedagogy described as a utopian project, I was slightly taken aback. *Utopia?* I pondered, thinking back to some of my adolescent literary encounters with utopias. Fantasies of the Western world flashed before me: Shangri La, a long-lost Himalayan valley of near immortality (Hilton, 1933/1960); Herland, a fully female, asexually reproducing society (Gilman, 1915/1998); and Rivendell, J. R. R. Tolkien's (1954/1995) Thomas Kincade–like refuge of elves. My connotations for utopia vacillated between the ethereal, the immortal, the pure, the lofty, much as heaven had been described to me as a child—a radiant, floating city of gold, crystal, and gemstones offering individual mansions and freedom from sickness and disease—and, alternately, the cold innovation one comes to expect from science fiction and Elon Musk's latest report on his Mars colonization efforts. Across these conceptualizations, utopias seem to offer figurative, and sometimes literal, escape from earthly life and all of its "inconveniences"—death, decay, defecation, and, perhaps in Elon Musk's case, the troublesomeness of life confined to one planet.

As utopias often signify our cultural yearnings, I am not surprised that many of my initial associations could be characterized by bodily transcendence and denial of ecological embeddedness. These ideals are deeply entrenched in Western thinking and language (Bowers, 2002; Stibbe, 2010), and the effects of these cultural strivings have only amplified under capitalism. Dominant anthropocentric discourses stressing individuality, human superiority, human exceptionalism (McDonald & Patterson, 2007), and unrelenting material progress clearly run counter to the goals of ecopedagogy. Ecopedagogy embraces deep ecology—a movement that decenters humans; positions them as deeply entwined in ecosystems; affirms the intrinsic value of all life; and, ultimately, advocates for an end to the anthropocentric domination of nature (Kober, 2013). Instead of otherworldliness, deep ecology, and, thus, ecopedagogy, advocates for recognition of our earthly tethering. And yet, ecopedagogy *could* be described as a utopian project (Antunes & Gadotti, 2006).

While many utopian visions cater to and amplify prevailing cultural desires, others have the potential to transform cultural aspirations altogether.

These revolutionary utopian projects cast visions of what is possible and disrupt the status quo to allow new ways of being to emerge. Ecopedagogy, a fusion of environmental education and critical pedagogy with arts education, falls within this socially radical category of utopian projects. Through education, it aims to establish more sustainable human civilization for improved ecological health and integrity (Norat et al., 2016), a project that, due to the complex, dynamic nature and interplay of education, society, and ecology, will always be ongoing.

The arts are central to these endeavors. Maxine Greene (1995/2000) explained the power of the arts for social transformation: "For me as for many others, the arts provide new perspectives on the lived world. As I view and feel them, informed encounters with works of art often lead to a startling defamiliarization of the ordinary" (p. 4). Sadly, this capacity of the arts—to enable fresh sight, to "defamiliariz[e] . . . the ordinary" (p. 4)—may never have been more needed on the Earth, as the "ordinary," for much of the planet, increasingly reflects environmental degradation. This state needs to be acknowledged and felt. Unchecked consumerism and economic growth have ushered in an incredible period of loss, characterized by air, water, and soil pollution; natural resource depletion; habitat destruction; ocean acidification; and biodiversity loss and wildlife extinction. Now, over 200 years since the Industrial Revolution began, it is easy to regard our planetary predicament as the familiar, "the ordinary." Unfortunately, our current environmental crises are anything but routine.

Accounting the full extent of the environmental degradation for which humanity is responsible is beyond the scope of this text. But we have all seen the headlines and heard the news: The Great Barrier Reef's coral populations have declined by half over the past 25 years due to record-breaking water temperatures (Cramer, 2021). Due to California wildfires over the past 5 years, approximately two-thirds of the giant sequoia groves have burned, double the amount that had burned in the previous century (Branch, 2020). Fires ravage the Amazon rain forests (Henao & Torchia, 2019); bee populations wane worldwide (McFall-Johnsen & Woodward, 2019); and the Arctic Ocean continues to see unprecedented declines in floating sea ice (Plumer, 2019).

These atrocities are not just faraway and global. We can all describe losses that are deeply and meaningfully felt as national and global trends play out on local stages with direct and personal impacts. For instance, in my hometown of Moore, South Carolina, I regretfully witnessed, throughout my 20s, sprawling housing and commercial development slowly eradicate the fields and forests near my home. During that time, land in the Upstate of South Carolina was developed at a rate five times the population growth, with approximately 700,000 acres of forest lost over a 2-decade period (Doughman, 2012). The land that I had cherished for over a decade, that once contained so many organisms and memories, is now an industrial park.

Likewise, in East Tennessee, where I now live, the effects of climate change can already be felt. In 2019, Knoxville experienced record-setting rainfall and widespread, historic flooding, closing businesses and schools (Riley, 2020). Over the past few decades, this region has seen heavier rains and longer drought periods (Capps, 2019; Lakin, 2019), a trend that likely played a role in the wildfires that raged across the Great Smoky Mountains National Park a few years earlier (McDermott, 2016).

Despite the dangers of climate change and the severity of the escalating ecological damage, both locally and globally, policymakers, industry leaders, and citizens, particularly in the United States, have shown inadequate inclination as a whole to take the steps necessary to avert further catastrophes, even when these disasters affect their own lives and the lives of their family members, neighbors, and constituents. Dominant cultural paradigms justify environmentally exploitive behaviors and the policies that enable them. Bowers (2002) described how cultural metaphors situate humans as separate from and above the biophysical world. Likewise, ecofeminists have explored how cultural dualisms, such as mind/body, masculine/feminine, and human/nature, intersect and create false hierarchies that perpetuate oppression (Li, 2007), including racism, colonialism, sexism, heterosexism, classism, ableism, speciesism, and "the subordination of nature" (Phillips, 2016, p. 59). When one sees oneself as distinct from another group, whether human or nonhuman, and superior to it, it is easy to rationalize mistreatment and exploitation. Thus, when humans position themselves as the rightful owners or conquerors of the Earth—the apex of Creation—they tend to give themselves license to subjugate and despoil it.

Despite these troubling social, cultural, political, and environmental realities, we have the ability to envision other futures . . . *better* futures. Greene (1995/2000) claimed, "We also have our social imagination: the capacity to invent visions of what should be and what might be in our deficient society, on the streets where we live, in our schools" (p. 5). I add that, equally, we have our ecological imagination: the facility to envision new ecological realities—more ethical ways of being in relation to the more-than-human world (Abram, 1996). The arts can allow us to conceive and convey "what might be" (Greene, 1995/2000, p. 5).

Eco-artists have been initiating dialogues about our role in the world and advancing pro-ecological perspectives and actions through their work since the late 1960s. For instance, in an ongoing experimental project, Kaitlin Bryson (2017) responded to a horrific environmental disaster in Silverton, Colorado: over three million gallons of toxic mine waste were accidentally released into the Animas River and spilled into waterways traversing Native lands (Hood, 2016; Morales, 2015). As time passed and Bryson (n.d.-a) saw that insufficient action had been taken to mitigate the pollutants, including lead, mercury, and arsenic (Hood, 2016), that had settled into the riverbeds, she felt compelled to act. Co-creating with fungal mycelium, Bryson (2017) formed a pair of fungal shoes she could wear to decontaminate the water; the vegetative part of the fungus forming the shoes would extract the heavy metals through a process called biosorption (Bryson, n.d.-a). In this mycoremediative work yet to be performed, the mycelium is set to become an extension of the artist's body, soaking in the harmful substances and cleansing the river. While *Mycelium Shoes for Remediation* likely is not intended to serve as a practical solution for restoring the entirety of the affected watersheds, like any good work of art, it shows us something worth seeing. Yes, it alerts us to the environmental disaster, but it also draws attention to sustainable, restorative solutions; models responsible multispecies interactions; explores themes of co-creation, interdependence, and reconciliation; and beckons us to rethink our own identities and accountabilities in relation to other organisms and the land. It offers alternative perspectives and visions for the future. Through her work, we see glimpses of a utopia—maybe not a simple, perfectly polished utopia. There are no pearly gates here. It's grittier. Messier. Complicated. Earthly. Works such as these, eco-artworks, can serve as an important foundation and inspiration for ecopedagogical curriculum, particularly in art classrooms, where art education could be reconceptualized as ecopedagogy.

Over the past half-century, art educators have been considering the role that environments and environmental education might play in art education (Anderson & Suominen Guyas, 2012; Barbosa, 1991; Bequette, 2007; Bertling, 2013, 2015; Blandy & Hoffman, 1993; Graff, 1990; Graham, 2007; Hofsess, 2020; Hunter-Doniger, 2021; Inwood, 2008; jagodzinski, 1987; Jokela, 2008; Lankford, 1997; Neperud, 1978, 1995; Thomson, 1978). One question that inevitably arises in environmental integration efforts is whether art content will be sidelined (Bertling & Moore, 2021a). Such questions are understandable, given the many challenges art teachers face. For instance, minimal annual class time might already be perceived as restricting students' opportunities to acquire disciplinary skills, knowledge, and understandings. However, we need not position art and environmental education as conflicting priorities. Thus, while ecopedagogy has the ability to transform art education, it also has the ability to enhance and enrich it—honoring and privileging the learning and understandings foundational to the discipline. Rather than competing with other curricular components as an add-on curricular component in already-crowded curricula, the environment can function as an integrating context for curriculum—a location to explore corporeally, materially, attentively, and, perhaps, affectionately; an arena to investigate critically and intersectionally; a site to free our social and ecological imaginations. This book is designed for art educators teaching in kindergarten through 12th grade (K–12) and can be adapted for a range of educators who are open to exploring ecopedagogical alternatives: new ways of teaching art that work toward sustainable, socially and ecologically just earthly futures.

This text, in Part I, begins by describing the foundations for art education conceptualized as ecopedagogy: Chapters 1–3 introduce the fields of ecopedagogy and eco-art and then establish how this text's curricular vision aligns with contemporary conceptions of art education. Subsequently, in Part II, Chapters 4–10 illustrate seven broad categories of interrelated goals, content, and strategies to teaching art education as ecopedagogy that K–12 art teachers might use or adapt as inspiration for their own curricular undertakings. Foundational methods for art education as ecopedagogy include emphasizing sustainability in art practice, studying eco-art, integrating ecological and environmental content, experiencing the outdoors, and making art that engages with ecological and environmental issues. These methods will be introduced and interwoven into the discussion of each curricular strand. Specific artists and curricular ideas are included within each of these seven chapters.

A developing body of research (Girak et al., 2019; Gray & Birrell, 2015; Staples et al., 2019), including research I once conducted as a middle school art teacher (Bertling, 2015), suggests that arts-based approaches to environmental education and related pedagogies can increase students' environmental knowledge, awareness, attitudes, attachment, and pro-environmental orientations. This research might give us hope that the forces we face are not immovable. Earthly utopian visions of social and environmental change can take root through art pedagogy and grow.

If there is anything I would impress upon you as you take up this text, it is a sense of agency and urgency. The visions we and our students have for the world matter. Philosophies matter. Actions matter. Education matters. Join me on this journey of reconceptualizing how art teaching might respond to the greatest challenges and opportunities of our time.

Part I

FOUNDATIONS FOR ART EDUCATION AS ECOPEDAGOGY

Part I is intended to provide the conceptual foundations for art education oriented as ecopedagogy. Each chapter will situate art education as ecopedagogy in relation to a central informing field: ecopedagogy as an education movement (Chapter 1), eco-art (Chapter 2), and art education (Chapter 3). In providing this foundation, the chapters will offer some historical background, outline philosophical foundations, and generally establish the context for the ecopedagogy proposed. As you read this text, I encourage you to refer to the glossary in the back of the book, which provides definitions of key words. Additionally, as each chapter will conclude with reflective questions, I hope that you will set aside time to evaluate your own experiences and teaching background in light of the chapter content related to this potentially new pedagogy.

CHAPTER 1

Ecopedagogy

Ecopedagogy is a critical environmental pedagogy. It is utopian in the sense that it seeks to transform social, cultural, economic, and political structures to construct a more just and sustainable society, while acknowledging that this process will always be incomplete (Antunes & Gadotti, 2006; Norat et al., 2016). Ecopedagogy is pluralistic in that it has been defined and promoted by various scholars and groups of practitioners over time with somewhat varying emphases. As Richard Kahn (2010) explained, "The movement for ecopedagogy is complex, heterogeneous, situational, both formal and informal, and a historical organizational force that is both prone to change and redefinition" (p. 26). Yet all forms of this burgeoning educational movement tend to share some key characteristics: they rely on critical frameworks; promote social, ecological, and climate justice; and avow the inseparability of social and ecological problems (Misiaszek, 2016).

Aligning with these common definitions, the ecopedagogy described in this text represents the confluence of multiple educational traditions, falling generally within three categories: critical pedagogy, environmental education (EE), and arts education (see Figure 1.1). In this chapter, I will attend to the first two traditions' influence on ecopedagogy, with arts education's role reserved for Chapter 3. Thus, first in this chapter, I will examine how critical pedagogy and EE have informed ecopedagogy's development and influenced its methods. Then I will delve into the diverse environmental philosophies, cultural onto-epistemologies, and ecological knowledges that can inform and infuse ecopedagogy. While emerging from distinct cultural and theoretical traditions that sometimes appear contradictory and incompatible, they share at least one vital characteristic—the ability to displace the damaging, dominant cultural philosophies and practices that have led to our global ecological predicament. Hence, this text embraces a pastiche of philosophies, knowledges, and practices, both Western and non-Western, Indigenous and non-Indigenous, that hold promise for challenging the status quo, troubling "what is taken to be the 'normal' world" (Greene, 1995/2000, p. 111), and bringing more relational, sustainable, and equitable modes of being into existence.

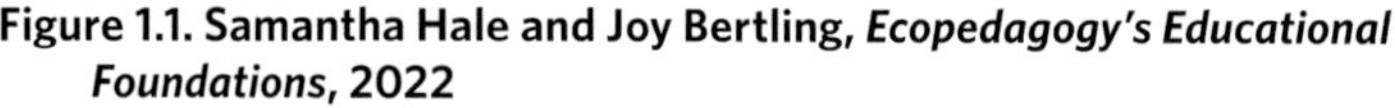
Figure 1.1. Samantha Hale and Joy Bertling, *Ecopedagogy's Educational Foundations*, 2022

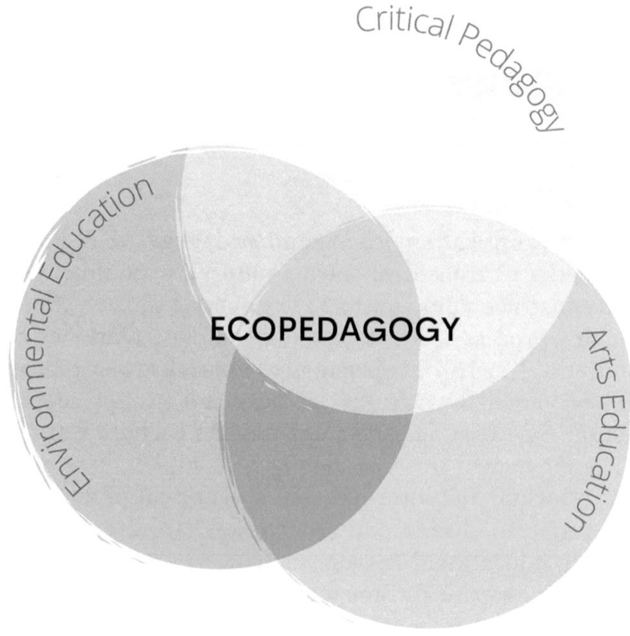

EDUCATIONAL TRADITIONS

While contemporary scholars (Kahn, 2010; Misiaszek, 2020) acknowledge that ecopedagogy has been influenced by a range of theories, the origins of the movement are widely ascribed to Latin American scholars and critical pedagogues in the early 1990s. In such cases, ecopedagogy is often positioned as an extension of Paulo Freire's (1968/2014) critical pedagogy: ecopedagogy expands the scope of critical pedagogy to consider the welfare of more-than-human life and the impact of environmental factors on human inequality. In Western countries where EE is already established, ecopedagogy might equally be understood as a critically oriented EE strand. A closer examination of both these legacies—critical pedagogy and EE—is important to understanding how ecopedagogy might function in K–12 classrooms today.

Critical Pedagogy

Critical pedagogy has a long and diverse tradition as an educational philosophy and movement, with Brazilian educator Paulo Freire generally credited as the founder. Drawing from critical theory, his groundbreaking book, *Pedagogy of the Oppressed* (1968/2014), exposed the exploitation that can occur through dominant social, political, and educational systems. Condemning such oppression, he advocated for new modes of education that might foster critical consciousness, an awareness of oppression and the structures that perpetuate it. A central goal of such pedagogy is praxis, the joining of critical reflection and action to transform societal structures.

Since Freire's (1968/2014) seminal work was published, educational theorists have expanded beyond his original focus on social class to include analyses of oppression in relation to other social constructs, such as race, ethnicity, gender, and sexuality (Kincheloe, 2012). Consequently, theoretical foundations for critical pedagogy can be diverse, to include postcolonial, queer, antiracist, and feminist theory. As critical pedagogy evolved in the late 1980s and early 1990s to consider multiple forms of injustice and as ecofeminists and environmental justice advocates illuminated how forms of domination are interconnected, critical pedagogy's evolution to confront environmental exploitation was a logical next step.

The 1990s represented a critical decade in ecopedagogy's development. In 1992, the Second Earth Summit, a series of United Nations–supported meetings attended by world leaders, was held in Rio de Janeiro, Brazil. While Brazilian intellectual circles were already directing attention toward environmental themes in the years preceding the summit, the heightened discussions in the months surrounding the summit were instrumental to ecopedagogy's emergence (Kahn, 2010; Norat et al., 2016). Later events in Latin America that decade, such as the First International Symposium on the Earth Charter in the Perspective of Education, held in Sao Paulo, Brazil in 1999, and other world events, including the drafting of the Earth Charter (Earth Charter Commission, 1994–2000), played critical roles in the movement's coalescence (Kahn, 2010). Over this time, Freire's work took an ecopolitical turn. Though his book addressing ecopedagogy was unfinished due to his death in 1997, the Paulo Freire Institute and other Latin American scholars carried on his ecopolitical legacy (Gadotti & Torres, 2009). Two years later, important founding theorists Francisco Gutierrez and Cruz Prado (1999/2013) published the book *Ecopedagogia e Cidadania Planetária* [Ecopedagogy and Planetary Citizenship], outlining a theoretical framework for the movement. With the First International Forum on Ecopedagogy in Porto, Portugal, the next year and development of the Ecopedagogy Charter (2000, as cited by Gadotti, 2000), ecopedagogy quickly circulated beyond Latin America at the turn of the 21st century.

Environmental Education

While ecopedagogy emerged more within critical pedagogy circles, it has always had close ties with EE. Having attended many of the early workshops in which ecopedagogy arose, Angela Antunes and Moacir Gadotti (2006) could attest that EE played an important role in these initial conversations. They explained that EE is foundational to ecopedagogy: "for ecopedagogy, environmental education is a premise" (p. 136). As ecopedagogy spread outside of Latin America, EE communities began to embrace it as a critical form of EE that might resolve persistent critiques of mainstream EE as it is enacted in K–12 school contexts (Kahn, 2010). For example, EE in practice has been critiqued as

- limited to science education (Bowers, 2006);
- technocratic—positioning science, including scientific assumptions, values, and methods, and technological advancements, as central solutions to environmental problems (Robottom, 1991);
- knowledge-based—assuming environmental knowledge is enough to produce improved environmental behaviors (Tsevreni, 2011);
- distant and abstract—focused on global problems—and, thus, not developmentally appropriate (Hicks, 1991; Sobel, 2008);
- oriented toward individual behavior change—advocating personal lifestyle modifications but disregarding the power of collective action (Kenis & Mathijs, 2012);
- culturally and politically neutral—not critically examining the social, economic, and political structures underlying environmental problems (Cole, 2007; Gruenewald, 2004); and
- Euro-Western universalist and settler colonialist—conceptualizing the environment as distinct and pristine, a place for White, middle-class leisure (Carter, 2018), and neither addressing colonialist legacies surrounding place (Tuck et al., 2014) nor attending to the origins of environmental hazards disproportionately impacting marginalized groups (Lewis & James, 1995).

Many of these critiques emerged from the way in which environmental education has been subsumed by science education in standards-based, formal educational contexts (Cole, 2007; Gruenewald, 2004).

Robert B. Stevenson (2007) identified this gap between espoused environmental education aims and actual practices as a "rhetoric-reality gap" (p. 139). He attributed this gap to the constraints of schooling, which tend to dilute transformative agendas and reinforce the status quo. Perhaps understanding these tendencies, Antunes and Gadotti (2006) asserted that ecopedagogy might be seen as a means for environmental education to achieve its ambitions. The ecopedagogy advocated in this text resolves the critiques of environmental education by

- embracing a transdisciplinary perspective (i.e., extending beyond the bounds of any one discipline although able to be integrated into disciplinary contexts, including art);

- facilitating direct experiences with place and building upon students' local knowledge and values;
- centering affect, imagination, and embodied experience;
- attending to human desire, including the role it plays in perpetuating the ecocrisis as well as its potential role, when redirected, in mitigating the ecocrisis;
- stressing creative inquiry and divergent modes of expression;
- encouraging collaboration and accentuating the power of collective action;
- acknowledging culturally diverse forms of knowledge, socioenvironmental perspectives, and ways of being;
- focusing on the deep changes that need to occur at social, political, and economic levels and promoting transformative action; and
- inspiring resistance to racism and colonialist legacies.

As such, the following educational approaches, which might also be seen as principally falling under the larger environmental education umbrella—outdoor education, slow pedagogy, critical place-based education, and ecojustice—intersect with and inform the ecopedagogy described in this text.

Outdoor Education and Slow Pedagogy. Outdoor education is a form of experiential education and, typically, environmental education where students engage firsthand, and primarily outdoors, with the biophysical environment. Thus, the outdoor environment, rather than the classroom, serves as the "laboratory for learning" (Hammerman et al., 1964/2001, p. 5), fostering connections between school-based learning and life outside school. Grounded in diverse philosophical and practical tenets, it can span a breadth of activities, to include adventure-based experiences (e.g., kayaking, camping, and expeditions), field investigations, outdoor play, and more traditional lessons held in outdoor classrooms.

As a strand of outdoor education, slow pedagogy distinguishes time as a factor in students' engagements with space and place (Payne & Wattchow, 2008). It serves as a counterpoint to modes of outdoor education that promote fast-paced, tiered demonstrations of skill, often in remote outdoor environments. Thus, rather than positioning the biophysical environment as a site to traverse and surmount expeditiously, it stages opportunities for students to slow down and linger in place and to experience place nonverbally—to imagine and discover (Payne & Wattchow, 2008, 2009). In so doing, slow pedagogy might promote place attachment and more relational understandings and consciousness.

Critical Place-Based Education. Place-based education is an educational approach dedicated to instilling place consciousness and, correspondingly, pro-ecological attitudes and behaviors, by rooting education within the local environment (Gruenewald, 2003; Smith, 2007). In such cases, environment is defined broadly, to include the social, cultural, economic, ecological, political, and historical arenas (Smith, 2002). As such, place-based educational experiences tend to be interdisciplinary, student-centered, and experiential, centering authentic problems and inquiry. This educational movement emerged toward the end of the 20th century in response to concerns surrounding globalization's negative impact on community life, the devastation of the environment, and standardized-curriculum mandates advancing decontextualized instruction (Gruenewald & Smith, 2014). Place-based education sought to infuse local content and experiences back into schooling to support more balance and correspondence between the local and global for renewed civic engagement. When oriented critically, critical place-based education has two defining goals: to "(a) identify, recover, and create material spaces and places that teach us how to live well in total environments (reinhabitation); and (b) identify and change ways of thinking that injure and exploit other people and places (decolonization)" (Gruenewald, 2003, p. 9).

Environmental Justice and Ecojustice Education. Influenced by the Civil Rights Movement in the United States, environmental justice arose in the 1980s as a grassroots social movement opposing the environmental injustices experienced disproportionately by disinvested groups, typically defined by race and class, and advocating for equal access to healthy environments (Environmental Protection Agency, n.d.; Murdock, 2020). Additionally, it highlights the often-unrecognized work of women of color as environmental activist leaders and recognizes the environmental burdens women face globally due to patriarchal social structures (Murdock, 2020). While environmental justice traditionally centers human groups' experiences of environmental exploitation, the ecojustice movement enlarges the scope of moral concern to consider the plight of other species amidst environmental abuses (Martusewicz et al., 2021). Foster et al. (2019) identified three integral components of ecojustice education:

1. Cultural analysis to explore how social and environmental violence is reproduced by cultural ways of thinking and being
2. Cultural revitalization to adopt cultural beliefs and practices that contribute to ecological health and integrity
3. Imaginative engagement to envision ethical living

As such, the ecojustice education branch of environmental education most closely aligns with the ecopedagogy proposed in this text.

CULTURAL AND PHILOSOPHICAL INFLUENCES

Ecopedagogy requires that teachers and students engage in significant rethinking surrounding cultural norms and practices and social structures. For instance, it demands that we question the primacy of Western science, the excessive consumption common to capitalist (and other) economies, and the policies that place low-income housing in closest proximity to pollution sites (Braubach & Fairburn, 2010). In the following section, I will explore environmental philosophies; cultural onto-epistemologies (i.e., cultural ways of perceiving reality and transmitting knowledge); and traditional ecological knowledge (TEK) that might inform ecopedagogy.

Environmental Philosophies

While numerous cultural and environmental philosophies shape ecopedagogy, in this text I will focus on two significant philosophical movements that can infuse how human–nature relations are conceptualized within an ecopedagogy curriculum. Ecofeminism and deep ecology share many similarities in decentering human experience, ascribing substantial value to nonhuman life, and appraising the intersections between culture and ecology.

Ecofeminism. The fundamental focus of ecofeminism is the interconnected system of oppression that harms humans and nonhumans alike. Specifically, ecofeminism, much like queer ecology, draws attention to an array of culturally sustained dualisms—male/female, culture/nature, human/animal, domestic/wild, mind/body, subject/object, matter/reason, good/evil, White/non-White, able/disabled, and I/other—that are deeply embedded in Euro-Western cultural narratives and practices (Kheel, 2008; Molina-Motos, 2019). Sadly, these dualisms construct artificial distinctions within and between groups and inevitably position one side as the ideal (e.g., human, male, and White) and more worthy of exerting agency, occupying space, receiving resources, exercising power, and so forth. As the nonprivileged points of these dualisms (e.g., nonhuman life and women) tend to culturally mingle (e.g., when female traits are ascribed to the Earth or women are compared to nature), exploitation is further reinforced (Molina-Motos, 2019). As such, ecofeminists see parallels between the patriarchy and a host of societal ills, including environmental violence (Kings, 2017; Molina-Motos, 2019). Through ecofeminism's commitment to intersectional analysis (Crenshaw, 1989), ecofeminism might offer ecopedagogy a means to examine critically how various forms of oppression and domination intersect and interact and, ultimately, prepare students to act for holistic change.

Deep Ecology. Deep ecology is an environmental philosophy and social movement affirming the intrinsic value of all life and, like ecofeminism, advocating for an end to human-induced environmental degradation (Kober, 2013). It is ecocentric in that it

- collapses anthropocentric value hierarchies that position humans as exceptional and superior (see Figures 1.2 & 1.3);
- decenters human needs to focus more holistically on ecological health and integrity;

Figure 1.2. Samantha Hale and Joy Bertling, *Anthropocentric Orientation Diagram*, 2021

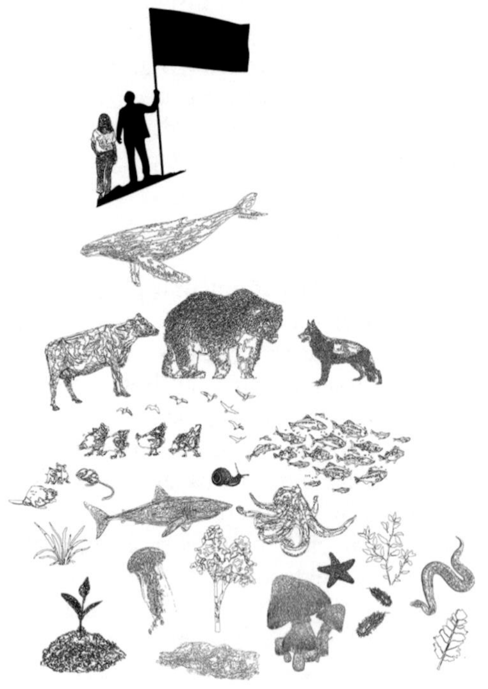

Figure 1.3. Samantha Hale and Joy Bertling, *Ecocentric Orientation Diagram*, 2021

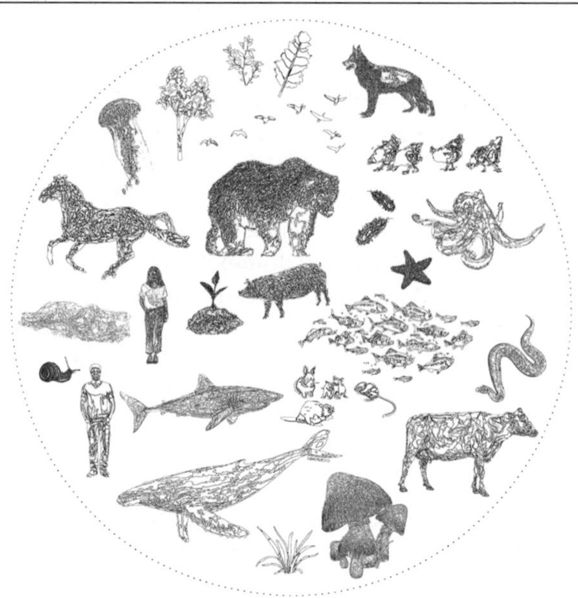

- underscores and celebrates humans' deep embeddedness in ecological systems; and
- equates ethical responsibility to ecological responsibility (Drengson et al., 2011).

As a natural outgrowth of these stances, deep ecology exhibits a sincere commitment to deep societal change, far beyond minor policy reforms and technological and scientific fixes (Drengson et al., 2011).

Cultural Onto-Epistemologies

The environmental philosophies articulated above and other related philosophies (e.g., critical posthumanism, Gaia, biophilia, and stoicism) can play important roles in helping students identify ecologically detrimental paradigms and conceive social-ecological relations anew. In addition, other cultural ways of knowing and being might be brought into conversation with these philosophies—"walking alongside" them (Sundberg, 2014, p. 33). Aligning with Donna Haraway's (1991) notion of "holding incompatible things together" (p. 149), Fikile Nxumalo and Stacia Cedillo (2017) discussed how Indigenous onto-epistemologies and Black feminist geographies, both offering decolonial perspectives, might be centered within and enrich place-based, environmental pedagogies. The approach they advocate that non-Indigenous communities adopt involves deep engagement with these cultural traditions in ways that are "non-appropriative" and "move beyond consumptive relations" (p. 101). As part of this engagement, the tensions, complexity, and fluidity of these cultural perspectives would need to be acknowledged. Thus, while these paradigms and knowledges should not be extracted or exploited, they might be imparted as ways to "restory places" and "disrupt settler imaginaries" (p. 103). Settler imaginaries are ideas, values, and forms of logic that settler societies draw upon to position themselves as uninvolved in the workings of colonialization and legitimize their claims to Indigenous land. Some of these myths and narratives include settler innocence, settler belonging to the land, national unity, and Indigenous authenticity (Bell, 2014). In keeping with this idea of unsettling settler colonial imaginaries and prompting deep engagement with more relational perspectives, Zhane Rhea (2018) asked: "Can students of the imperialized and colonized world of the twenty-first century enter the world of sentient nature and learn to hear old, and develop new, resonant languages and practices that will cocreate ecological harmony?" (p. 113).

Indigenous Onto-Epistemologies. Living sustainably on ancestral lands, sometimes for millennia, distinct groups of Indigenous peoples have developed complex and diverse stories, histories, modes of conceptualizing reality and time, and ceremonial practices that emphasize the relationality between humans, nonhumans, and the land (Brown et al., 2020; Nxumalo &

Cedillo, 2017). For the Abenaki Nation in North America, these notions of relationality infuse sacred ceremony, where members ascend the Green Mountains (many of the mountain names in the Algonquian and Mahican dialects have been lost [Holschuh, 2019]). They approach the peaks not as conquerors, but as relatives (Walker, 2019). Writing about this experience, Melody Walker claimed, "We are all made of the same source of life—power runs through all things and binds us together as a family" (p. 15). Correspondingly, Apache scholar Sharon Gloshay (2020) described how, in the Apache worldview, energy exists in all things and "thereby, rituals and ceremonies can bring inanimate objects to animacy, or transformations can occur, but all things must be done in the right format, right stage of mind, body, and soul, because non-compliance could be disastrous" (p. 20). While Indigenous perspectives are diverse, Andrea Vásquez-Fernández and Cash pii tai poo taa (2020) explain that they tend to share a relational conception of respect, extending to the land and the entirety of its inhabitants, exceeding common Euro-Western notions. As such, they enact "an ethic of biocentric relationality" (Ritchie, 2013, p. 395). Such Indigenous paradigms offer vital ecological perspectives and demonstrate how sustainable relationships might be conceptualized and made possible.

Black Feminist Geographies. As colonialist discourses put limitations on who qualifies as fully human and set up false dichotomies between humans and nonhumans, Black feminist geographies disrupt these formulations, challenge the notion of Black experience as placeless, and explore the complexities of living in racialized sites (Nxumalo & Cedillo, 2017). While works of art may engage with these geographies, literature can be valuable in portraying the complexity of Black–life–land relations, as it often presents other ways of being and invites students into continued empathetic imagination of these alternate realities. Zora Neale Hurston's *Their Eyes Were Watching God* (1937/1998) represents one such geography (Nxumalo & Cedillo, 2017). Throughout the novel, the main character, Janie, exhibits a strong connection to the biophysical world, through her early experiences with a pear tree, which come to define her later decision-making, and through her direct experiences with the land while living in the then-verdant Florida Panhandle (Panzeca, 2014). Andrea Panzeca explained how Janie refuses an anthropocentric paradigm:

> In doing what she must to realize her dream, Janie resists oppressive divisions both within society and between society and nature. Instead, Janie "becomes another wisp;" she hears "the words of the trees and wind" and wishes seeds soft landings (25). (p. 3)

Such ways of being, as articulated through literature or other arts forms, might play a vital role in modeling diverse affirmative place relations, particularly for students belonging to groups often wrongly conceptualized by dominant groups as not belonging to place.

Traditional Ecological Knowledge

Just as Indigenous onto-epistemologies and Black feminist geographies might disrupt the hegemony of anthropocentric worldviews, so TEK has an important role to play. TEK signifies a form of knowledge production (Whyte, 2013) whereby dynamic bodies of knowledge, situated in place, are developed through people's close, relational dealings with the biophysical world and passed down over generations (Drew, 2005). This knowledge often has cultural and spiritual significance for the Indigenous knowledge-holders, which differs appreciably from the ways Euro-Western scientists typically regard data (Chisholm Hatfield et al., 2018). For instance, Aboriginal peoples in the Australian Northern Territory have long understood the ways in which predatory birds can manipulate fire for hunting purposes (Elbein, 2018). This knowledge, while only recently recognized by Western scientists (Bonta et al., 2017), has long been embedded in their complex lore and Dreaming ceremonies involving the firehawk, who first brought embers to people through a flaming stick (Elbein, 2018).

Despite the significant differences in TEK's and Euro-Western science's philosophical traditions and uses, many scholars are beginning to attend to how they might co-exist and complement each other (Datta, 2015), particularly as they relate to common issues such as climate change (Chisholm Hatfield et al., 2018). This co-existence is bound to bring difficult tensions, but TEK's rich, embodied ways of knowing, focus on local knowledge, and commitments to ecological reciprocity and sustainable practices (Maffi & Woodley, 2010) need to be recognized. Moreover, they are critically important for effective ecopedagogy. Mindfulness of common pitfalls, such as essentializing Indigenous knowledges (Tuck et al., 2014) and unconscious "imposition of Western norms" (Datta, 2015, p. 106), will be vital for non-Indigenous instructors and students during these learning processes.

CONCLUSION

Informed by a diverse group of educational, environmental, and cultural philosophies, the ecopedagogy proposed in this book looks for the possibilities that emerge as distinct traditions are brought together for ecopedagogical aims: to promote an "ecological consciousness," "ethic of compassion and care," sense of "planetary citizenship," and "sustainable culture" (Norat et al., 2016, pp. 183–184). While this chapter attended to the general educational and philosophical origins of ecopedagogy, the subsequent two chapters will explore eco-art and art education as important foundations for and influences on this educational tradition.

QUESTIONS FOR EDUCATOR REFLECTION

1. Think back to a situation where you became aware of a specific environmental harm, small or large (e.g., when you realized polystyrene trays were the only tray option in the school lunchroom or learned a local landfill was approaching its capacity).
    a. List the many ways you could have reacted proactively to that scenario.
    b. Identify the responses likely to have been successful and to have the widest impact. Circle the two to three most effective responses.
    c. Consider the characteristics of these strategies. Do they share anything in common?
    d. What are the implications of these effective strategies for how environmental education should be conducted?
2. How do the critiques of environmental education practice as described in this chapter align with your own knowledge of how environmental education is being enacted in schools, such as the schools you have attended or the schools where you have taught?
3. If you have witnessed any of these pitfalls of environmental education in practice, what changes seem necessary to avoid them?
4. What texts have shaped your own ideas about the environment?

CHAPTER 2

Ecological Art

In many respects, the environmental and cultural perspectives advocated in the previous chapter are revolutionary; they demand that dominant society significantly rethink what it means to be human and inhabit the world. This shift has weighty implications for the way human life is performed on the planet. Given the significance of this shift in consciousness, from anthropocentric to ecocentric, all human dealings might be seen as eligible for revision. Known for their creativity, innovation, and attention to affect, artists and designers have a central role to play in spurring and supporting this sustainable societal conversion (Weintraub, 2012). Such cultural workers are often termed "eco-artists."

Ecological art, or eco-art, is art that works toward ecological health and integrity. Such efforts can impact ecology directly, as when artists revitalize ecologically impoverished areas, construct sculptural habitats for small animals, or minimize their environmental footprint by using nonmanufactured materials. However, equally often, eco-art operates at the cultural level to encourage ecological relationships and inspire public awareness surrounding ecological dynamics and human-produced degradations. Thus, eco-art approaches are diverse; eco-artworks address a myriad of environmental topics, encompass numerous art genres and media, and employ a range of strategies. This chapter will provide an overview of this broad and flourishing art movement, with particular attention to the issues surrounding eco-art and the qualities that make it particularly poignant when integrated into an ecopedagogical curriculum.

ECO-ART IN RECENT HISTORY

While multiple art and design movements overlap with and inform eco-art, in this section, I will focus on three: land art, environmental art, and sustainable design. An examination of these three movements will provide some historical context for eco-art and help refine conceptions of eco-art and the issues surrounding it. Here I will provide a synopsis of each of these intersecting, or overlapping, movements and then delve into the issues surrounding eco-art in the subsequent section.

Land Art

Often used interchangeably with "earthworks" and "Earth art," land art is an art movement that arose in the 1960s and 1970s, originally in the United States, where land often served as both site and medium for art-making (Kurtaslan, 2016; Malpas, 2007). Key influences included a desire to circumvent the overly commercialized art world, passion surrounding the burgeoning environmental movement, interest in spirituality, and embrace of minimalist aesthetics (Kurtaslan, 2016; Mikash, 2009). One of the most well-known examples is Robert Smithson's *Spiral Jetty* (1970), a spiraling stretch of earth, salt crystals, and rock stretching out into a salt lake in Utah. Another notable work is Agnes Denes's *Tree Mountain—A Living Time Capsule* (1992), an artificial mountain in Ylöjärvi, Finland, with 11,000 trees, planted by 11,000 people, swirling in a mathematically arranged pattern down from the center of the mountain (Kalela, 1996). While many of these land art projects, or earthworks, required ecologically intrusive practices in rural areas, such as momentous excavation and imposition of formal designs on the landscape, some works have been restorative and employed more ecological aesthetics. For instance, Alan Sonfist's *Time Landscape* (1965) involved the reintroduction of various native plants to New York City, planted as an urban forest and public memorial to the more-than-human world in lower Manhattan (Klosterwill, 2019). Additionally, more temporal installations, such as Shona Wilson's (2015) works using found organic materials, only minimally interfere with the landscape.

Environmental Art

While the term "environmental art" is sometimes used synonymously with "land art," environmental art is a much larger genre. Environmental art, as commonly defined, can include all forms of art that represent environmental subject matter or engage with environmental topics. Thus, environmental art approaches can range from traditional to contemporary, and orientations can span from ecocentric to anthropocentric. Hence, environmental art could include works with nature as the subject, such as Katsushika Hokusai's (1832) ukiyo-e prints of Mount Fuji and Deborah Butterfield's (2017) bronze sculptures of horses. However, it also could include more socially and politically oriented works that might be designated "eco-art," such as Natalie Jeremijenko's (2011) X-Design Environmental Health Clinic, where art "serve[s] as a healthcare provider for an ailing planet" (Weintraub, 2019, p. 288). As less ecologically oriented works related to the environment are grouped alongside eco-art, environmental art is a more inclusive and value-free term than eco-art.

Sustainable Design

In the early 1970s, designer-activists such as Victor Papanek (1984/2009) began to criticize unsustainable product development and call for more responsible design, and in the 1990s, this movement took further hold as designers sought scientific and technical solutions to sustainable design problems (Keitsch, 2012). Sustainable design objectives include "reduc[ing] consumption of non-renewable resources, minimiz[ing] waste, and creat[ing] healthy, productive environments" (United States General Services Administration, n.d., para. 1). Thus, environmentally sustainable design can involve a host of activities, spanning all design areas, to include the redesign of various commercial products, built environments, services, communications, and product-production systems. For instance, designers and business leaders might conduct life-cycle assessments of products to examine the environmental impact of a product over its lifetime, from its fabrication to its use and eventual disposal (Jedlicka et al., 2018). Some considerations include:

- Materials usage—choosing sustainably sourced materials that can be recycled, reused, or refurbished.
- Supply footprints—aiming for minimal material transportation.
- Regional manufacturing regulations—opting to manufacture in regions with strong environmental regulations.
- Waste—aspiring toward zero manufacturing waste.
- Product durability—producing products that will last and not need to be replaced quickly (Steves & Silver, 2018).

In seeking ecological sustainability, designers and engineers often engage in biomimicry, imitating natural cycles and systems to identify sustainable design solutions (DeLuca, 2018). For instance, kingfishers' beaks and diving behaviors have informed wind turbine redesigns to increase renewable energy production (Biomimicry Institute, 2022). Moreover, human-centered sustainable design attends to the ways that products, services, and environments might facilitate and motivate people toward sustainable actions (Hanington, 2018). For instance, newer kitchen trash cans often contain multiple compartments to encourage recycling and composting.

The industrial and business aspects of sustainable design (e.g., mapping supply chain footprints or testing product material durability) may stray from the typical interests and practices of eco-artists and art educators. Yet especially relevant to these fields are the biomimetic and human-behavioral aspects of design, particularly as they inform the development of products and built environments (e.g., studying termite mounds to design more energy-efficient built environments [Biomimicry Institute, 2022]; see Figures 2.1 & 2.2).

Figures 2.1. and 2.2. Mike Pearce, Designs for *Eastgate Harare*, 1996

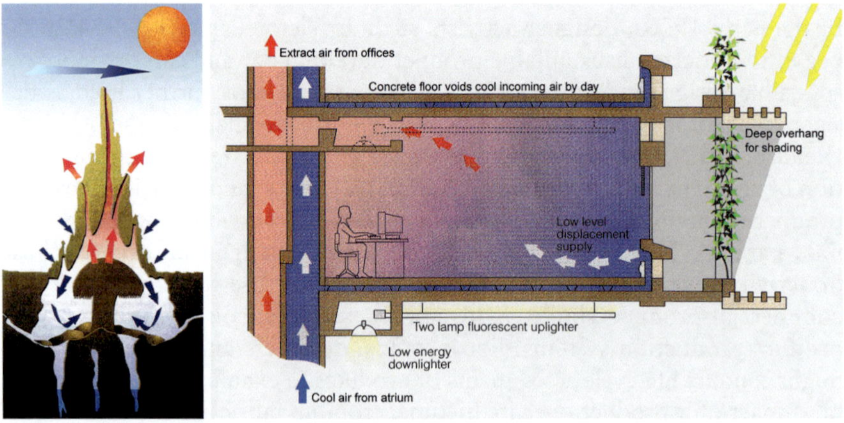

© Arup

ISSUES SURROUNDING ECO-ART

In eco-art's seeking to promote healthier social-ecological relations and states of being, various tensions and issues arise. These matters are pertinent to art education, as they inform the artworks teachers elect to present to students as well as spur student dialogues about art's role in the ecological crisis. This section addresses some of these concerns: the relationship between traditional practices and eco-art; ethnic and racial diversity in eco-art practice; the ecological responsibilities of eco-artists; and the level of urgency and extent of activism surrounding these works.

The Relationship Between Traditional Practices and Eco-Art

As the ecopedagogy proposed in this book looks for the potential in bringing together diverse traditions for ecopedagogical purposes, the relationship between eco-art and traditional artistic practices that model sustainable relations should be considered. The lineage of eco-art differs significantly from the traditional Indigenous practices that had been occurring and evolving prior to this era. The term "eco-art" tends to describe an art genre that emerged in the 1960s, initially influenced by ecofeminism and responding to concerns of human degradation of the environment. Hence, the philosophical foundations of eco-art, as it is commonly defined, and traditional art practices diverge in some key respects, for instance, in their level of emphasis on innovation and social justice. Yet we can consider how practices that operate from relational, ecological paradigms, whether contemporary or traditional, could be brought alongside one another in an ecopedagogical curriculum.

Increasingly, these traditional practices are intersecting with contemporary art practice. Walking methodologies, explored further in Chapter 4, represent one such contemporary eco-art practice, where artists draw upon, and sometimes reinterpret, traditional walking practices of moving mindfully through outdoor environments (McCaw & Smith, 2021). As discussed in Chapter 1, the tensions brought about by such pairings and intersections are important to recognize and navigate with care and respect.

Ethnic and Racial Diversity in Eco-Art Practice

Of the artists featured in 18 major United States museum collections, Topaz et al. (2019) estimated 85% of the artists were White and 87% were men. The same issues of underrepresentation apply to mainstream eco-art: in particular, the perspectives of Black and Indigenous peoples are not receiving adequate recognition in the field. While a myriad of factors play a role in this situation, narrow definitions of eco-art are part of the problem. For instance, the number of Black and Indigenous artists working in this vein expands greatly when conceptions of eco-art are reoriented to include works that acknowledge colonial occupation; integrate social and cultural experiences of place, particularly those of Black communities; allow for fraught land relations; and include a stronger emphasis on environmental justice (Aagerstoun, 2021). Including traditionally underrepresented artists in the curriculum will involve additional homework on the part of teachers, as underrepresented artists and their works are not often included in online eco-art resources. However, these searches will be well worth the effort as richer, more complex ecological narratives emerge that resonate with diverse student bodies and critically educate students from historically privileged groups. This text attempts to support teachers in these efforts by presenting artists from a range of ethnic, racial, and cultural backgrounds as well as women and LGBTQIA+ eco-artists (see also Appendix A).

The Ecological Responsibilities of Eco-Artists

As eco-art operates in a moral domain by advocating more ethical socioenvironmental relations, artists creating eco-art might be held to a higher ethical standard. Questions that arise include: Can an artwork made primarily from nonrecycled, nonbiodegradable materials, set to be deposited in a landfill after its exhibition, be considered eco-art? Can an artwork that removes topsoil and upsets eco-systems be considered eco-art? Eco-artworks, as generally defined, span a range of practices from small works composed of found natural materials (e.g., Amanda Cotton's [2012] necklace made from her own earwax and hair; see Figure 2.3) to large installations requiring manufactured materials (e.g., Florentijn Hofman's [2012] towering sculptural slugs made from thousands of plastic bags attached to a massive metal frame; see Figure 2.4). One important question surrounding those works that leave an environmental footprint, whether through material manufacture, extraction, transportation, or disposal, is whether the ends justify the means. Is the environmental toll of the work justified? Is the work materially modeling the ecological principles it appears to espouse conceptually? Can a work be classified as eco-art if the methods are environmentally injurious?

Figure 2.3. Amanda Cotton, *Earwax Necklace*, 2012

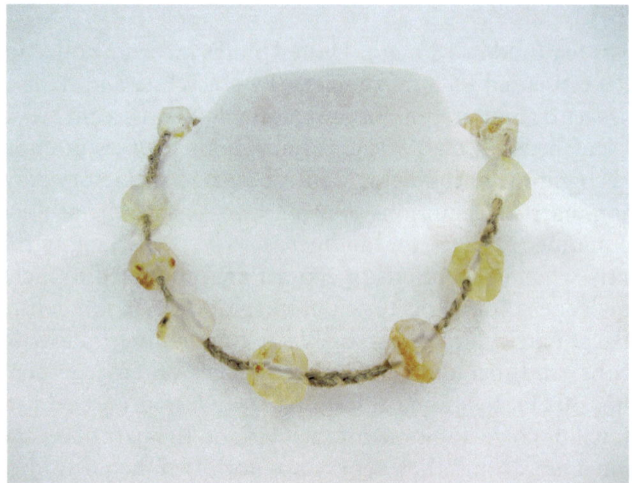

Figure 2.4. Florentijn Hofman, *Slow Slugs*, 2012

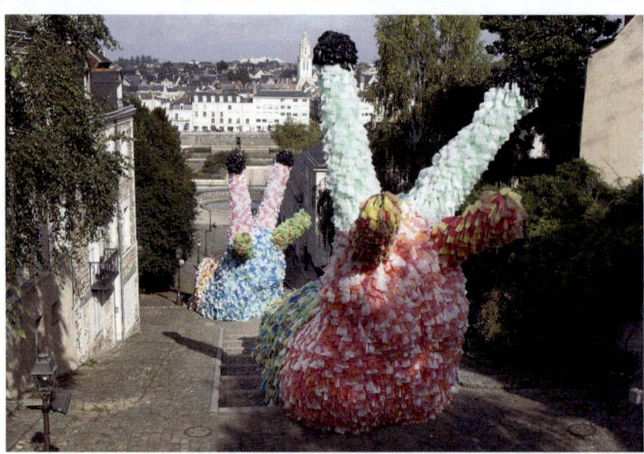

Courtesy Studio Florentijn Hofman. © Ville d'Angers—Thierry Bonnet

These are important questions for teachers to consider as they curate works for presentation in the art classroom. Works where artists attend to materiality, and their artistic material interactions align with their ecological intentions, might be especially poignant when incorporated in art curricula. However, less materially attuned eco-artworks may also serve an educative purpose; they can be presented in such a way as to incite dialogues surrounding the nature of eco-art, ethical responsibilities associated with materials usage, and common contradictions between stated values and behaviors.

Linda Weintraub (2019) offered a good/better/best model for evaluating the materiality of artworks. For instance, an example of a "good" practice would be to "avoid manufactured art supplies that squander natural resources"; "better" might be to "use discarded and reprocessed mediums"; and "best" might be to "utilize an excessive product" like an invasive weed or "detoxify a polluted resource" (p. 21). She also applied this model to consider other aspects of materiality, such as the work's disposal, tool usage, transportation, and site impact. As we all encounter ethically multifaceted, environmental dilemmas daily, from whether to visit zoos, consume meat, camp, drive an electric car, or even buy a printed copy of this book, these types of interrogations and models can be valuable in helping students perceive and navigate socioenvironmental complexities.

Level of Urgency and Extent of Activism

As discussed previously, the term "eco-art" implies a certain adherence to ecological values and a fundamental desire to achieve harmonious relations between social and ecological systems. As such, eco-art can take on political and activist roles, particularly as these works react to the severity of our human-induced environmental calamity. For instance, John Jordan and Isabelle Frémeaux's Laboratory of Insurrectionary Imagination (2008) has coordinated "playful" acts of civil disobedience, such as the outfitting of a band of artist-turned-pirates with a boat to block a coal-fired power station. However, the extent to which works classified as eco-art embrace activism and convey a sense of urgency can vary drastically. For instance, Andy Goldsworthy's (1987) ephemeral installations of leaves placed carefully in outdoor environments appear more formalistic, and their only claim to radicality is tenuous (i.e., through their use of natural materials, an approach that has been used in eco-artworks for over half a century).

Works that appear less politically attuned are sometimes accused of self-indulgence, romanticizing the environment, being out of touch with the environmental conditions associated with late capitalistic, postindustrial society, and deflecting attention away from serious environmental atrocities and their perpetrators (Malpas, 2007). These critiques should be weighed. However, like the issues with material usage discussed in the section above, I would not go so far as to recommend the removal of all "apolitical" works from art curricula. From an educational and psychological standpoint, these works could have an important role to play at the K–12 level, particularly in the early stages of ecopedagogy, as affective relationships between students and their biophysical environments often need to be forged and can be built upon as sustenance for later activist undertakings. As Phillip Payne et al. (2018) argued, humans have a need for "affectivity, nostalgia, and aesthetic sensibility" (p. 96), and these proclivities are deeply intertwined with ecopolitics and environmental ethics. Thus, all three components—the aesthetico-emotional, political, and ethical—could be attended to in ecopedagogical curricula.

CONCLUSION

To meet the needs of students to engage with the ecological concepts at multiple levels (i.e., aesthetico-emotional, political, and ethical), curricula will need to integrate a range of eco-artworks. Diverse forms of eco-art will be examined in more depth in Part II, where each chapter will introduce a strand of eco-art and consider ecopedagogical implications. However, to fully understand the nature of these possibilities, it is important to explore ecopedagogy's relationship to art education first. Chapter 3 will articulate current movements in art education and demonstrate how ecopedagogy might function within these frameworks.

QUESTIONS FOR EDUCATOR REFLECTION

1. Do you think eco-artists have more of a responsibility to use ecologically sustainable methods than artists working in other areas? Can a work of art be considered eco-art if it does not employ sustainable methods?
2. Should all eco-art be explicitly activist? Why or why not?
3. Are there ways your own definitions of eco-art might be expanded or troubled to allow for diverse cultural experiences of the land and place?
4. What other issues and tensions seem inherent to eco-art? How might you respond to these issues through the curricula you design and implement in your classroom?

CHAPTER 3

Contemporary Art Education

Over the past 2 centuries, the field of art education has evolved in response to educational discourses, art movements, and social, cultural, and political conditions. These same influences are present in the field's burgeoning movement toward ecologically responsive forms of education, to include eco-art education (Inwood, 2008), critical place-based art education (Bertling, 2015; Graham, 2007), E*arth* education (Anderson & Suominen Guyas, 2012), arts-based environmental education (van Boeckel, 2015), and, now, ecopedagogy. Since at least the early 1970s, ecologically responsive art education has been shaped by movements within and outside the field, including the rise of environmental education, eco-art, and environmental politics. Consider the year 1970, an important year for environmental progress in the United States (U.S.), the year the first Earth Day was held, with an estimated 20 million participants (Rome, 2003), and the National Environmental Education Act (1970) was passed. That same year, the first major art education publication addressed the topic; the *Journal of Aesthetic Education* published a special issue (Smith, 1970) exploring the relationship between ecological concerns and aesthetic education. For instance, in this issue, Ralph and Christiana Smith (1970) argued that aesthetic education could help students identify with the natural environment. This time frame, the late 1960s to early 1970s, also coincided with the emergence of eco-art as a powerful art movement. Within that same special journal issue and subsequent writings in art education (e.g., Anderson & Suominen Guyas, 2012; Bertling, 2013; Blandy & Hoffman, 1993; Golańska & Kronenberg, 2020; Graham, 2007; Haley, 2021; Inwood, 2008), eco-artworks have been cited as inspiration for ecologically responsive pedagogies.

In addition to influences outside the field, internal debates have played a role in supporting ecologically responsive pedagogies as the discipline shifted from modern to postmodern approaches to art education. Since the 1990s, scholars (e.g., Gablik, 1991; Milbrandt, 1998) have called for art education to move away from insular, modernist aesthetics to engage with the world. Within this context, ecologically minded art education theorists have identified the environment as one ideal site for art engagement (Blandy & Hoffman, 1993; Graham, 2007; Jokela, 2008). Additionally, they have explained how various ecologically oriented pedagogies, including

- Environmental design education (Neperud, 1978, 1995);
- Ecological Vision (Graff, 1990);
- Art education of place (Blandy & Hoffman, 1993);
- Ecological stewardship in art education (Lankford, 1997);
- Ecological design for transformative education (Gradle, 2007);
- Art education informed by a critical place-based pedagogy (Graham, 2007);
- Eco-art education (Inwood, 2008);
- E*art*h Education (Anderson & Suominen Guyas, 2012);
- Critical place-based art education (Bertling, 2013, 2015); and
- Art-based environmental education (Hunter-Doniger, 2021; Schneller et al., 2021)

align with other contemporary approaches to art education.

This chapter will provide an overview of current art curricular trends in the United States with attention to how ecopedagogy might align with and be informed by these contemporary curricular movements. To provide context for these discussions, I will reference my recent survey research (Bertling & Moore, 2021a, 2021b) examining the current emphasis of these approaches in U.S. K–12 art education. Through this discussion, ecopedagogy's current and potential future role in contemporary art education will be explored.

CURRENT ART EDUCATION MOVEMENTS

Over the past half-century, U.S. art education has seen the progression of major curricular movements. While the creative self-expression movement (Korzenik, 1990) was a dominant art educational approach throughout the early- and mid-20th-century U.S. art education, it eventually yielded ground to a more structured approach to art education—discipline-based art education (DBAE). Discipline-based art education defined the structures of art as a discipline: aesthetics, art criticism, art production, and art history. It represented a shift from supporting the self-taught young artist to teaching using a "formal, continuous, sequential written curriculum" (Greer, 1984, p. 212). In the early 1980s, DBAE consolidated as a formal movement with support from the Getty Center for Education in the Arts (Dobbs, 1992). However, with persistent critiques of DBAE over the next 2 decades (e.g., Delacruz & Dunn, 1996), other approaches were proposed, resulting in the plethora of curricular frameworks we have today (Carpenter & Tavin, 2010; Coats, 2020).

Within this context of diverse curricular discourses, a colleague, Tara Moore, and I wanted to understand the extent to which the varied educational approaches discussed in art education literature were informing art education and the manner in which ecological/environmental education, the approach most aligned with ecopedagogy, compared to these other approaches. From late 2019 to early 2020, we conducted a national descriptive survey study (Bertling & Moore, 2021a, 2021b), sending a questionnaire to 3,000 art educators in the United States (1,000 educators from each National Art Education Association [NAEA] division associated with K–12 art education: elementary, middle, and secondary), with 742 art educators responding. In this questionnaire, we asked art educators to rate their emphasis of 10 common educational approaches in art education. These approaches were presented in alphabetical order on the questionnaire, but are listed below by level of art educator emphasis (1 = most emphasized; 10 = least emphasized):

1. Visual/material culture
2. Multicultural education
3. Interdisciplinary education or arts integration
4. Design education
5. STEM/STEAM (science, technology, engineering, arts, and mathematics)
6. DBAE
7. Choice-based art education/teaching for artistic behavior (TAB)
8. Social justice
9. Community-based education
10. Ecological/environmental education

As seen above, visual/material culture, multicultural education, and interdisciplinary education were the most dominant approaches, though multiple other approaches also appeared to be playing an important role in the field. While we (Bertling & Moore, 2021b) were somewhat dismayed to find that ecological/environmental education was emphasized lower than all other educational approaches surveyed, responses to other questionnaire items were more encouraging. For instance, we found that teachers rated the importance of implementing ecological/environmental art pedagogies in their classrooms 3.48 out of 5, a rating between important and highly important. Additionally, their accompanying comments were heartening. For instance, participants stated, “I think we need to push as much awareness as we possibly can about environmental issues, and the art room is a place where it is often safe and expected that we do so!” “Extremely [important]. Children are very interested and want to make a difference,” and “I feel that it’s my duty to introduce environmental awareness to my students since they are the future of our planet’s well-being” (Bertling & Moore, 2021a, p. 392).

In addition to examining the emphasis levels of each approach individually, we also explored correlations between the various educational approaches (Bertling & Moore, 2021b). In relation to ecological/environmental education, we found significant positive correlations (at the $p < .0011$ level; adjusted for Bonferroni correction for multiple tests) with four other educational approaches (social justice, multicultural education, design education, and community-based education), which suggested some pairing or intersection of ecological/environmental education in practice (see Bertling and Moore's [2021b] Table 3 for Spearman's Rank-Order Correlation Coefficients). These correlational findings raise questions about the compatibility of ecological/environmental education (i.e., ecopedagogy) with other common modes of art education. In this section, I will focus on some of the most prominent educational approaches impacting art education in the early 21st century (Bertling & Moore, 2021b).

Social Justice Art Education

Garber (2004) identified social justice art education as representing a melding of various educational approaches, including visual culture, critical pedagogy, community-based education, social reconstructionism, and environmental education. In prioritizing environmental justice and ecojustice, ecopedagogy allies with social justice art education's aims: "to create awareness about sociopolitical issues, challenge common sense attitudes, mobilize civic participation, take action to shift unequal power relations in our society, and work to change policies" (Desai, 2020, p. 13). Because our environmental crisis is equally a social predicament (Anderson & Suominen Guyas, 2012), and since social equity work must address environmental matters when supporting communities disproportionally burdened by environmental devastation, social and ecojustice work are fundamentally intertwined.

Critical Multicultural Art Education

Also aligned with social justice art education, critical multicultural art education represents a form of multicultural education that, like ecopedagogy, engages in social critique. It builds upon multicultural education's aim to acknowledge students' diverse knowledges, cultures, and histories (Kraehe & Acuff, 2013); however, it differs from multicultural art education in that it actively decenters a European, middle-class perspective (Kraehe, 2010). As such, critical multicultural art education, much like ecopedagogy, involves the interrogation of power and privilege. When coupled, critical multicultural art education and ecopedagogy might manifest as critical place-based art pedagogies that honor cultural ways of being and cultural narratives that trouble categories of what is human and disrupt anthropocentric relations with the land (Nxumalo & Cedillo, 2017). Such approaches would be inherently nonanthropocentric, decolonial, and antiracist (Bertling & Moore, 2022).

Visual and Material Culture Studies

With robust movements toward interdisciplinary curricula and visual and material culture since the turn of the century (Bertling & Moore, 2021b), scholars have noted the intrinsic interdisciplinarity of ecological/environmental art education (Inwood, 2008; Parsons, 2004) and explored the role visual culture might play in these pedagogies (Graham, 2007; Illeris, 2012). Visual and material culture have played an important role in broadening art studies to include a wide range of cultural images and objects (Freedman, 2019). As visual and material culture frequently involve critical pedagogy (Bolin & Blandy, 2003; Tavin, 2003), these educational approaches aim to empower students to analyze and question cultural artifacts and, ultimately, critique popular culture (Graham, 2007). As such, they offer ecopedagogy a means of interrogating ecologically injurious cultural narratives.

Community-Based and Critical Place-Based Art Education

Known for its interdisciplinarity, much like the approaches discussed above, community-based art education situates learning in an inherently interdisciplinary arena—the local community. When community is conceptualized broadly to include more-than-human communities (Blandy & Hoffman, 1993; Graham, 2007), community-based art education is often synonymous with place-based art education. As such, both pedagogies aim to promote students' awareness and appreciation for local communities and environments as students study local content and engage with their communities inside and outside the bounds of the classroom. Just as ecopedagogy emphasizes experiential learning and the value of the local environment as a starting point for learning, community- and critical place-based art education can offer vital methods for "inclusive, engaged, socially just pedagogical practices" (Lawton, 2019, p. 209) centered in the particularities and diversities of local communities and environments.

Design Education and STEAM

While just as interdisciplinary but slightly less inclined toward social reconstructionism than the educational approaches mentioned previously, design education and STEAM tend to be more grounded in academic curricular aims (McNeil, 2014). Oriented toward 21st-century innovation, design education, an approach increasingly focusing on functional design (Berk, 2016), and STEAM (Liao, 2016), an arts-infused revisioning of the transdisciplinary STEM educational model, frequently connect through their common emphasis on authentic, transdisciplinary problem-solving. As this creative problem-solving can be directed toward difficult, complex, persistent societal problems—often labeled "wicked problems" and including environmental concerns such as climate change—design education and STEAM can provide ecopedagogy with methods for responding proactively to such dilemmas.

Choice-Based Art Education

As various approaches to art education are enacted, choice-based art education offers a means for art education to respond to student interests and proclivities. Douglas and Jaquith (2018) claim that choice-based art education prioritizes students' authentic artistic decision-making. Namely, choice-based art education offers students a range of artmaking choices, to include media, techniques, processes, formal qualities, subject matter, and themes explored in their art; artmaking pacing; and student collaborations. Art education research suggests student choice can support student motivation and ownership of learning (Dravenstadt, 2018; Hess, 2018), including student choice in ecologically responsive art education programs (Bertling, 2015; Creel, 2005). As student engagement and sense of ownership of learning are essential for effective ecopedagogy, student choice can be an integral element of such curricula.

Gates (2016) explained how the choices in choice-based art education tend to unfold in one of two ways:

- through *big ideas*, where the teacher organizes the curriculum by big ideas and students can select which aspects of these ideas to explore and how they want to respond artistically to these ideas; or
- through a *teaching for artistic behavior model*, where the classroom is oriented more as a studio space (with centers) and students can pursue drastically different artistic agendas with minimal whole-group instruction.

While I recognize the value of student choice in ecopedagogy, in this book I recommend placing more of an emphasis on the first approach: student choice centered on big ideas. Big ideas are relevant transdisciplinary themes often selected by teachers based upon their knowledge of students, including their developmental levels, interests, and pro-environmental orientations (Sparks et al., 2022). In an ecopedagogical curriculum, these big ideas can serve as important foci for students' ecopedagogical dialogues and artistic engagement. As students explore these themes together, this theme-based approach contains an important communal element that might support group transformation and united action. Conversely, other choice-based art-educational approaches like TAB, which prioritize individuality, immediate student interests, and existing student proclivities while deemphasizing whole-group instruction and engagement (Douglas & Jaquith, 2018), could miss opportunities to engage in the most powerful and transformational aspects of ecopedagogy. I encourage art educators to reflect upon the ways in which they might facilitate extended student dialogues, collaborative art-making, and reflections surrounding critical topics while also honoring their students' unique ideas, viewpoints, and backgrounds.

ECOPEDAGOGY AS ART EDUCATION

Art education when conceptualized as ecopedagogy is ecologically focused and critically oriented at its core, yet fluid and capable of heterogeneity: it can be influenced and enriched by many compatible art-educational approaches. For instance, the ecopedagogical curricular ideas described in Part II embrace multiple authentic modes of orienting student art production associated with various traditions: theme-based approaches common to choice-based art education, inquiry-based approaches often seen in arts-based research, and problem- and project-based approaches found in design and STEAM education. Additionally, this ecopedagogical orientation to art education places a strong emphasis on student collaboration and choice to support motivation and collective action, much like the strategies one might see in social justice and community-based art education. Due to this potential of ecopedagogy to borrow, adapt, and integrate, it does not necessarily compete with the educational approaches described above, crowd curriculum with new add-on content, or hinder art educators' ability to "cover" academic standards. Ultimately, it honors disciplinary imperatives and existing curricular frameworks while also recognizing the need for reorienting processes in view of our global crises. The following chapters delve deeper into how art education might operate to foster more sustainable socioenvironmental relations.

QUESTIONS FOR EDUCATOR REFLECTION

1. Which art education movements tend to inform your teaching? Which factors have influenced this emphasis in your teaching?
2. Which movements have had little impact on your teaching? Why?
3. Which movements appear to complement ecopedagogy?
4. How do you see different educational approaches influencing your art education as ecopedagogy practice?

Part II

CONTEMPORARY ART AND ECOPEDAGOGICAL CURRICULUM AND METHODS

As ecopedagogy represents a confluence of goals, ecopedagogical curricula can operate in a myriad of ways. In Part II, I have distinguished some of the ways in which ecopedagogy might manifest with the idea that these various approaches could come together to form a well-rounded ecopedagogical curriculum. Each of the following chapters introduces a different curricular strand that can be distinguished by its pedagogical aims; content, to include eco-art content; and, in some cases, methods. These curricular strands or clusters are not meant to be comprehensive, nor are they intended to represent fully formed curricular plans. Rather, the ideas might serve as inspiration for art educators' curriculum design efforts and instruction, informed by knowledge of students, including student needs and development stages, and teaching contexts, including place and local ecology.

Part II chapters are arranged in a fairly sequential fashion, presented in the order in which they might be most likely to unfold in an ecopedagogical art curriculum. The earliest chapters focus on helping students acquire important ecological sensibilities, such as a sense of nature connectedness, deep awareness of ecological relationships, and ecological paradigms. These sensibilities can serve as important affective and psychological foundations that might spur and support outward-oriented pedagogical endeavors in the future. Accordingly, the later chapters, focus more on empowering students to make changes in their schools and communities. Although helping students form a relationship with the biophysical world before asking them to protect it is a common environmental-education principle (e.g., Smith & Sobel, 2014), the urgency of our current environmental condition should also be considered: immediate and direct actions are needed around the globe. Given this urgency, ecopedagogical curriculum should be paced to allow time for students to reach and inhabit these valuable later stages. In so doing, teachers may be surprised to discover how students' socio-politico-ecological acts might further foster and reinforce the affective foundations the earlier chapters prioritized.

When ecopedagogy unfolds within the discipline of art education, multiple methods can support it. Core methods for art education as ecopedagogy might include studying eco-art, emphasizing sustainability in studio art practice, integrating ecological and environmental content, experiencing the outdoors, and making art that engages with ecological/environmental topics and issues. Each of these core methods might integrally infuse instructional units in the following ways:

- *Studying and making eco-art.* Since studying and producing art are established, central components of most art curricula, these common disciplinary approaches might easily be directed toward the ecological—to encompass the study of eco-art and making of ecological/environmental art. While traditional environmental artworks, like landscape paintings, likely have ecopedagogical value, contemporary eco-artworks are more strongly recommended for study, as discussed in Chapter 2.
- *Emphasizing sustainability in studio art practice.* As art students inevitably engage in artmaking, the materiality of these activities presents opportunities for students to identify, engage in, and reflect upon sustainable artmaking practices. Teachers might support these activities by setting aside time for dialogue; modeling sustainable artmaking practices; only offering materials, techniques, and processes in the classroom that are more sustainable; openly advocating for sustainable practices (when the teacher has strong rapport with students); and establishing classroom procedures that contribute to sustainability, such as recycling, waste reduction, and energy-saving practices.
- *Integrating ecological and environmental content.* Contemporary art often surpasses disciplinary boundaries as it "connects to diverse worlds outside the classroom" (Marshall & Donahue, 2014, p. 7). When art educators seek to incorporate these powerful approaches into the classroom, interdisciplinary and transdisciplinary learning naturally unfold. Indeed, such approaches are generally considered best practices in the field (Guyotte et al., 2014; Marshall & Donahue, 2014). In embracing these practices, teachers might choose to orient curriculum around ecological/environmental

themes, introduce eco-artworks into the curriculum, and foster student inquiry surrounding socio-ecological topics. In such cases, engagement with ecological/environmental content would further student understanding of these works and support deeper student inquiry.

- *Experiencing the outdoors.* While outdoor experiences may not be possible in all teaching contexts, teachers at schools where outdoor engagement is permitted might take advantage of the ecopedagogical possibilities inherent to those spaces. Ideally, lessons would involve outdoor learning experiences directly related to the biophysical environment, such as designing a garden or studying biotic phenomena in preparation for an artwork. Secondarily, students also might benefit, in terms of motivation and, perhaps, pro-environmental orientations, when general art classroom activities (i.e., not necessarily connected to environmental topics, such as critiques) are moved outdoors.

As the following chapters expound upon ecopedagogical aims, introduce eco-artworks allied with these aims, and present curricular ideas, I would encourage readers to recall these core methods and reflect upon how they might be adopted, adapted, and structured to facilitate these various approaches to ecopedagogy. The next seven chapters illuminate some of the paths art education as ecopedagogy might take, and the methods above offer the mechanics for accomplishing these vital ambitions.

As educators respond to these chapters and reflect upon how they could design these various forms of ecopedagogical curricula, I suggest that they gather information about their students' relationships with and feelings toward the more-than-human world, pro-environmental orientations, and action competences. Such understandings can enable teachers to adopt appropriate strategies, pacing, and instructional supports. While dialogues with students and other common classroom activities can provide teachers with valuable insight into their ecological proclivities, surveys can also be useful in quickly and systemically assessing students on various cognitive and behavioral dimensions. Such questionnaires include the following:

- Connectedness to Nature Scale (Mayer & Frantz, 2004)
- Connection to Nature Index (Cheng & Monroe, 2012)
- Inclusion of Nature in Self Scale (Schultz, 2002)
- Environmental Identity Scale (Clayton, 2003)
- Love and Care for Nature Scale (Perkins, 2010)

- New Ecological Paradigm Scale for Children (Manoli et al., 2007)
- Climate Change Hope Scale (Li & Monroe, 2018)
- Motivation Toward the Environment Scale (Pelletier et al., 1998)
- Self-Perceived Action Competence for Sustainability Questionnaire (Olsson et al., 2020)

When selecting a questionnaire, teachers should consider grade level and whether the questionnaire is suited for that age group; the phenomena the questionnaire is designed to assess and whether that phenomena aligns with the focus of the curriculum; and the length and intensity of the program, as certain phenomena are more likely to change in a short time period than others (Salazar et al., 2020). Administering such questionnaires before and after ecopedagogical curricula can allow teachers to assess students' growth in these dimensions and make inferences into the impact of their ecopedagogical curricula. To support teachers interested in attempting similar teacher research into ecopedagogical impacts, whether for personal motivation, to inform curriculum design, or to disseminate results to stakeholders, two questionnaires are provided in Appendixes B and C.

CHAPTER 4

Cultivating Relations and Fostering Empathetic Encounters

When is the last time you paused and attended to your sensorial experiences of the land? When is the last time you experienced awe or wonder? When is the last time you felt viscerally connected to more-than-human life? The ecological landscape is replete with multilayered phenomena and rich life worlds. David Abram (1996) described how openly and intensely experiencing the sights, sounds, smells, and tactile sensations of the "many-voiced landscape" (p. ix) can allow humans to enter into relations with the land and recognize the multiple, intertwined relations and intelligences that exist there. Additionally, environmental scholars (e.g., Dunlap et al., 2000) have argued that a deep recognition of the interconnectedness of all life—an ecological paradigm—is necessary to move past the harmful anthropocentric schemas that have defined dominant human society's relations with the Earth. As an ecological paradigm involves a comprehension of the self as part of a larger, more complex whole, it requires an expanding of consciousness for other living things and the environments upon which they depend.

To construct relational dispositions toward the Earth, direct, affective experiences with the biophysical environment are critical. Beyond theoretically identifying connections with the more-than-human world, students need to experience and feel them. Writing of human relations with the land, Aldo Leopold (1966) claimed, "We grieve only for what we know" (p. 48). Sadly, one problem is that we often do not "know." David Abram (1996) described modern Euro-Western culture's perceptual failures: "a real inability to clearly see, or focus upon, anything outside of the realm of human technology, or to hear as meaningful anything other than human speech" (p. 27). This perceptual obliviousness to the more-than-human world stands in contrast to diverse Indigenous ways of being that demonstrate acute sensitivity to the subtleties of and changes occurring in the more-than-human world and establish close, familial bonds with nonhuman animals, plants, and sites.

As art educators, we might ask ourselves how students' empathetic, awe- and wonder-filled experiences and understandings of ethical relationality with the land can be fostered through art education. How can students connect with organisms and life worlds seemingly different from their own? How can students find affinities with rocks, rivers, and mountains? How can the intellectual distance between human and nonhuman dissolve and kinship become clearer? In many ways, the discipline may be uniquely suited for cultivating these relations. First, many art genres lend themselves to outdoor engagement. Consider traditional art activities, such as clay harvesting, Raku firing, en plein air painting, landscape photography, stone sculpting, and basket weaving, which require that artists operate outdoors. Moreover, students can engage in direct, intentionally empathetic encounters with the biophysical world through works of eco-art, like ephemeral installations and ecoperformances. As such, art as a subject can intersect with outdoor education and can be particularly poignant when it unfolds as slow pedagogy—students pausing and immersing themselves in outdoor spaces (Payne & Wattchow, 2008). Secondly, art's affective, emotional nature, particularly as it tends to encourage introspection and reflection, is conducive to such relational acts. Aesthetic experiences with the more-than-human world can be cultivated and built upon in art curricula.

A diverse body of works and modes of engaging in art can foster the relationality described above. These works can range from traditional practices that have resurged and been reinterpreted by artists to more contemporary practices that engage closely with environmental phenomena. Each section of this chapter introduces specific works of contemporary art that model such attendance to local environments and emphasize relationality. Themes that could arise in relation to these works include attentiveness and relationality/reciprocal relationships. In each section below, I identify some possible approaches to engaging with these themes in the classroom (see Table 4.1 for a curriculum outline).

BEING PRESENT

Over time and across the globe, various art forms have centered attention to sensory experience and mindfulness. Consider the Western tradition of natural history illustration over the past 4 centuries, where artist-scientists have studied plants and animals in their natural habitats and carefully recorded their firsthand knowledge. Or consider the traditional arts of Zen Buddhist practitioners, who, since the 12th century, have engaged in calligraphy, painting, and tea ceremonies as forms of meditation. As many traditional art forms require attention to the present, modern and contemporary artists have drawn from; reimagined; and, in certain cases, as with natural history illustration and landscape painting, decolonized these practices.

Table 4.1. Some Curricular Applications of Themes of Attentiveness and Relationality

Big Ideas	Grade Levels	Ecopedagogical Goals	Key Concepts	Discussion/Reflection Prompts	Possible Artistic Responses
Attentiveness	K–12*	Sensing, closely noticing, and empathizing with the more-than-human world Experiencing wonder and awe	When we sense the world, we are physically connecting with it. Art can allow us to be more present and perceive the world more closely.	When is the last time you observed something closely? What senses did you use? What did you learn? How was that knowledge different from the knowledge you might find in a textbook? Have you ever felt connected to the more-than-human world? What did it feel like?	Walk mindfully Macro photograph biotic and abiotic matter Document bodily experiences in a somatic journal Map animal trails or other patterns in animal movements (e.g., birds or insects) or water-flow patterns Audio record more-than-human sounds
Relationality/ Reciprocal Relationships	K–12*	Identifying webs of relationships Expanding ideas of ethics to include the more-than-human Attuning to Indigenous and ecocentric perspectives	People have an ethical responsibility to the people, places, and things in which they are in relation: these relationships can involve mutual caretaking. Many Indigenous cultures emphasize reciprocal relations and kinship with the land and its inhabitants.	How are you in relation with the animals, plants, and matter around you? How might this relationship be reciprocal? How can one act ethically toward the land and its inhabitants? How can you mutually caretake? What do various Indigenous cultures and ecocentric perspectives teach us about our relationship with the Earth?	Reflect on relationality in visual journals Create artworks, installations, and performances that make human and more-than-human affinities visible Visualize stories of place that decenter human perspectives

*The wording of key concepts and prompts will likely need to be modified for use with elementary students.

Artists Sensing and Corporeally Exploring

Walking methods have emerged as one such presencing practice. Equally a kind of perception and type of art (O'Rourke, 2016), walking methods draw upon diverse artistic, cultural, and spiritual traditions, including various spiritual pilgrimages (Scrivens, 2021); Indigenous traditions of meditatively moving through place (Bidwell & Winschiers-Theophilus, 2012); and the Situationist artists' wanderings through European cities (O'Rourke, 2016). Correspondingly, the practice of walking has been conceived in varied ways: as research practice (O'Neill & Roberts, 2020), socially engaged public performance (Pujol, 2018), and aesthetic and spiritual pedagogy (Irwin, 2006). In this chapter, I am conceiving of "walking" broadly to include pausing in spaces; diverse forms of locomotion, such as dancing; and movements performed by diverse and differently abled bodies, including movements achieved through mobility aids. This stance aligns with critical walking methodologies (Springgay & Truman, 2019). In the following I will focus on walking as a form of eco-art practice or ecoperformance while considering its aesthetic, spiritual, contemplative potential and its possibilities for transformation.

While walking itself can be a stand-alone art practice, artmaking can be intimately tied to these experiences (Irwin, 2006), whether integrated throughout the process or enacted as culminating acts of reflection. Karen O'Rourke (2016) described how contemporary walking artists often outline their methods in walking protocols that others might follow. In this chapter, I define "walking protocol" broadly to include prescriptive written protocols as well as artists' loose, fluid sets of walking habits. Consider Canadian artists Rhonda Neufeld and Rodney Konopaki's collective artistic meanderings (e.g., Konopaki & Neufeld, 2013). Over the course of several years, the artists have come together to observe and traverse various outdoor Canadian environs. As they reflectively pass through "mountain trails, urban streets, rural fields, boreal forests and shoreline" (Infrastructure, n.d., para. 3), they walk in unison, joined by an art surface they carry, often a drawing board or printing plate (Priegert, 2012). Neufeld and Konopaki's cooperative journeys are aimed at sensorially experiencing place; the artists use their drawing movements to record "the surface of the land" (Infrastructure, n.d., para. 3) and their exchanges with other organisms. Their performative works often produce jostling, blind-contour-line drawings, punctuated marks, and layers of color, visually demonstrating the artists' meditative experiences of the land (Priegert, 2012; "Suggestions," 2014; see Figure 4.1).

The walking protocols walking artists employ can differ dramatically. For instance, rather than integrating visual art into their meditative practices like Neufeld and Konopaki, the Imagining Climates' (2021) *Inose/ Field Trip* supports public participation through aurally guided walking. Anishinaabe leaders Yolanda Bonnell, self-identifying as a "Queer, 2 Spirit

Figure 4.1. Rhonda Neufeld and Rodney Konopaki, *Claybank Hills*, woodcut, 24″ x 39″, edition of 11, 2013

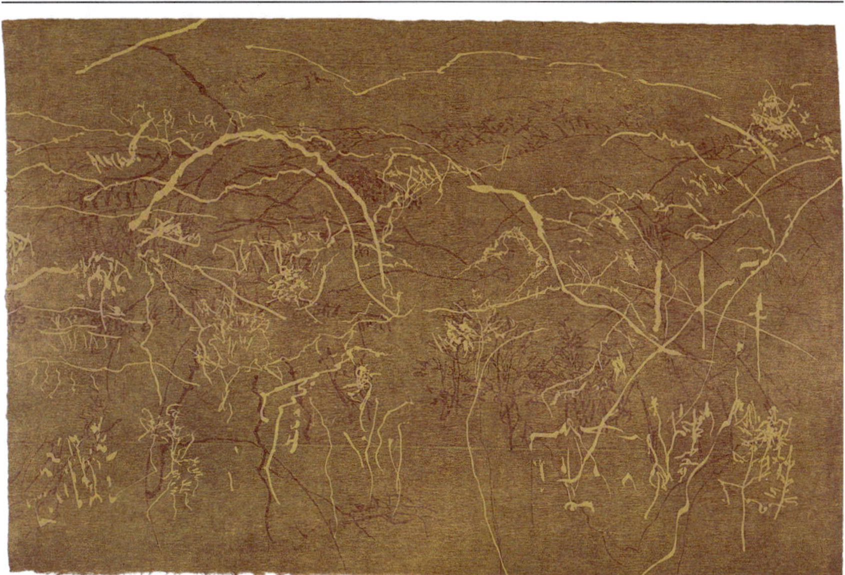

Photo credit: Blaine Campbell

Anishinaabe-Ojibwe, South Asian [and] Scottish" (Bonnell, n.d., para. 1), and Jesse Popp, a member of Wiikwemikoong Unceded Territory (Popp, n.d., para. 1), organized this guided sound-walk project (Bush & Richardson, 2021). Working with other artists, they produced a 26-minute sound recording, or "walking meditation," listeners could play during outdoor walks to inspire profound reflection on "the land we walk upon and the diverse living things we encounter" (para. 1). The work's title, *Inose/Field Trip*, incorporates the Ojibwa word *Inose*, meaning "to walk in a certain way, to a certain place" (Bush & Richardson, 2021, para. 2), emphasizing the intentional, place-specific nature of such walking.

Curriculum of Conscious Attendance

Art forms and works capable of cultivating conscious attendance do not always conform to traditional Euro-Western notions of art. In many cases, they operate largely outside of the art market—not producing a finished product or commodity. In that sense, they challenge and expand notions of what art could be. One way to introduce students to the idea of art as conscious attendance is to ask students to participate outdoors in walking, loosely following a protocol established by a contemporary artist or artist group. Throughout this process, students can be encouraged to adopt the dispositions, stances, and movements the artists have modeled, particularly those that align with slow pedagogy, such as attentive participation, unhurried movements, and conscious breathing (refer to Table 4.1). Such conditions set the stage for students' affective and ecological learning.

As students experience other artists' approaches, they may begin to grasp the many possibilities of walking and the ways in which various approaches embody diverse values and foster different dispositions. With these understandings, they can begin to develop their own walking protocols. They can reflect upon the experiences such protocols may cultivate and the ideas communicated. Eventually, students may engage their school community in participating in these walking experiences. To prepare, students can choreograph movements, develop signage identifying native plants, produce sound guides, construct labyrinths (with minimal ecological footprints), or weave rope from invasive vines to link walkers. They may also look to various forms of literature, such as environmental philosophy, ecospiritual texts, or ecopoetry, for material to inspire walkers on their journeys. Black feminist geographies and Indigenous texts might be particularly poignant to consult. Additionally, students can consider whether and how artmaking might infuse these experiences. For instance, walkers may keep a somatic journal, where they sketch their bodily experiences; sketch native plants in a field journal; closely photograph the smaller life forms and matter they encounter; audio-record cicada choruses; chart geese movements; or map ant thoroughfares. As these experiences unfold, students' new understandings and sensibilities can be explored and extended through dialogue and visual reflection.

In taking students outdoors, a common teacher concern is the nature of the environment surrounding their school, especially if the school is situated in an urban or suburban zone and has experienced significant ecological devastation, as is often the case. While sites with more ecological diversity might be worth seeking out on campus and in surrounding areas for walking field trips, any outdoor environment offers encounters with the more-than-human world (e.g., pigeons, squirrels, and bees) and, as such, presents more affective learning opportunities than can be found inside a typical classroom.

EMPHASIZING RELATIONALITY

In Western countries, Romantic ideas associated with an art and literary movement of the late 18th century, among other dominant cultural conceptions of nature, tend to infuse aesthetic encounters with the biophysical environment. It can be beneficial to note the limitations of these notions of nature, such as

- nature as separate from society/culture/humanity;
- nature as feminine;

- nature as a site primarily for White, middle-class pleasure and leisure (Carter, 2018); and
- place as ahistorical and unaffected by colonial legacies (Tuck et al., 2014)

We can recognize how easily these notions intersect with and perpetuate sexism, classism, racism, speciesism, and colonialism. Wonder- and awe-filled aesthetic encounters with the more-than-human world need not rely on misguided cultural conceptions, such as oversimplified Romantic notions emphasizing "nostalgia for a lost unity with nature" or "rhapsodic celebration of beautiful scenery" (Harrison, 2006). Instead, reciprocal relationality might be foregrounded, where humans are seen as part of nature, ecologically damaged spaces and colonial inheritances are acknowledged, Indigenous and ecocentric perspectives are centered, and reciprocity is emphasized. The following section will present contemporary artists whose works embody such relational practices and do not shy away from the intricacies of these relations.

Artists Engaging With the Complexity of Land Relations

As social and environmental violence have been enacted in various ways at sites across the globe, land relations can be fraught, particularly for members of historically oppressed groups. Consider how the landscape has been, and often still continues to be, a site of toil (i.e., enslaved or exploited labor), sexual assault, environmental degradation, and racial terror (e.g., lynchings and police brutality). Artist Torkwase Dyson, who has scuba-dived in the ocean as part of her artistic process, explained how these intersections have manifested in the way she approaches bodies of water:

> I think about the oceans as a commons. Being in the ocean, I try to understand the ecosystem—how the creatures, materials, minerals, caverns, and light interact. I don't have a particular kind of melancholy when I do it. Over the centuries, individuals—Black people, in particular—have been sacrificed on the ocean, because people have used it as a superhighway. I'm aware that there are energy particles—ancestorship—that belong to a commons with all of the other sentient beings living there. When I'm there, I try to be in the moment, really conscious of what's around me, allowing my individual senses to open up and be present and aware that I'm not alone. As a Black woman, I belong to the distance between solitude and the commons. I'm aware of it when I'm in the water, and I feel a sense of belonging when I'm there that I take with me when I'm not. (quoted in Binlot, 2021, para. 16)

In a manner similar to Dyson's, the following artists present works that acknowledge traumatic histories and present states while simultaneously foregrounding deep immersion in more-than-human environments and modeling relational paradigms.

The works of Brooklyn-based artist Athena LaTocha, raised in Alaska and of Lakota and Ojibwe heritage, reflect an understanding of the land's storied history and demonstrate deep bonds with it (Mitter, 2021). Unlike traditional landscape paintings that tend to reinforce the idea of nature as distinct, her expansive mixed-media works situate humans firmly in the landscape. Her site-responsive installation, *In the Wake of . . .* (2021), attends to both the geological and human history of the Manhattan terrain going back to prehistoric times (Mitter, 2021). Incorporating materials she gathered from the area, LaTocha repeatedly soaked and scrubbed ink and earth into a 17-meter-long, resin-coated paper and used local refuse, like tire remnants and bricks, to move the materials and transfer marks (BRIC, n.d.; Mitter, 2021). Lead impressions of local geological formations overlay portions of the emotive work, and ambient urban sounds, captured at construction sites and in subways, resonate through the space (Mitter, 2021).

Her process involves research as well as on-site immersion, involving photography, sound recording, lead-sheet molding, and reflection, at the sites she is representing (Mitter, 2021). LaTocha explained:

> How do you understand something? You put yourself in it; you surround yourself; you embed and immerse yourself into it to try to gain intimate knowledge of something through a physical relationship of being present in that space. (quoted in Green, 2022, para. 12)

One curator articulated how this immersive process was evident in the work: "It's hands-on, not like this distant viewing eye. It's actually in the landscape, touching it, embedded in it" (quoted in Mitter, 2021, para. 10). By bringing the land forward, into our consciousness, she emphasizes human–land relations, and by making the industrial histories an integral component of her works, she confronts the unsettling social and cultural patterns that have played out there. She explained how it is important for us to understand "what we've done as a species in these places" (para. 12).

Similar to the way LaTocha foregrounded the land, visual artist Allison Janae Hamilton positions the rural landscapes of the American South as the central characters in her works. Imagination and memory infuse Hamilton's dreamlike explorations of place and Black experience, with each work "contain[ing] narratives that are pieced together from folktales, hunting and farming rituals, African-American nature writing, and Baptist hymns" (Hamilton, 2022, para. 2). In *Three Girls in Sabal Palm Forest II* (2019b), three girls in white dresses and red head wreaths mythically perch on a fallen tree trunk (see Figure 4.2). In her underwater photograph, *Floridawater III*, Hamilton (2019a) floats in a white dress, illuminated, among underwater vegetation (see Figure 4.3). However, her underwater surroundings are not

Figure 4.2. Allison Janae Hamilton, *Three Girls in Sabal Palm Forest II*, 2019b

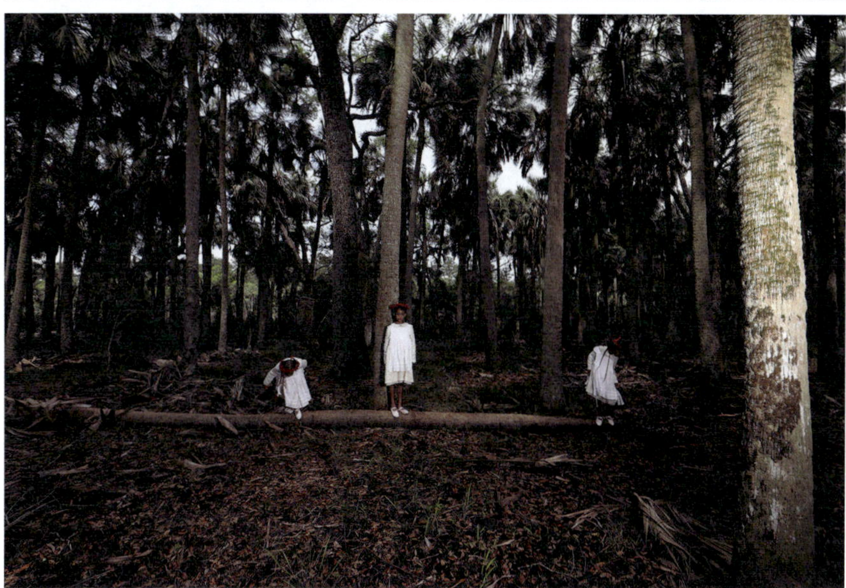

Courtesy of the artist and Marianne Boesky Gallery, New York and Aspen.

untouched by human presence: in the photograph, a large metal grate has replaced the river floor. This river is the Wascissa River, a river system where enslaved Black people were once required to dig a canal that was never used. Evocative works such as these draw us into the landscape but also testify about the contemporary social and political realities found there, particularly those affecting Black communities. The land itself becomes "a storyteller and witness highlighting issues such as ownership and loss, sustainability, and climate change" (Goodalle, 2019, para. 1). In telling these stories, or positioning the land to tell these relational stories, both Hamilton and LaTocha made no attempt to conceal unpleasant sociohistorical truths.

Indigenous art collective Postcommodity have also managed to navigate the complexities of referencing the land's troubled colonial history while revealing and venerating deep relationality (see Figure 4.4). In the installation *Do You Remember When?* (2009/2012), interdisciplinary artists Raven Chacon, from Fort Defiance, Navajo Nation (Chacon, n.d., para. 1); Cristóbal Martínez, of "Northern New Mexico Mestizo roots" (Martínez, n.d., para. 8); and Kade L. Twist, of the Cherokee Nation (Twist, n.d.), removed a portion of Arizona State University Art Museum's gallery floor to uncover a square of earth. A microphone reaches down to the soil as sounds fill the space, as if the land's voice is being broadcast. In this "psychosocial soundtrack" (Schmelzer, 2017, para. 4), a mix of animal calls and songs of

Figure 4.3. Allison Janae Hamilton, *Floridawater III*, 2019a

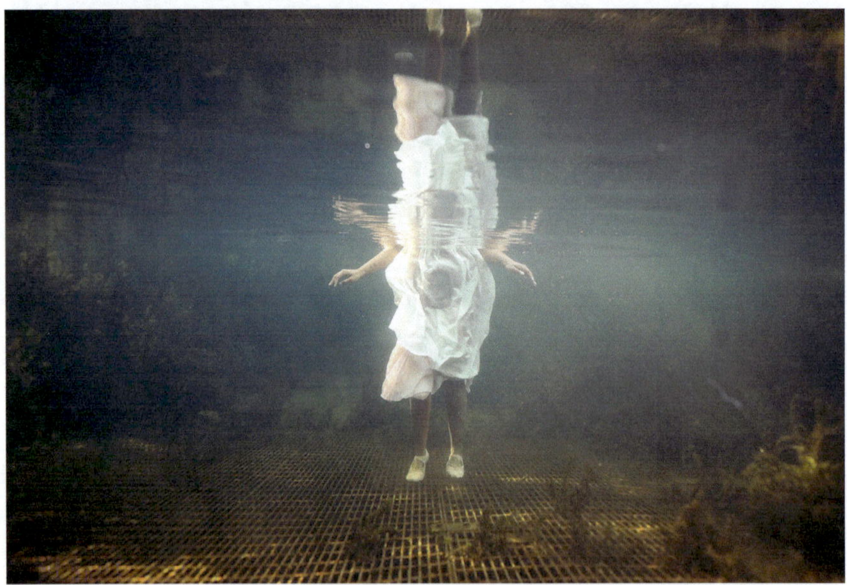

Courtesy of the artist and Marianne Boesky Gallery, New York and Aspen.
© Allison Janae Hamilton

Figure 4.4. Postcommodity, *Do You Remember When?*, 2009/2012

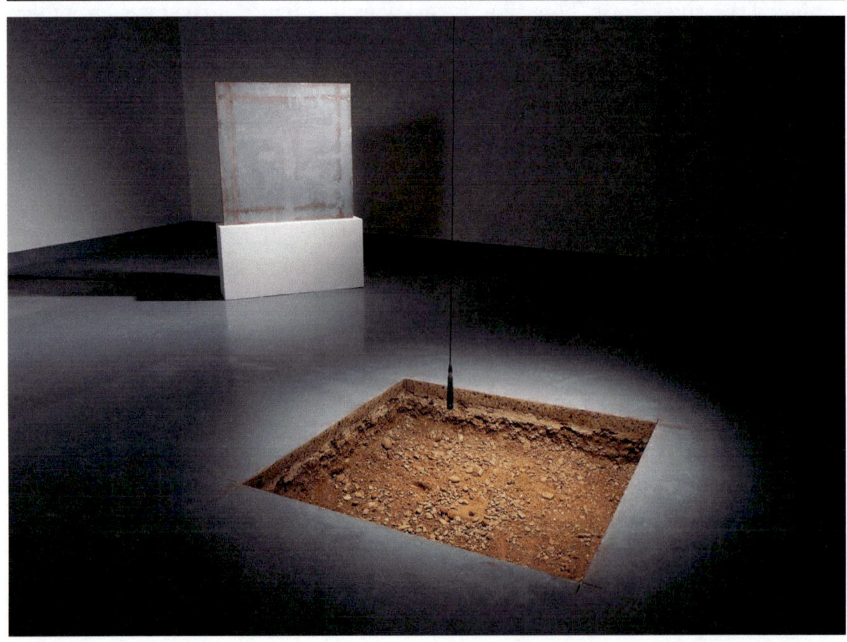

Indigenous voices are in dialogue with the earth. Schmelzer identified this installation as creating "a passage between worlds": "a doorway to the exposed earth, and to spiritualities and cultures tied to it, below" (para 4). As such, this installation visceralizes relational, Indigenous ways of being, and metaphorically reclaims the land. By exhibiting the second iteration of this work in Sydney, Australia, and incorporating Aboriginal voices and traditions in the soundtrack, this decolonizing work is "trans-Indigenous" (Watson, 2015, p. 144)—drawing attention to Indigenous alliances and centering dynamic Indigenous perspectives that emphasize reciprocity with the land.

Curriculum of Reciprocal Relationality

In fostering reciprocal relationality, teachers can encourage students to adopt aspects of the artistic process similar to the artists' methods described above (refer to Table 4.1). Like Torkwase Dyson and Athena LaTocha, students may deeply immerse themselves in the outdoor environments they encounter. Various activities can support this immersion (e.g., walking methods, photography, or meditative deep-breathing practices). To further comprehend webs of relations, students can participate in a series of reflective exercises and dialogues associated with these outdoor experiences. Students may begin by reflecting upon their own perceptions of the land: visual journal prompts can ask students to reflect upon the feelings they experience, the associations that arise, and the personal and cultural experiences that inform these experiences. Visual and literary artists can provide models for these reflections on human–land relations. After initially exploring their own relations with these spaces, students can attend to their firsthand knowledge of the phenomena unfolding there. In so doing, they can explore curiosities, learning with the land. Like LaTocha's artistic process, they can supplement personal, close noticing with online research related to place, including the various histories (e.g., geological, ecological, sociocultural, and colonial) that have unfolded there.

As the "reciprocal" in the term "reciprocal relations" emphasizes a mutual exchange, obligation, and caretaking that can be applied to human–land relations (Diver et al., 2019), students can explore ideas of relational accountability and seek opportunities to exhibit caring responses toward the more-than-human world. Given that many Indigenous worldviews emphasize webs of kinship with animals, plants, and sites, or animism (Diver et al., 2019; Harvey, 2019), Indigenous stories and poetry can play an important role in such curricula. Students might artistically reflect upon the underlying ideas of responsibility and relationality that can inform their own interactions with the world. A myriad of artistic responses could arise: ecoperformances uniting "human and more-than-human movements, gestures, and sounds" (Nxumalo & Tepeyolotl Villanueva, 2020, p. 220); visual stories of place that decenter human perspectives; or other artworks and installations that make human and more-than-human affinities visible.

CONCLUSION

As students experience and awaken to the world, wonder, joy, awe, and *transcendence* are possible. Not the transcendence of leaving one's earthly station to engage with a higher power or achieve a higher state—vertical or absolute transcendence—but the transcendence associated with horizontally reaching toward, and recognizing our inherent embeddedness in and belonging to, the more-than-human world—"horizontal transcendence" (Johnson, 2007, p. 14). As educators, we can impart these joyful, transcendence-inducing relationalities to our students, or at least create the conditions for them to begin to recognize these relationalities themselves.

QUESTIONS FOR EDUCATOR REFLECTION

1. Think back to a time when you paused and attended to your sensorial experiences of the land. What did it feel like? How did that experience impact you? How could such experiences be important for students?
2. Think back to a time you experienced awe or wonder surrounding the more-than-human world. How was that experience similar or different from how you have felt when you encountered a particularly meaningful work of art?
3. List as many webs of relation in which you find yourself in this moment (e.g., family, food, air, watershed). How could respect and care (i.e., reciprocity) infuse some or all of these relations?
4. Walk the school campus and surrounding areas. Identify areas that might be more biodiverse. Consider how these sites could be educative. What types of learning could happen there? How could art experiences facilitate such learning?

CHAPTER 5

Embracing Natural Cycles and Processes

How often do you viscerally feel your own mortality or that of others? How often do your students have experiences that allow them to sense the mortality of the beings around them? Perhaps a lot less frequently than if they had lived a century or so ago. Affifi and Christie (2019) described how "diverse accomplices" (p. 1144) within capitalist societies progressively work to shield us from experiencing and dwelling upon mortality. Advances in cosmetology and medicine allow us to "hide" or "fix" evidence of the aging process. Aging relatives' care is often relegated to health care professionals and nursing homes (Oaks & Bibeau, 1987). Collective rituals surrounding death, common to cultures around the world, are increasingly minimal or anesthetized in Western countries (Affifi & Christie, 2019). Euphemisms gloss over death: someone "slipped away" or is "at rest" (Oaks & Bibeau, 1987, p. 420). We are more and more removed from our meals' biological origins; multinational corporations often play the starring role in food production, processing, and preparation. Even visual cues of our foods' animal or plant origins are frequently lost—visualize prepackaged chicken nuggets and smiley-face potato fritters. Moreover, in limiting our time outdoors, we distance ourselves from more-than-human communities that innately offer rich, abounding displays of mortality (Affifi & Christie, 2019). For better or worse, half-eaten frogs and cracked robin's eggs are rarely found inside malls or trampoline parks.

This collective propensity toward death disavowal is relatively new in human history and has ecological consequences: Existential anxiety can lead us to retreat from our biological identities and position ourselves as distinct from and superior to other species (Marino & Mountain, 2015). Abram and Jardine (2000) described this fear: "The terror of being vulnerable, and the consequent wish to disembed oneself, to stand forever outside the sensuous world" (p. 174). Sadly, this anxiety-ridden stance reinforces exploitive behavior toward the environment. A large body of research suggests that latent mortality anxiety can exacerbate materialism and consumption in members of Western capitalist cultures (see, for example, Arndt et al., 2004; Kasser & Sheldon, 2000). Students who are reminded of death are more likely to find money (Solomon & Arndt, 1993, as cited in Arndt et al., 2004) and high-status objects, such as luxury cars and watches (Mandel & Heine, 1999), appealing and to deplete scarce natural resources in the pursuit of wealth (Kasser & Sheldon, 2000; see also Becker, 1973).

Psychological studies show intensified awareness of death through contemplation can be incredibly beneficial for individuals (Vail et al., 2012). As modern capitalist cultures deny corporeality and the frailty of the human body, some contemporary artists' works offer us the chance to rediscover our embodiment. Additionally, their work challenges the speciesist hierarchy that privileges human life by calling attention to the existence of species outside of our daily perception and foregrounding their life-and-death drama.

Each section of this chapter begins by presenting contemporary works of art that illuminate and revel in the decadence, decay, and potential for regeneration imminent in the decomposition of organic matter. When integrated into art curriculum, the ecological and aesthetic experiences these works incite can be built upon to inspire further eco-aesthetic engagement and reflection. Some themes that naturally arise include conceptualizations of beauty, the potential of multispecies interactions, and cultural acknowledgments of mortality. In the following sections, I pose some possible approaches to engaging with these themes in the classroom (see Table 5.1 for an outline).

REDEFINING BEAUTY

Notions of beauty are continually changing and shifting, but, ultimately, what or whom we consider beautiful is an indication of our values; we find beauty in the people, objects, and settings that most embody our ideals. Thus, as we come to appreciate these biological and ecological processes, we may find ourselves more aesthetically attracted to the organisms and states of matter that we most equate with these processes. A moldy blueberry unexpectedly houses a fascinating blend of colors and textures in its transient state. A spongy mass of fungi is suddenly delicate, exquisite, and lovely. . . .

Artists Observing Decay Processes

Some contemporary artists have drawn attention to the transience of existence by observing and representing evidence of biodegradation processes (Matsuura, 2015), while others have set up the conditions to allow these cycles to unfold in real time (Makoto, 2015). Whether audiences witness this decadence firsthand or experience it vicariously through the artist's photographic lens, they have the opportunity to grapple with its more discomfiting elements as well as its charms.

Table 5.1. Some Curricular Applications of Themes of Beauty, Co-Creation, and Mortality and Culture

Big Ideas	Grade Levels	Ecopedagogical Goals	Key Concepts	Discussion/Reflection Prompts	Possible Artistic Responses
Beauty	K–12*	Experiencing the beauty of natural processes, including death Acknowledging death as an aspect of life Expanding perceptions of what is worth caring for	Our knowledge, values, and experiences can impact the way we perceive beauty. Aesthetic experiences can allow us to expand our perceptions of beauty (and reverse certain perceptions of ugliness). Artists can help people see the beauty of objects, environments, and ideas, like interdependence.	What makes something beautiful? Can people have different ideas about what is beautiful? Is there something you think is beautiful that others may not (yet)? What is it, and what makes it beautiful to you? Name something you value that others may not. Why do you think you see it differently?	Photograph or illustrate decomposing organic material, whether plant life or food waste. Create an installation with perishable materials. Create an artwork communicating beauty others may not recognize (yet)—that may challenge societal norms.
Co-Creation	K–12*	Acknowledging the agency of other organisms Cultivating attentiveness and embracing uncertainty	Artists can enter into multispecies artistic relations and co-create works of art. Multispecies relations require immersion, attentiveness, and patience.	What might be some examples of multispecies communities? How might artists acknowledge and ethically work with other species to create art? How might this process be different from traditional artistic processes with non-living media?	Create agar art. Perform (ethical) multispecies experiments (could be as simple as promoting bacterial growth).

(continued)

Table 5.1. Some Curricular Applications of Themes of Beauty, Co-Creation, and Mortality and Culture (*continued*)

Big Ideas	Grade Levels	Ecopedagogical Goals	Key Concepts	Discussion/Reflection Prompts	Possible Artistic Responses
Mortality and Culture	10–12	Honoring life and death Honoring animal life Critiquing cultural practices (as appropriate)	Western consumer culture often works to shield us from dwelling upon mortality (the mortality of humans and nonhumans). Artists can communicate alternative ways to think about and deal with mortality.	What is mortality? Do you think of your mortality or others' mortality often? When? Sometimes culture can shield us from thinking about mortality. Can you think of cultural practices that make mortality more hidden? Where do you wish mortality might be more visible? How might cultural practices go further to acknowledge we are a part of natural systems and cycles?	Use contemporary creative strategies, such as juxtaposition, to challenge a cultural value or norm indirectly or directly surrounding mortality. Invent a new cultural practice indirectly or directly related to mortality: design the materials necessary for it and/or perform it.

*The wording of key concepts and prompts will likely need to be modified for use with elementary students.

Japanese artist Tomoya Matsuura (2015), in his *Withered Plant* series, observed processes of decay already advancing by capturing deteriorating botanical life with a scanning electron microscope. In these black-and-white images, desiccated petals and stems twist and peel, revealing their organic intricacies before they disintegrate into oblivion (see Figure 5.1). The microscope, with a resolution of a few nanometers, allowed Matsuura (n.d.) to achieve a level of detail in these images, only a few millimeters in size, which would not have been possible otherwise. Matsuura explained, "One seems to catch a glimpse of the mystery and dynamism connecting the cycle of life in the finely etched traces of existence in the microscopic world" (para. 2). The artist expressed his intention to draw attention to the magnificence of the "micro-world" (Matsuura, n.d., para. 3) and the cycles integral to its continuation so that viewers might begin to situate themselves within these webs of existence.

Azuma Makoto, a Japanese artist well-known for his eccentric botanical sculptures, has also turned his attention to the process of biodegradation, placing it on full display. In his ephemeral, sculptural installation *Box Flowers* (see Figure 5.2), Makoto (2015) formed a cube with over 200 vibrant varieties of flowers "bursting with excitement" (Loffeld, n.d., para. 3). Initially, the work exuded vitality and abundance: viewers could experience

Figure 5.1. Tomoya Matsuura, #37, 2015

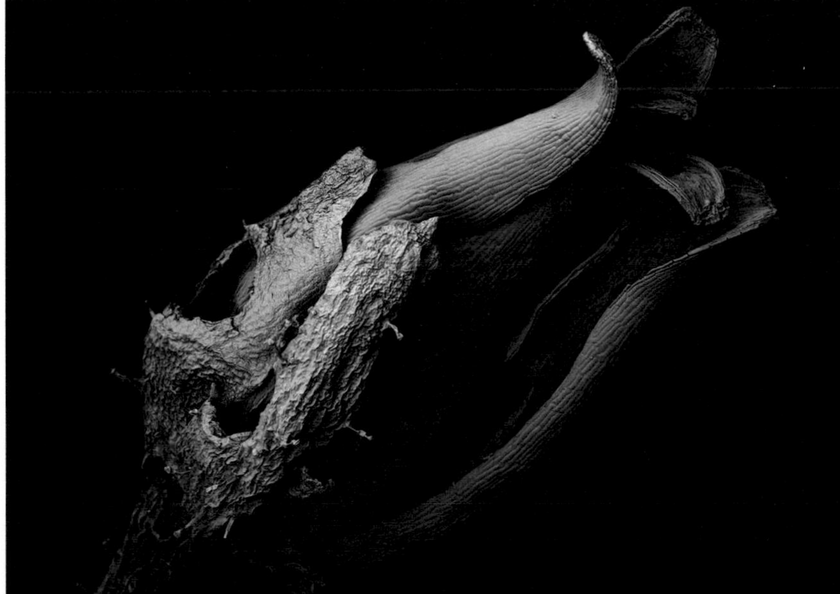

Figure 5.2. Azuma Makoto, *Box Flower* (image from a later stage), 2015

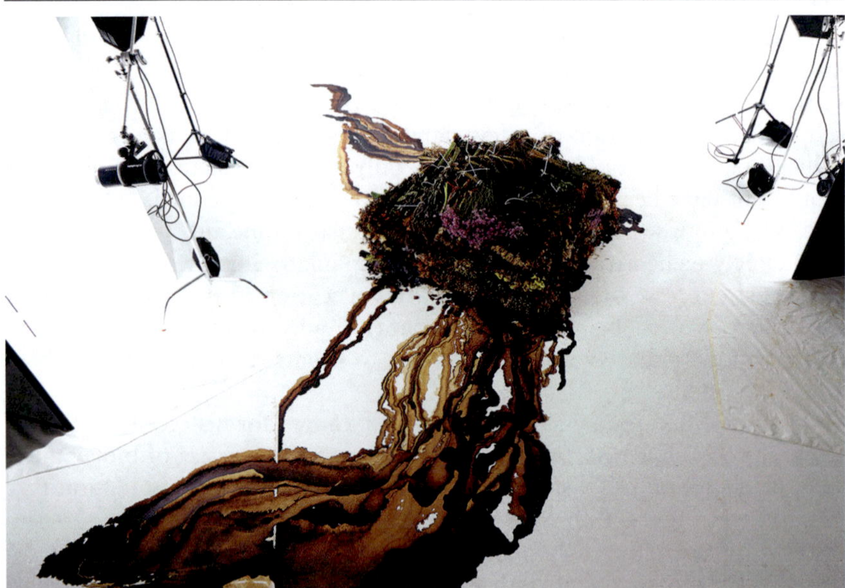

© Azuma Makoto, © Shiinoki/AMKK

the opulence of the vegetation in the rich hues of the large-scale work. However, as the blossoms reached the height of their fertility, their doom was imminent. The flourish of their deaths played out in its lurid beauty. The floral cube compressed, and tacky fluid oozed and pooled. Makoto (personal communication, December 8, 2020) characterized his work as "a lump of life" and discussed how it was inspired by the ideas behind *kusōzu,* a centuries-old Buddhist series of paintings where a cadaver was set outside and then graphically depicted in various stages of decomposition. First introduced in eighth-century Japan, *kusōzu* images incite contemplation on the temporality of the material world, among other themes (Fukaya, 2016). According to Makoto (personal communication, December 8, 2020), *Box Flowers,* with all of its beauty, narrates that there is an evanescence, grotesqueness, unpleasantness, and also forcefulness to life. Such works might lead us to question cultural conceptions of beauty by allowing us to find it beyond the idyllic, in the messiness of the perishing process.

Artists Illustrating and Interpreting Evidence of Decay With Unexpected Media

Other artists (Brown, 2014; Ryan, 2019; Thomas, 2018) observe these processes, noting the organisms that flourish as others decline—the mold feeding on rotten lemons and the bacteria growing in petri dishes—and then translate these observations through unexpected media, provoking viewers to see them anew. These intricate and unexpected works offer new aesthetics for decay. Rather than inspiring fear and revulsion, they can comfort, dazzle, inspire, and critique.

New York–based artist Kathleen Ryan has constructed oversized sculptures of fruit (see Figure 5.3). However, rather than presenting produce in their "pure" and unblemished states, she portrayed them in the fullness of their garish deterioration, as mold spores anchor into the acrid peels and flesh and begin to take on a life of their own. Thousands of glass beads and semiprecious stones bedazzle the organic foam forms, mimicking the mold configurations she studied in her Manhattan studio (Newell-Hanson, 2019). Her choice of media in the glittering gems amplifies the sense of marvel and dread in the works. Ryan expressed this tension: "The sculptures are beautiful and pleasurable, but there's an ugliness and unease that comes with them" (quoted in Newell-Hanson, 2019, para. 2). While the bejeweled moldy fruit might allude to societal decadence, they also offer novel and, perhaps, pleasurable associations for biological decline.

Correspondingly, Rogan Brown's ethereal paper sculptures and Elin Thomas's endearing woolen works conjure new perceptions of mold and bacteria. Rather than faithfully illustrating these microorganisms, these British artists use them more as inspiration for their petri dish works. Brown explained, "Inevitably, [my sculptures] mix factual reference and flights of pure imagination" (Fleerackers & Brown, 2019, para. 3). In his 2014 installation, *Outbreak*, he explored the human microbiome through painstakingly hand-cut relief sculptures constructed from layered, achromatic paper cutouts and foam board spacers (see Figure 5.4). Using cozier media, Thomas (2018) employed various crochet, needle felting, and embroidery techniques to signify

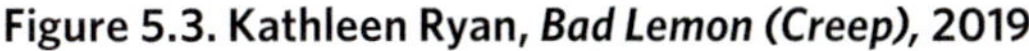

Figure 5.3. Kathleen Ryan, *Bad Lemon (Creep)*, 2019

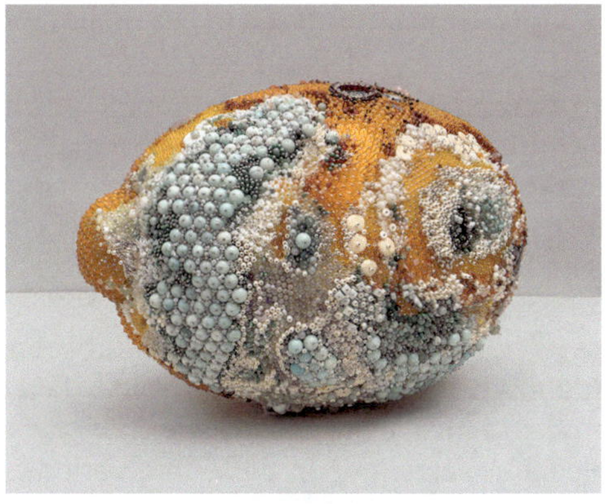

© and courtesy of Kathleen Ryan

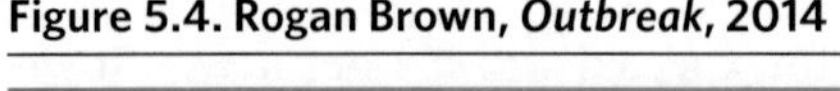

Figure 5.4. Rogan Brown, *Outbreak*, 2014

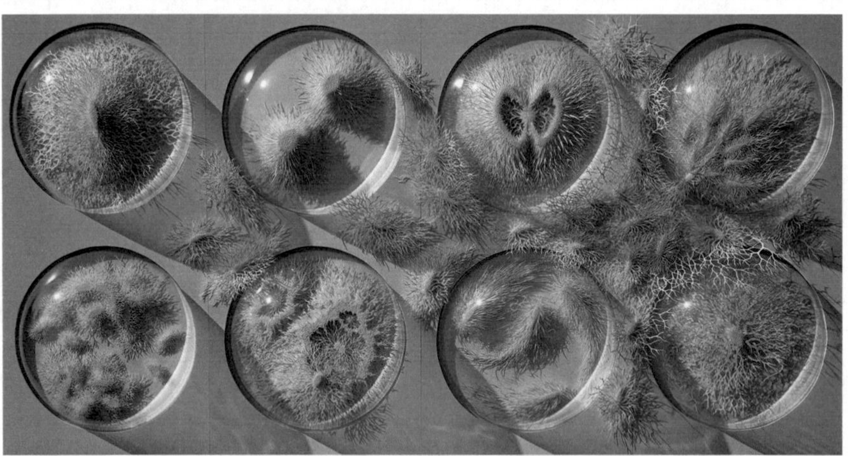

fuzzy fungal growth with a clear sense of whimsy. Her delicate felt fiber art, burgeoning with textural mold and lichen formations, evokes nostalgia and presents these growths as adorable and potentially loveable. Likewise, Brown positioned the organisms as exquisite, stating, "My objective was to create a piece that showcases the beauty of the bacterial world in order to modify our negative perception of bacteria, as the overwhelming majority of the microbes that inhabit us are beneficial" (Duru, 2014, para. 3).

Curriculum That Redefines Beauty

One way to expose students to the same types of natural processes examined in eco-artists' works and to allow them to explore this materiality firsthand might be to compost as a class; the act of composting itself is an exercise in embracing decadence and hastening biological decay (refer to Table 5.1). Some artists, such as Heikki Leis (2016), might serve as inspiration for these activities, as they have begun to experiment artistically with processes akin to composting—leaving out food remains and then exploring the surfaces of the overmature, moldering matter (see Figure 5.5). Like Leis, students can photograph the leftovers, or, similar to *kusōzu* artists, illustrate the remnants they observe. As the English term "still life" literally translates to "dead nature" in Romance languages (Hulsey & Trusty, n.d.), these activities are not as far removed from the European art genre's *vanitas* traditions, alluding to the impermanence of life (Berger, 2011), as one might think. As students engage in such artistic endeavors, they can benefit from documenting and reflecting upon their observations, impressions, and unfolding sensibilities.

Figure 5.5. Heikki Leis, *Beet Mold*, 2012

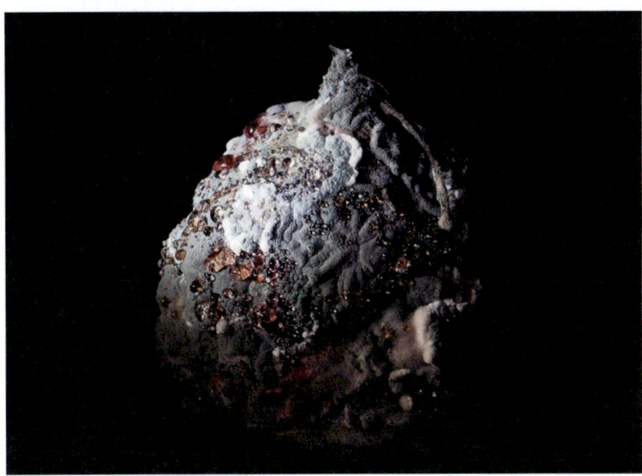

CO-CREATING WITH AGENTS OF DECOMPOSITION

Instead of artistically rendering the organisms that thrive in decomposing matter, some artists collaborate directly with them, allowing them to function as media and co-creators. Ever since Alexander Fleming, the discoverer of penicillin, "painted" with bacteria nearly a century ago onto an agar-filled petri dish, scientist-artists have been experimenting with this art form (Tsang, 2019), which is now supported by the American Society for Microbiology's Annual Agar Art Competition (Amsen, 2019). While agar artists (i.e., microbial artists) tend to exploit these organisms' illustrative powers, some contemporary artists use this media more conceptually to encourage reflection on our bacterially and fungally rich relationships with the world.

Artists Collaborating With Decomposers

By incorporating the human microbiome in their nontraditional agar art portraits, Portuguese artist Joana Ricou (2013), in *Other Self Portraits (Bellybutton Portraits)*, and British artist Mellissa Fisher (2015), in *Microbial Me*, challenged notions of the human body as discrete and pure, untouched by continual and manifold processes of generation and degeneration. As a twist on traditional agar art in offering a participatory experience, Ricou (n.d.), working with scientists, swabbed over 500 public members' navels and allowed the flora to grow in petri dishes. Through this project, they found over 2,400 species, averaging 67 species per participant. Similarly, Fisher

(2015), working with a scientist, constructed three-dimensional microbial self-portraits cast from her own face, where multiple microbial colonies grew (see Figure 5.6). In both artists' cases, their living portraits represented a unique culture of the bacteria and other organisms growing on the human body—perhaps just as much a part of the individual as any appendage. Ricou (n.d.) explained, "We are made of many things, and many types of things. Most of these things are alive, and not human. Our human and non-human selves coexist, collaborate, compete or ignore each other" (para. 1). In Fisher's (2015) work, the microbes from her own skin flourished on the surface, interacting with the bacteria already active in the environment, before eventually dying, performing the biological life cycle.

Embracing the agents of decomposition commonly shunned, Dutch designer Aniela Hoitink developed her own sustainable, living fabric from fungal mycelia—mushroom roots—which she then used to produce custom-made biodegradable garments. Working with universities and fashion designers, she plans to mass-produce these products in the near future

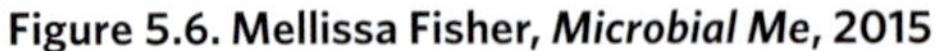

Figure 5.6. Mellissa Fisher, *Microbial Me*, 2015

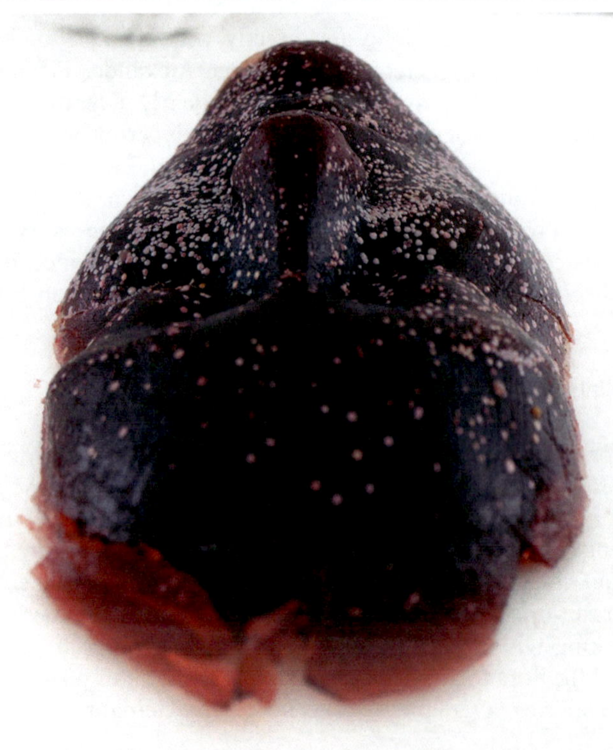

(Feitelberg, 2018). Her proof-of-concept fungi dress consisted of dozens of disc-shaped, skinlike mycelia meshes she shaped onto a dress form. Due to the organic nature of this waste-free process, this attire (see Figure 5.7) could be adapted and repaired as necessary, and eventually, when the fabric had become thoroughly worn, it could be composted. Not only does Hoitink's apparel inspire musing on materiality, it might also lead us to rethink our own identities and ways of being in relation to cycles of growth and decline (Nai & Meyer, 2016).

Curriculum Involving Co-Creation With Other Organisms

While, in popular culture, the artist may still be conceptualized as a solitary individual expressing a unique and profound inner vision, for several decades now, many contemporary artists have been placing relationality at the center of their art (Bourriaud, 1998/2002), both in content and practice. Some eco-artists, such as the ones described above, take this emphasis on relational entanglement further by actively cultivating and working within multispecies communities of microorganisms, fungi, plants, and animals. In such cases, traditional artistic processes with nonliving media are replaced with living media/co-producers that exert agency in the artmaking process.

Figure 5.7. Aniela Hoitink, *MycoTEX Dress*, 2016

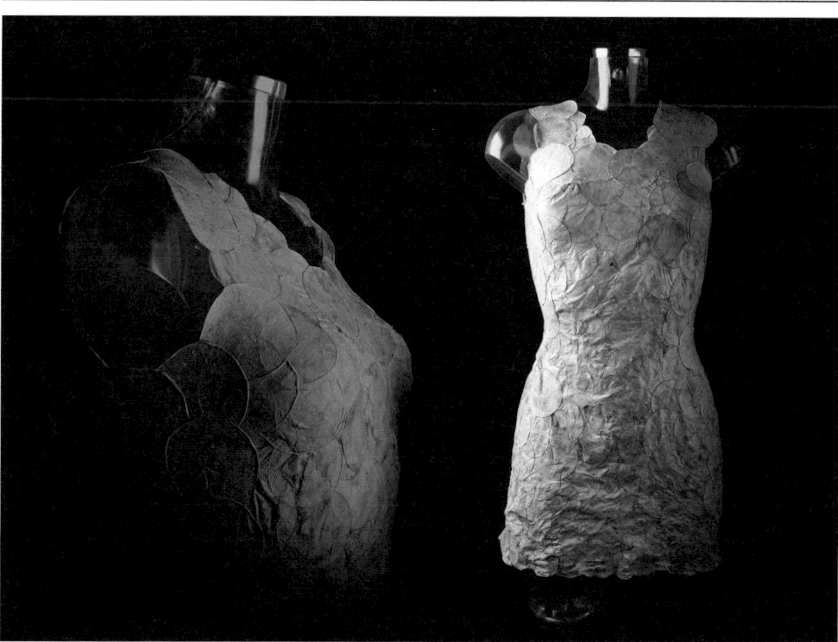

Due to this complex relationship, with the potential to produce unexpected results, such works are often positioned as artistic experiments.

While many of these artists' processes might appear to require specialized scientific knowledge and expensive equipment, interdisciplinary collaborations and partnerships can support acts of co-creation in K–12 learning contexts (refer to Table 5.1). For instance, art and science classes could join together to create agar art (microbial art) in school science labs. Additionally, co-creation could occur through smaller, scaled-down experiments in the art room, particularly at the elementary level. Microbial self-portraits could be created simply by strategically licking food items, sealing them in a reused sandwich bag, and observing the microbial colonies over time as they physically transform the food surfaces. With careful planning, students could design and perform their own ethical multispecies experiments, giving them the opportunity to begin to cultivate attentiveness and embrace uncertainty (van Dooren et al., 2016).

CULTURALLY ACKNOWLEDGING MORTALITY

Beyond multispecies interactions, cultural practices offer another avenue for cultivating dispositions of attentiveness and acceptance of biological processes, including our own mortality. Across the globe and over centuries, cultural communities have developed profound and often intense rituals and customs "to make sense of the mysteries surrounding death" (Hoy, 2013, p. 1). As modern, Western cultures increasingly depart from such rich traditions, art offers an avenue for perceiving these distancing practices and exploring alternative cultural modes of engaging with mortality—both human and nonhuman.

Artists Questioning Our Lust for Immortality

In their own way, each of the works in this chapter might be seen as promoting a subversive message by flaunting biological decay, a topic bordering on indecent in capitalist cultures. The following two artists go further down this path, challenging and exposing societal practices and cultural norms related to life and death. While the works presented up to this point could be incorporated into curriculum at any grade level, K–12, the following works might best be reserved for secondary grades or above due to their more mature themes and deeper cultural metaphors.

Korean artist Min Jeong Seo (2005), in her installation *To Live On*, presented the scene of a minimalist cathedral: under a large stained-glass window, she suspended dozens of cut-rose stalks in neat rows (see Figure 5.8). The churchlike window and the formal arrangement of the stalks below it, as choir members or organ pipes might be positioned, reinforce associations with

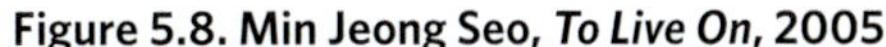

Figure 5.8. Min Jeong Seo, *To Live On*, 2005

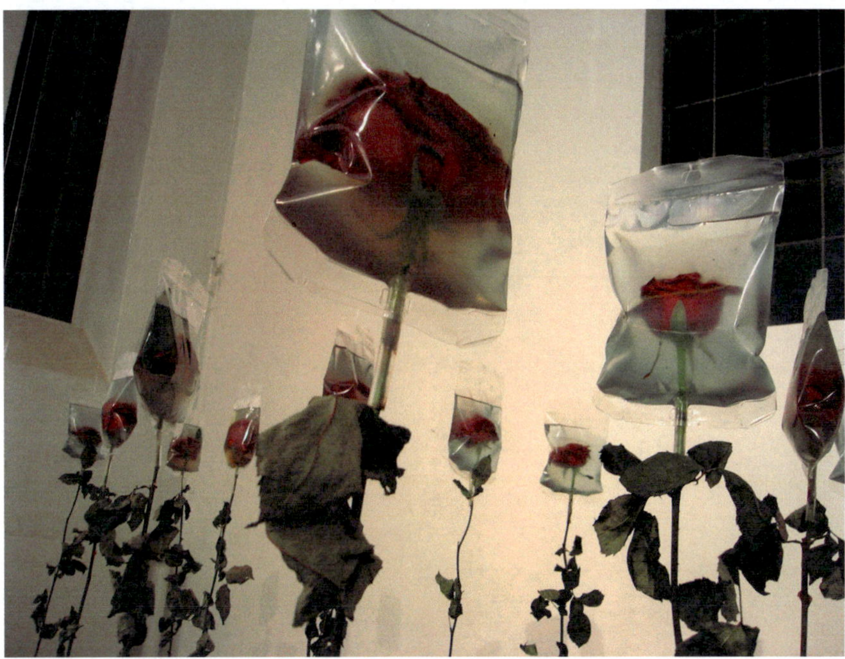

mortality already evoked by the precarious status of the roses. Significantly, Seo encased each crimson blossom in a fluid-filled medical infusion bag. The fluid from the plastic bags temporarily preserved the roses in the installation, extending their life in an "artificial and codependent" state (Nolte, n.d., para. 2). As the roses' plight might easily be equated to human efforts to prolong life, this work engages with ethical questions surrounding the continuation of life using medical advancements, particularly in relation to quality-of-life concerns (Nolte, n.d.). Additionally, Nolte (n.d.) claimed that the work, more generally, might "[persuade] us to confront our fears concerning sickness and death and our constant pursuit of youth" (para. 3).

While still engaging with conceptions of death and youth, Polish artist Andrez Wasilewski's (2008) *Pin-Ups Fruits* project embraces an even more lavish, decadent aesthetic. His series of paintings from this somewhat controversial project appropriate the visual culture of vintage pin-up girl posters, with each painting representing a single voluptuous woman (see Figure 5.9). As these figures cavort in the excesses of nature, in implausible landscapes of massive souring fruit, Wasilewski's images intermingle carnal pleasure with death. The women seem to eroticize the produce surrounding them, while the dwindling fruit project a temporality onto the women's physical forms: the grotesque becomes enthralling and the glamorous unsettling.

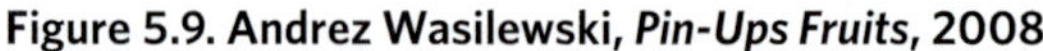

Figure 5.9. Andrez Wasilewski, *Pin-Ups Fruits*, 2008

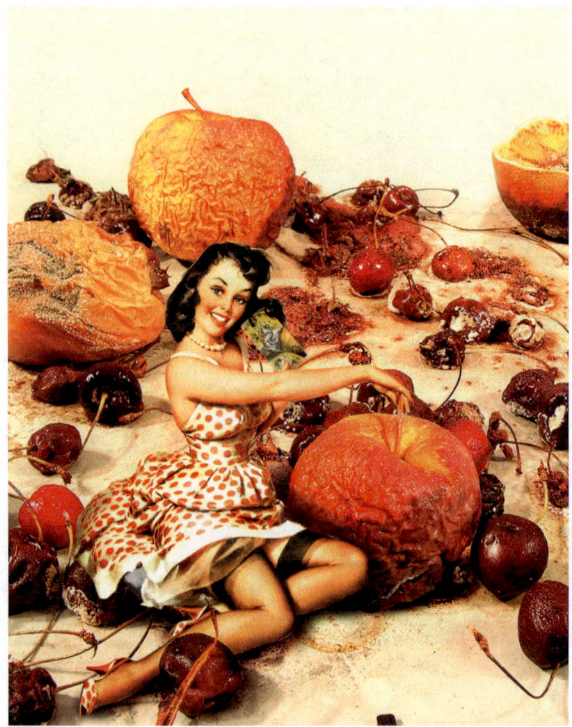

Warnke (2018) saw these images as a cultural critique: "[Wasilewski] is rebelling against pop culture, particularly advertising, by making things we would rather forget seem alluring" (para. 17). While the paintings might expose the underside of cultural desires, they might also offer viewers a more ecologically oriented avenue to direct desire—toward the succulence of our own earthliness.

Artists Confronting Us With the Mortality of Nonhuman Animal Life

Thus far, the artworks featured in this chapter have focused on the decomposition of plant life and existence of microbial and fungal life, which bask in decomposition, with connections to human life. Nonhuman animal life could also be an important area to explore in seeking to cultivate students' ecological sensibilities, although this arena is fraught with complexities (Kallio-Tavin, 2020). K–12 art teachers should reflect upon a range of sociocultural and ethical concerns when selecting artworks that engage with this topic. For instance, the fact that humans regularly inflict harm, both directly and indirectly, on nonhuman animal populations in the service of human endeavors, including art, is worth considering. Additionally, community members, including parents, administrators, and students, may be uneasy about the subject of death in classrooms. While I personally would appreciate seeing students, parents, and administrators unaffronted by exposure to all forms of life in various stages of composition and decomposition, as could naturally be experienced in outdoor spaces, teachers must also be attuned to students' psychological readiness, particularly as research (e.g., Arndt et al., 2004; Kasser & Sheldon, 2000) suggests that inciting awareness of mortality in students who do not yet have an ecological framework can exacerbate environmentally harmful behavior. Ernest Becker (1973), in outlining his Terror Management Theory, made the case that even the presence of nonhuman animals can serve as an existential threat, a reminder of our own creatureliness. Thus, care must be taken when introducing these images and issues in classrooms. Some ethical and pedagogical parameters for the selection of artworks include the following:

1. Nonhuman animals were *not* harmed in the making of the work. For example, Damien Hirst's works of taxidermied animals, where animals were killed to create the works (Voon, 2017), would not meet this standard.
2. Animal death is *not* handled in a clinical or perverse manner, even if the work might seem to encourage other important ecological understandings. For example, Sarah Perry's (2009) sculpture "Skin Deep," where a skinned mouse is strung up inside a transparent plastic human anatomical toy, would be excluded despite its potential to inspire reflection on the similarities between human and nonhuman animal forms.
3. Animal death is *not* presented in a way that might alarm students or encourage a spirit of voyeurism, even if this response is not the artist's stated intent. For example, Craig Stecyk's (1983) stark black-and-white photographs, in the style of Weegee's gritty crime scene photography of the 1930s and 1940s, depict animals killed on highways. Because of their shocking style and methods, which included skinning the corpses, these works would be unlikely to cultivate students' relational understandings of mortality or ease their existential anxieties despite Stecyk's (n.d.) claims that the works "pay homage" to the animals (para. 2).

The following two artists' works serve as examples of works that could meet the criteria described above as they address the mortality of nonhuman animal life, but do so in ways that inspire empathy and reflections on relationality over feelings of shock and estrangement.

In the installation *As Above, So Below*, Kaitlin Bryson (2015) constructed a tomblike structure resembling the form of a hive—a "microcatacomb"

(Bryson, n.d.-b, para. 1)—from plant and animal products to honor the deaths of 189 bees (see Figure 5.10). Affixed to this conical structure, fluffy, wool-lined, beeswax dishes serve as final resting places for the 189 small bee bodies. According to Courtney (2015), the work commemorates the honeybee ritual of removing deceased bees from the hive. As bee populations have continued to decline sharply in recent years (McFall-Johnsen & Woodward, 2019), this memorial holds special significance, with implications for human–nonhuman animal relations.

Emma Kisiel (2011) likewise drew public attention to animal welfare concerns while commemorating death. In her photographic series *At Rest*, the artist documented the deaths of animals hit by moving vehicles on American roadways. In one image from the series (see Figure 5.11), a dead fox rests on the roadside surrounded by a ring of flowers and stones the artist arranged. The artist explained that she did not move or alter the bodies of the animals documented in this series in any way (Kisiel, 2012). Rather, she assumed the practice of a person attending a human death-related ceremony, such as a funeral or body viewing, by quietly and respectfully visiting the deceased animal and assembling a memorial. Kisiel claimed that her works highlight the "the sublime, the grotesque, the lure of the macabre" (para. 2), while emphasizing "the sacredness of all things" (para. 3).

In using biodegradable materials that bees and other nonhuman animals featured in the works might encounter on a regular basis, these artists' works attempt to honor them in life and death. Both works tap into our collective desire to acknowledge life and loss. I witnessed this human propensity when my own children, upon encountering a quivering bird embryo in a cracked eggshell, spontaneously constructed their own makeshift memorial to the life

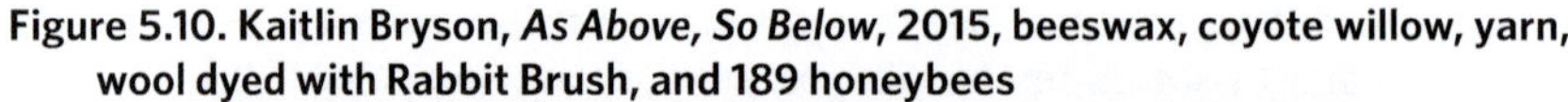

Figure 5.10. Kaitlin Bryson, *As Above, So Below*, 2015, beeswax, coyote willow, yarn, wool dyed with Rabbit Brush, and 189 honeybees

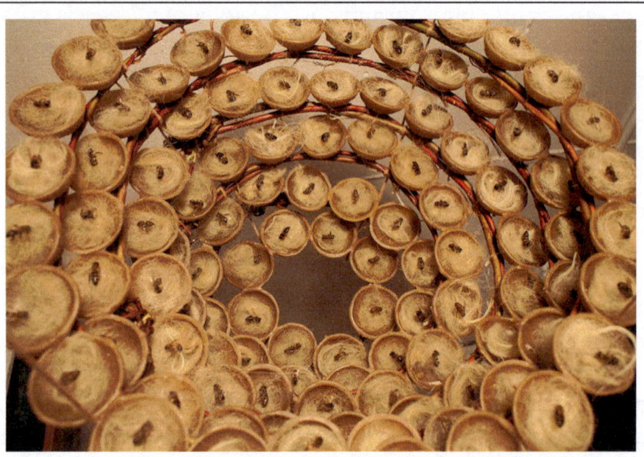

Figure 5.11. Emma Kisiel, *At Rest*, 2011

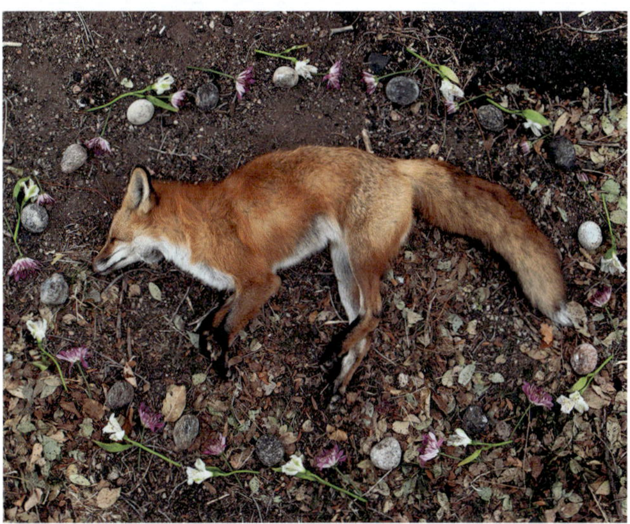

Emmakisiel.com

slowly extinguishing before them (see Figure 5.12). Many of the artists in this chapter present mortality to us so that we might mature and authentically acknowledge the mortality that defines our existence. However, when mortality already feels present, as was the case with my daughters when they happened upon the egg on the road, such art might offer us an avenue to contend with and emotionally process the transience of life.

Curriculum Culturally Acknowledging Mortality

Given that rich death traditions are increasingly absent or limited in Western countries, secondary students may be encouraged to grapple with the issue of how society might better acknowledge mortality, death, and those who are grieving (refer to Table 5.1). For instance, students could be asked to challenge a cultural value or norm surrounding mortality in an artwork or to invent a new cultural practice related to mortality. In addition to human deaths, the loss of nonhuman animals could also be acknowledged. When engaging with topics more generally or indirectly related to mortality such as the capitalist practices mentioned at the beginning of this chapter (e.g., food preparation and cosmetic procedures), the corresponding artistic responses need not be wholly solemn; contemporary artists are known for their divergent thinking, playfulness, and irony in critiquing convention. Whether lighthearted or somber, such artistic engagement by students is likely to spur crucial dialogues on how to recognize and value our embeddedness in natural systems and cycles.

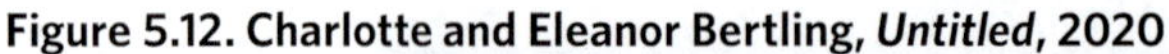

Figure 5.12. Charlotte and Eleanor Bertling, *Untitled*, 2020

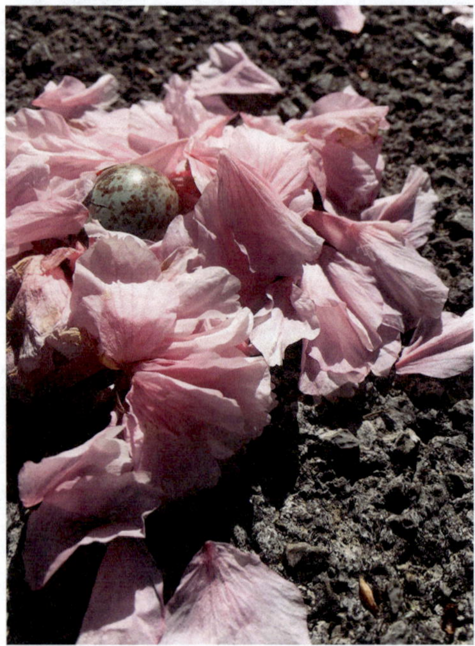

CONCLUSION

The artworks and curriculum highlighted in this chapter make the mortality and multiplicity of life physically present, able to be sensed and experienced in all of its soiled splendor, so that students can comprehend it, honor it, and, perhaps, rejoice in facets of it. Destabilizing cultural narratives of individuality and superiority, survival and competition, art education as ecopedagogy can emphasize interdependence and shared biological experience. In conclusion and in the spirit of (com)postmodernity, let's consider how art curricula might inspire us all to derive comfort from, or at least courageously accede to, the biological rhythms and cycles that surround us.

QUESTIONS FOR EDUCATOR REFLECTION

1. What are your associations with death and mortality? How comfortable do you feel discussing these topics?
2. How comfortable do you feel in the presence of decomposition? What are your associations with decomposition?

3. How might we learn to cherish the impermanence of life? How might we begin to see beauty in *all* the stages of life? How might these perceptions be important socially and ecologically?
4. How might art teachers help students embrace their biological identities and see themselves as deeply embedded in natural systems and cycles without inspiring unhealthy levels of fear and anxiety?
5. How might art teachers acknowledge and cultivate multispecies communities, particularly involving agents of decomposition, inside and outside their art classrooms?

CHAPTER 6

Collecting and Visualizing Data for Awareness

What might ancient Assyrian relief sculptures of conquests, mythology, and court life have in common with Incan quipus, strings encoding numeric values as knots, or 20th-century Hmong story quilts? People across time and culture have translated stories and information into easily accessible forms that can be experienced or used by the public. Notably, many cultures have designed objects and images to communicate information, both scientific and magico-religious, surrounding the more-than-human world. Ancient Babylonians inscribed geographic knowledge as maps inscribed in clay, 11th-century Chinese astronomers designed celestial atlases, and Paleolithic peoples communicated their knowledge of large mammals through naturalistic animal paintings on cave walls.

Now in the era of big data and media saturation, the public is often inundated with massive quantities of information. Large databases, including those housing environmental data, are easily accessible online. To combat feelings of data deluge, confusion, and apathy, artists and designers have sought to story, or humanize, data—to communicate information to the public in meaningful ways. In so doing, they have turned to data visualization, "the visual representation of data in order to uncover and understand trends and patterns" (Klein, 2014, p. 27). Similarly, eco-artists, scientists, and designers have turned to a subset of data visualization practices, termed "eco-visualizations." These visualizations, or artworks, engage with ecological, environmental, and sustainability data and surrounding issues with the goal of educating the public and inciting sustainable attitudes and behaviors (Holmes, 2009).

Comprising dense scatter plots, striking infographics, interactive online tools, and multisensory works of contemporary art, eco-visualizations utilize diverse strategies and media. Though multidisciplinary teams are commonplace, eco-visualization practices tend to most align with the disciplinary backgrounds of their creators (Dean & Bertling, 2020). Thus, eco-visualizations originating in STEM fields are more likely to use conventional graphics to communicate information quickly and accurately, while the eco-visualizations of contemporary artists tend to employ more emotive, immersive, metaphoric strategies to contextualize content, facilitate audience engagement, and provoke nuanced readings of data (Bertling et al., 2021).

Just as eco-visualizations differ by form, eco-visualization content varies, addressing a range of environmental topics and issues. While most eco-visualizations highlight environmental concerns, some works draw attention to unique organism and ecosystem capabilities, particularly those that might play a role in mitigating ecological harm. These works raise public awareness of present phenomena and point toward projected futures.

Capable of captivating, educating, and inspiring viewers and their creators, these visualizations can serve multiple pedagogical functions. This chapter will introduce several contemporary eco-visualization artists whose work unsettles anthropocentric modes of being in the world, renders ecological relationships visible, and emboldens sustainable acts. Subsequently, this chapter will offer guidance for empowering students to engage in collecting and visualizing such data toward these purposes as part of an ecopedagogical curriculum. Some themes to be explored in the art classroom include consumption and progress (see Table 6.1 for an outline).

VISUALIZING THE PRESENT

As the biosphere is currently experiencing unprecedented threats due to human enterprise, the present offers unlimited data for artists and designers to decipher and impart to audiences. Pollution levels, energy consumption, and mining impacts are only some of the topics data artists are exploring and illuminating. In so doing, artists give us all an opportunity to see aspects of our lives, communities, and actions in new ways—from the food we eat, the energy we consume, and the products we purchase to the ecosystems in which we are enmeshed.

Artists Consuming Data

Unexpectedly using food as a medium for information, Data Cuisine collaborative research workshops have engaged students and teachers with local foods and local data, including data related to environmental issues. For instance, one Bostonian Data Cuisine indirectly addressed food-distribution-related carbon impacts through a "smoothie drinking performance" (Rosenstock, 2016, line 3). In *Deconstructed Food Miles Smoothie*, a performer consumes a deconstructed smoothie, slurping each disparate smoothie ingredient simultaneously (see Figure 6.1). The length of each straw equates to the distance the ingredient traveled to reach Boston. Based upon the exaggerated straw length and corresponding labels, the thousands of miles the ingredient traveled before arriving in the smoothie are

Table 6.1. Some Curricular Applications of Themes of Consumption and Progress

Big Ideas	Grade Levels	Ecopedagogical Goals	Key Concepts	Discussion/Reflection Prompts	Possible Artistic Responses
Consumption	3–12*	Developing awareness for human acts of consumption, both sustainable and unsustainable. Recognizing ecological processes that sustain life and biodiversity.	Consumption can be sustainable or unsustainable. Ecological processes can sustain life and biodiversity. Data visualizations, or eco-visualizations, can draw attention to sustainable and unsustainable systems and inspire ecologically sustainable actions.	When is consumption beneficial? When is consumption not beneficial? To whom is it beneficial or not beneficial? How can consumption be sustainable? What sources might we draw upon to learn sustainable ways of being? (Traditional ecological knowledge? The workings of local ecosystems?)	Visualize local/regional data surrounding • an unsustainable human practice, • a sustainable human practice, and/or • a beneficial nonhuman act of consumption, through graphical means, digital photograph manipulation, sculpture, or site-specific installation.
Progress	9–12	Recognizing EuroWestern ideas of linear progress can perpetuate harm (e.g., colonialism and ecological destruction). Considering the implications of climate change for more-than-human communities.	Change does not always lead to progress. "Progress" can be interpreted differently; a sign of progress to one group might be an act of violence to another group, species, or ecosystem.	What associations do you have with the idea of progress? How has the notion of progress played out in our country's history? How are cultural ideas of progress played out on the land? How does climate change relate to progress? How can data visualizations show the progression of time? How can data visualizations make climate change's progression felt? How might certain non-Western ideas of time lead us to rethink linear progress?	Visualize regional environmental projections as • Two-dimensional works with projected environmental impacts symbolized through subject matter and design choices • A site-specific installation in the school/community

*The wording of key concepts and prompts will likely need to be modified for use with students in earlier grades.

Figure 6.1. Joshua Pablo Rosenstock, *Deconstructed Food Miles Smoothie*, 2016

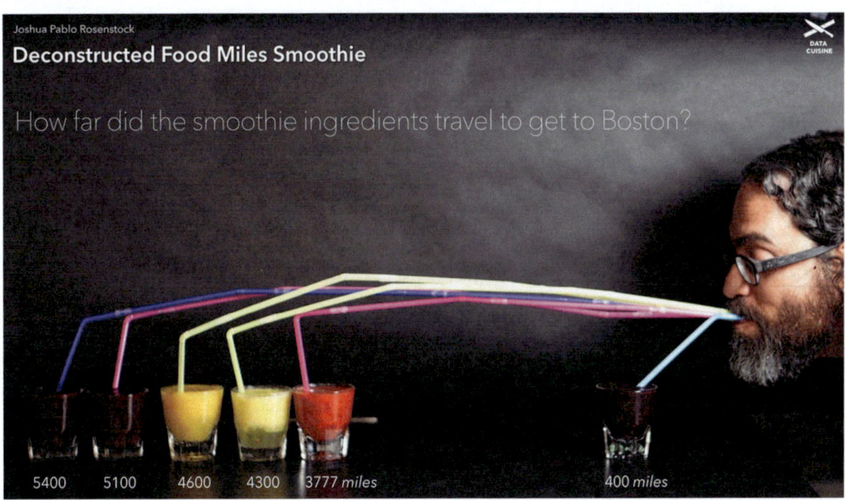

Figure 6.2. Ben Snell, Steven Braun, and Ann McDonald, *Unequal Exposure*, 2016

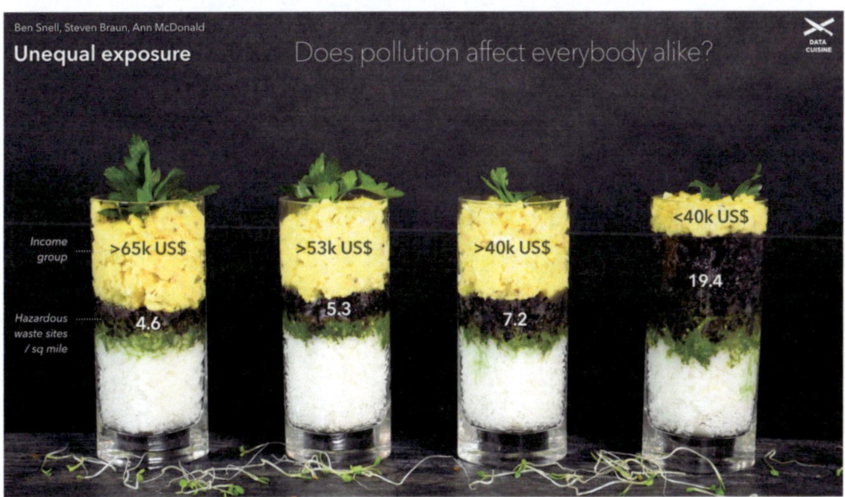

clearly visible. Another Data Cuisine (Snell et al., 2016) from the same Boston workshop tackled an environmental justice issue: unequal proximity to environmental hazards based upon income level (see Figure 6.2). Four layered rice dishes demonstrate these class-based inequities. As each dish to the right signifies a lower income group, the density of hazardous-waste sites per square mile increases from 4.6% to 19.4%. Correspondingly, the size of the black rice layer, symbolizing the density of hazardous waste sites, increases. In the last dish on the right, green pesto leeches further through the white rice, embodying the heightened pollution exposure that lower-income households are more likely to face.

Artists Accentuating Consumption

In *Nuage Vert*, Finnish artist duo Helen Evans and Heiko Hansen, known as "HeHe" (2008), collaborated with Helsinki Energy to visualize the power plant's changing energy output as a green cloud—a green laser light reflecting off water vapor the plant emitted (see Figure 6.3). As residents reduced their energy consumption each evening, prompted by a community initiative to unplug devices between 7:00 and 8:00 p.m., the light projection strengthened. While the cloud initially might have functioned as an emblem of collective energy consumption, Evans (2008) suggested that as the cloud grew and energy consumption decreased, the glowing vapor eventually visualized the power of collective community effort. The aesthetic spectacle of real-time energy data raised awareness surrounding urban emissions and mobilized community participation in the energy-saving initiative.

Two eco-visualizations, Dillon Marsh's (2014) copper mine visualization and Semiconductor's (2014) visualization of forest carbon capture,

Figure 6.3. HeHe (Helen Evans and Heiko Hansen), *Nuage Vert* (Green Cloud), 2008

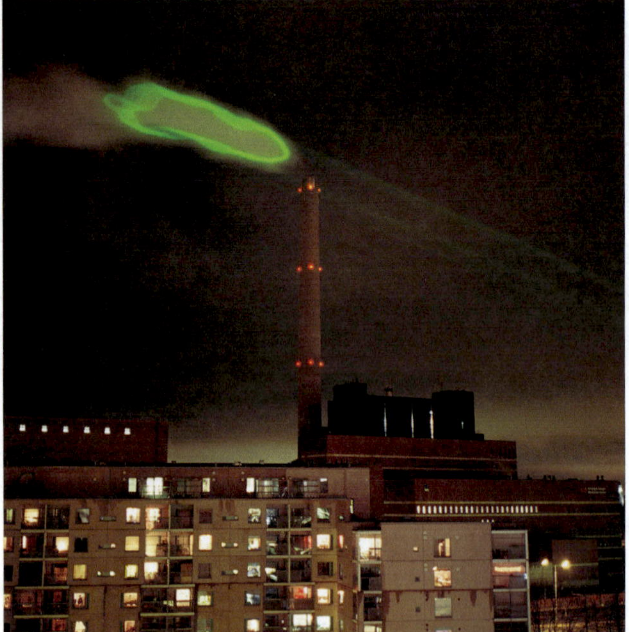

have striking visual similarities. Taught in conjunction, the works can inspire dialogues surrounding our relationship with the Earth. While a large sphere plays a prominent role in each work, the environmental processes and practices that have unfolded in relation to each sphere are radically different. In Marsh's (2014) work, the copper ball symbolizes copper ore extracted from one South African mine (see Figure 6.4). Through Marsh's digital insertion of this proportionally accurate orb into the mine photograph, viewers can see the devastation the hunt for ore has wreaked on the landscape and might question whether the material was worth the environmental harm. In contrast, Semiconductor's (2014) work, produced by Ruth Jarman and Joe Gerhardt, manifests the carbon captured by one United Kingdom forest annually as a large, textured sphere resting in the forest (see Figure 6.5). Fabricated from wooden hexagonal and pentagonal plates inscribed with carbon release and absorption data, this spherical data object serves as a physical reminder of the vital work forests and other ecosystems perform. Whereas Marsh's (2014) visualization highlights ecological tolls, Semiconductor's (2014) foregrounds ecological restoration and possibility.

Figure 6.4. Dillon Marsh, *Nababeep South Mine—302,500 Tonnes of Copper*, 2014

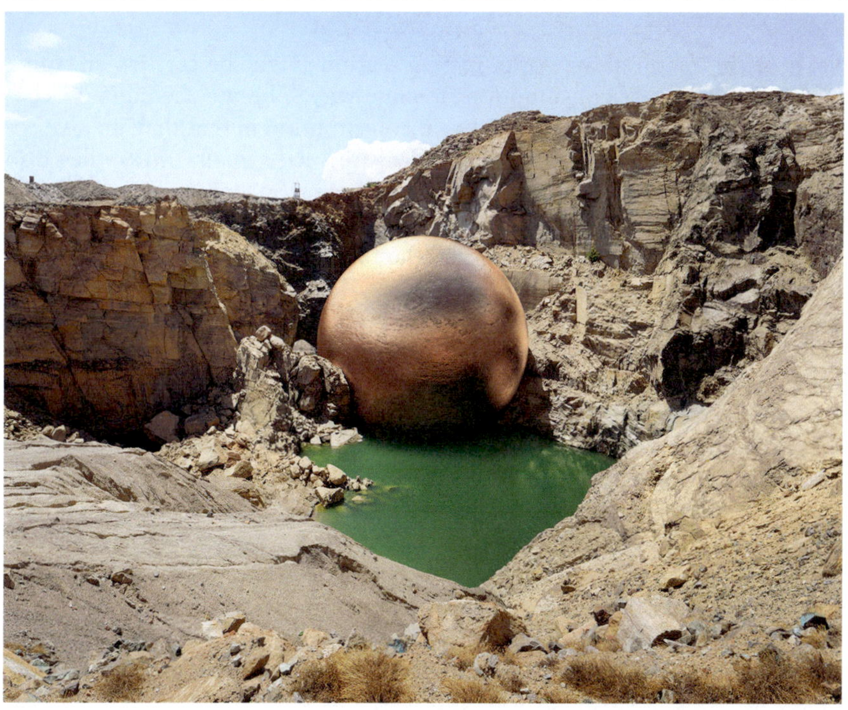

Figure 6.5. Semiconductor: Ruth Jarman and Joe Gerhardt, *Cosmos*, 2014

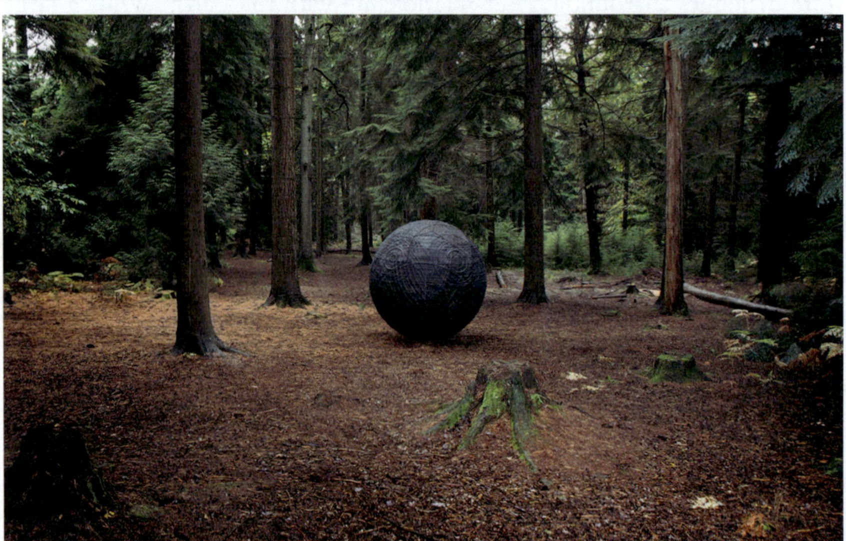

Curriculum Visualizing Consumption

Each of the featured artworks in this section might be seen as engaging with the concept of consumption in some way. Though the culinary eco-visualizations allude to actual physical consumption in that they involve edible materials, like many of the other featured eco-visualizations, they also tackle consumption in a more abstract sense: energy consumption, natural resource consumption, and the involuntary absorption of environmental hazards into our bodies. Conversely, the forest biomass engages in an ecologically beneficial form of consumption by sequestering carbon.

In the K–12 art classroom and other art education contexts, students could explore consumption as a theme and consider ways in which it manifests in their lives and more-than-human communities, particularly through the lenses of ecology, sustainability, and equity (refer to Table 6.1). Students in earlier grades could consider more concrete examples of consumption, such as pesticide ingestion and plastic waste, while secondary students may be ready to explore more figurative forms, as in natural disasters "consuming" natural and built environments. Such exploration need not focus exclusively on troubling topics: Students could also explore equitable and sustainable acts of consumption. For instance, students can investigate the vital activities various species and ecosystems carry out: bees provide pollination services as they feed on nectar and pollen, sunflowers absorb and neutralize heavy metals and toxins in soil, and wetlands sequester carbon. Likewise, students can examine more sustainable human acts of consumption, such as crop rotation and renewable energy usage.

As one approach to engaging with these topics, students could take on the role of artist inquirer and researcher by developing questions for inquiry, collecting data aimed at answering these questions, analyzing the data, and visualizing it for the school and community. Such data collection would often occur locally and outdoors, for instance, as students conduct bird or butterfly counts, test water quality in local water bodies, or survey local parks for invasive plants. These types of projects could also function as citizen science, public engagement in scientific research. They could involve community-driven projects or align with more global research investigations. Since students may study science-related content and use statistical skills in data-analysis phases, interdisciplinary collaborations, particularly with STEM classes, could support these activities.

The final visualization component falls clearly within the realm of the arts. When communicating data trends and patterns to audiences, students could employ various artistic conventions, such as elements and principles of design or contemporary creative strategies (Marshall & Donahue, 2014), to communicate meaning. Eco-visualizations can story the data by situating it in a context that closely relates to its origins, such as carbon-absorption data located in a forest (refer to Figure 6.5). Alternately, eco-visualizations could integrate data into entirely new contexts, such as environmental hazard exposure data in rice dishes (refer to Figure 6.2), to create visual metaphors that inspire new associations and dialogues surrounding the topic. Irrespective of the contextualization strategy, one important goal for students would be to facilitate audiences' comprehension of and empathy with the phenomena.

VISUALIZING OUR FUTURE

Despite the magnitude of current ecological challenges, which are being felt already across the globe, future projections are grimmer. Climate disruption, biodiversity decline, human population growth, and unchecked consumption foretell a planet that can no longer support complex life in the coming centuries. Many contemporary eco-artists are recognizing the severity of this more-than-human predicament and finding ways to make this gravity palpable. These works seek to awaken the public to these trajectories and catalyze ecologically responsible action.

Artists Visualizing the Extinction Crisis

Within our current environmental context of escalating avian extinction rates, Krista Caballero and Frank Ekeberg's (2013–2018) installation series envisages the past, present, and future of this crisis. As birds have played a vital role in foretelling weather changes and disasters historically, in *Birding the Future*, birds are harbingers of this human-induced environmental crisis as well as its victims. Site-specific installations, held at locations around the globe, convey locally and regionally specific ornithological data while making connections to larger extinction trends.

Through audio, video, stereographs, and sculpture, ecological data become a visceral experience. Stereoscopic cards showcase images, scientific information, and poetic text. Sounds of local bird species' songs, some of which are translated into Morse code, filter through installation spaces. The timing and sequencing of these audio recordings is particularly poignant; Caballero and Ekeberg (2014) explained that each recording is timed to the length of the exhibit, matching the progression of time until the century's end. As the recording progresses, the sounds decline as more species are silenced in accordance with their expected extinction date. Each installation beckons visitors to revisit their relations to birds; contemplate their profound contribution to cultural histories, mythologies, and ontologies; and consider the unfathomable tragedy their extinction would represent.

Artists Visualizing Climate Change

Similar to Caballero and Ekeberg's (2014) engagement with species-extinction projection data, many eco-artists are visualizing climate change data. While some artists are showing how climate change is already occurring, such as the Tempestry Project (n.d.), where annual climate data is knitted into wall tapestries and can be compared with previous years' tapestries, other artists are visualizing the future impact of these trends. Such artists employ a range of media and strategies to make these climate futures feel imminent and tangible.

Site-specific installations and performances, through their physicality and situatedness in the places viewers inhabit, may be particularly effective in making climate change projections palpable. In recent years, several artists have undertaken this type of eco-visualization project, with specific attention to sea-level rise. Adam Kuby's (2017a) *Sea Level 2080* project documents projected sea levels using stretched fabric. When Kuby open-sourced the project in conjunction with the 2019 United Nations Climate Summit, artists, students, and activists across the globe had the opportunity to take ownership. In 27 countries, participants stretched and staked, held, or walked large swathes of blue fabric to the height of projected 2080 sea levels (Micro Galleries, 2020). With similar aims, Kuby's (2017b) site-specific installation *Sea Level Clock #1* drew attention to future sea levels (see Figure 6.6). Emerging from the ocean's surface, the spiraling structure served as a point of reference for fluctuating sea level heights. The steel and

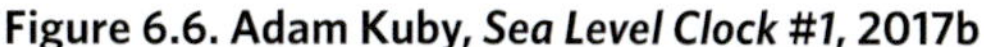

Figure 6.6. Adam Kuby, *Sea Level Clock #1*, 2017b

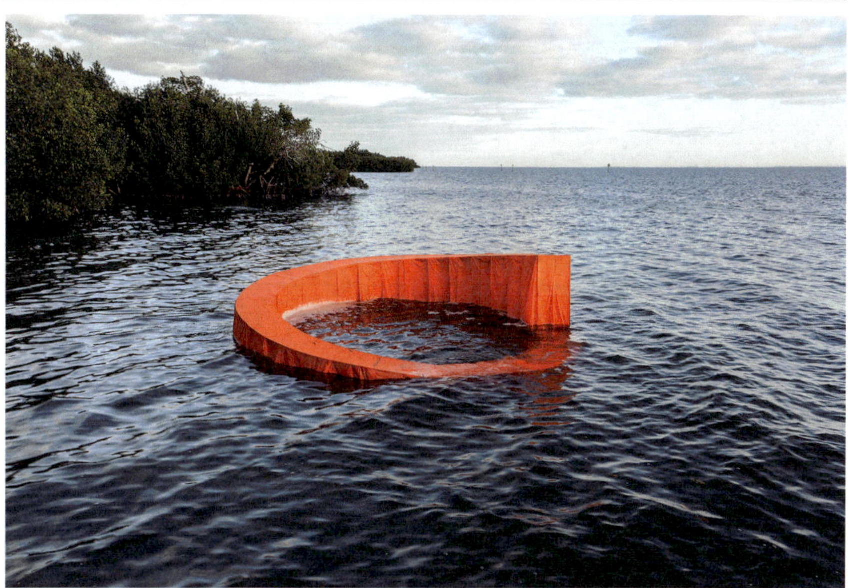

fabric form was intended to serve as a prototype for a more permanent sculpture that could track climate-change-related sea level rises over time. Even so, the work's temporary presence serves as a visual reminder of sea-level-change trajectories.

Like Adam Kuby in *Sea Level Clock #1,* Timo Aho and Pekka Niittyvirta (2018) have inserted visual reminders of future sea levels into the landscape. Their site-specific light installation *Lines (57° 59′ N, 7° 16′W)*, set in a remote Scottish coastal town, makes climate change impacts unmistakable: future storm surge heights, expected within the century, are represented as searing, glowing lines, scarring the built environment (see Figure 6.7). In *Coastline Paradox*, the artists (2020) expanded the scale and complexity of this data visualization strategy using online media (see Figure 6.8). Merging multiple climate-change datasets surrounding population displacement, temperature change, and sea-level rise; elevation models; and three-dimensional rendering via Google Maps and Street View, this global interactive online platform allows users to select global locations and years between 2000 and 2300 to see how specific coastal areas will be affected (Aho et al., 2020). As with *Lines,* glowing lines traverse the various sites in *Coastline Paradox*. But as various cities are compared, with an array of impacts described for each site, the online platform emphasizes the geographically disproportionate impacts of climate change: while the entire globe will be affected, certain regions are especially vulnerable.

Figure 6.7. Timo Aho and Pekka Niittyirta, *Lines (57° 59′ N, 7° 16′W)*, 2018

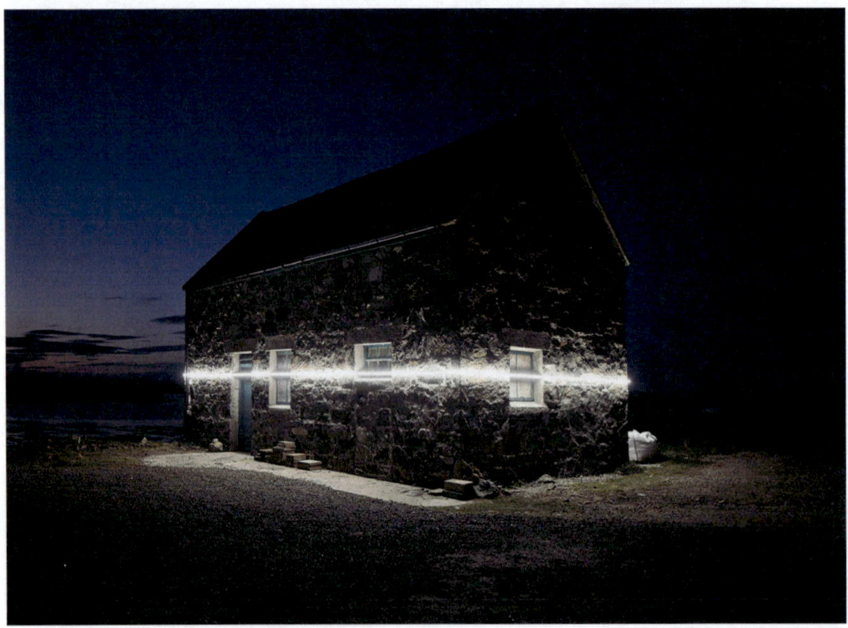

Photo credit: Pekka Niittyvirta

Figure 6.8. Timo Aho and Pekka Niittyirta in collaboration with Google Arts and Culture, *Coastline Paradox*, 2020

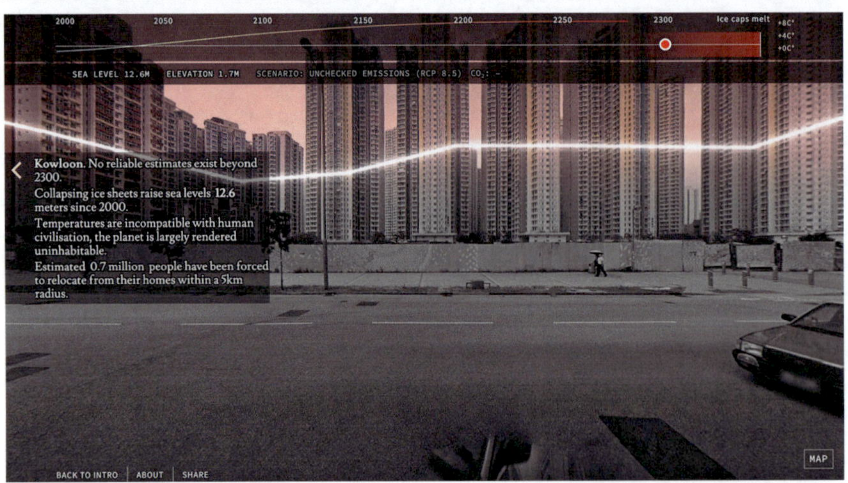

Like the works described above, Jill Pelto's (2021a) work *Rising Mitigation* visualizes sea-level-rise data, via the blue line traversing the work, and includes future projections, signified by dotted lines (see Figure 6.9). However, in visualizing these data, Pelto looks for solutions or, at least, strategies to mitigate these trajectories, with attention to renewable-energy usage. Her mixed-media work depicts a typical Maine coastal wetland scene with a house situated along a shoreline. Beyond the house's solar-paneled roof, a stacked bar graph extends into the sky, symbolizing Maine's energy usage between 1960 and 2018, including renewable-energy usage (Pelto, 2021b). Overlapping the scene, the sea-level data show three varying trajectories, with the least-severe 2100 projection dependent upon human mitigative actions, such as renewable-energy adoption. The difference between the 8-inch sea-level-rise prediction and the 19-inch prediction is substantial

Figure 6.9. Jill Pelto, *Rising Mitigation*, 2021a

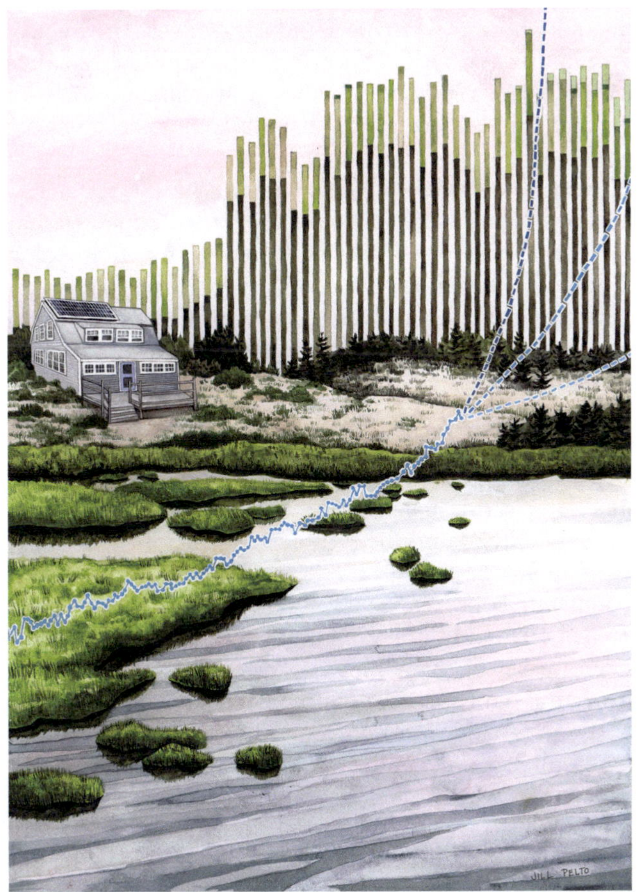

(Pelto, 2021b), foregrounding the importance of immediate action to preserve Maine coastlines. Due to her use of media typically available in K–12 art classrooms, watercolor, colored pencil, and acrylic paint, and her use of standard graphic techniques with which students might be familiar from their math classes, her work may be particularly accessible and appropriate for K–12 school contexts.

Curriculum Visualizing Progress

By focusing on the future consequences of human actions, these works present a world where human "progress" has led to catastrophic ends. These visualizations may lead us to question fundamental Euro-Western settler colonialist notions that assume change is good and always leads to progress (Bowers, 2002). In relation to the ecological health and integrity of the Earth's ecosystems, modern "progress" has hardly been positive. Consider the ecological toll of the Industrial Revolution, mining, industrialized farming, fracking, and, now, private space-industry travel. The by-products—air and water pollution, ocean acidification, soil degradation, deforestation, biodiversity and species-extinction crises, and climate change—have compounded danger and suffering. We have all experienced profound loss, whether we realize it or not.

Students need to comprehend and contend with this state of affairs (refer to Table 6.1). Secondary students could begin their exploration of progress by examining historical artworks associated with settler colonialism. In the United States, 19th-century Hudson River School landscape paintings or other works associated with westward expansion and Manifest Destiny would apply. As settler colonialism, the subjugation of Indigenous peoples, land exploitation, and our current ecological condition are deeply intertwined, students might consider how colonialist ideals and practices focused on infinite growth have played out on the land and continue to shape the present. Foundational understandings of environmental colonialism can enrich students' later eco-visualization activities as they consider how these trajectories might extend into the future.

Prior to visualizing ecological data, students could play a role in identifying environmental concerns, especially those heavily impacting their communities. Both human and nonhuman impacts can be explored, from rises in tick-borne diseases to dwindling frog populations. To assist students in locating projection data surrounding the environmental topics they identified and to streamline the research process, art educators could compile a list of relevant online sources and databases. Visualizations might take many forms; students can work independently or with partners to create two-dimensional visualizations of impending change, in keeping with Jill Pelto's approaches, or work as a class to produce a large-scale public installation drawing widespread attention to an issue of particular community concern.

CONCLUSION

Misiaszek (2020, 2021) discussed how environmental devastation is often perceived erroneously as distant: distant geographically, happening far afield; historically, transpiring in the distant future; and socially, only impacting "less than human" others. Eco-visualizations can perform an important, "de-distancing" (Misiaszek, 2021, p. 2), ecopedagogical function. Not only can eco-visualizations counter cultural misconceptions by foregrounding scientific data, they can also establish, on an emotional level, our proximity to and interconnection with ecological systems. This educational process can be particularly effective when eco-visualizations are situated locally (i.e., engaging with local issues, visualizing local or regional data, and displayed in the community) and employ the divergent practices of the arts (e.g., evocative qualities, metaphor, and multisensory elements). While the works featured in this chapter can support students' investigations of themes of consumption and progress, the works in the following chapter build upon these ideas to delve further into cultural critique.

QUESTIONS FOR EDUCATOR REFLECTION

1. What social and environmental issues affect your students' lives? What notable ecological processes are occurring locally?
2. What local or regional online databases might students access to investigate these issues or ecological processes?
3. What school or community resources or features could support data collection (e.g., a school parking lot could be tested for water-runoff toxicity)?
4. What interdisciplinary connections seem inherent to the issues or processes identified above? How could you integrate this learning (e.g., guest speakers, virtual field trips, or collaborations with other subject-area teachers)?
5. If you teach at the secondary level, how comfortable do you feel interpreting or conducting descriptive statistical analyses (e.g., mean, mode, median, and range) and simple graphical analyses? What are some ways you might refamiliarize yourself with these statistical concepts and skills?
6. What are some ways students might humanize, story, or visceralize data—making their eco-visualizations evocative and emotionally impactful?

CHAPTER 7

Confronting Capitalocene Violence

What drives dominant human society to destroy the very ecosystems that support them? Various terms have been used to describe the era in which we find ourselves: Anthropocene (Crutzen & Stoermer, 2000), Plantationocene (Haraway, 2015), Necrocene (McBrien, 2016), Homogenocene (Mann, 2011), and Capitalocene (Moore, 2017), to name a few. Each of these terms identifies specific ideological and behavioral patterns associated with ecological degradation. While the term "Anthropocene" emphasizes the damaging effects of humans philosophically separating themselves from nature, "Plantationocene" and "Capitalocene" focus on the social, cultural, political, and economic systems that intersect in environmental degradation. Specifically, Capitalocene brands capitalism as a major contributor and defines our present age as "shaped by the endless accumulation of capital" (Moore, 2017, p. 596). While acknowledging that humans perpetuated environmental violence prior to the birth of capitalism, Capitalocene emphasizes the ways in which this economic system has accelerated the scale and speed of this destruction greatly, imperiling biodiversity across the planet. Since many Indigenous communities lived sustainably on the land for millennia, widespread ecological destruction does not have to be perceived as a fundamental human trait.

Unfortunately, cultural patterns are often so engrained they are not readily visible. Yet they infuse nearly every aspect of our daily lives—from the stories we tell to the products we use and the environments we inhabit, visual and material culture are replete with them. As visual-culture and material-culture art education expand the study of art to include a wide range of cultural images and objects (Blandy & Bolin, 2018; Freedman, 2019) and overlap with critical pedagogy (Bolin & Blandy, 2003; Smith, 2011; Tavin, 2003), these approaches can empower students to analyze such cultural artifacts and critique popular culture. Art education as ecopedagogy can draw upon these approaches to engage students in interrogating environmentally harmful cultural narratives for ecojustice purposes. Contemporary artists who expose and confront capitalist cultural practices that exacerbate environmental problems can serve as inspiration for these pedagogical endeavors. This chapter explores the role visual-culture art education and critical-arts pedagogy can play in ecopedagogy, introduces eco-activist artists, and outlines some specific curricular approaches that engage students in eco-activist art critique and production.

The contemporary artworks described in this chapter range from more "traditional" contemporary works of art, installed in galleries, to works more closely resembling popular culture. In many cases, artists have appropriated elements of visual culture to engage in cultural commentary—surprising audiences, subverting expectations, and destabilizing cultural narratives. Some themes that could be explored in relation to these works and inform students' own artistic exploration include cultural desires, identity stories, and accountability. See Table 7.1 for a curriculum outline of potential ways these ideas might be examined.

EXPOSING CULTURAL DREAMS AND DESIRES

One major concern with Capitalocene life is the way our longings are often at odds with sustainability: Our cultural dreams and desires tend to be oriented toward the collection of capital. McGown (2016) explained these troubled human–object relationships:

> The capitalist subject is a subject who never has enough and continually seeks more and more . . . Capitalist accumulation envisions obtaining the object that would provide the ultimate satisfaction for the desiring subject, the object that would quench the subject's desire and allow it to put an end to the relentless yearning to accumulate . . . The key to capitalism's staying power lies in the fact that this ultimately satisfying object doesn't exist. (p. 21)

As cultural narratives sustain these unhealthy tendencies, artists can play an important role in dismantling them.

Artists Making Desires Visible

Maxine Greene (1995/2000) asserted, "informed encounters with works of art often lead to a startling defamiliarization of the ordinary" (p. 4). As many of us are daily immersed in narratives of cultural cravings that are ecologically harmful, art can allow us to recognize these patterns and see them in new ways. The Indigenous art collective Postcommodity, introduced in Chapter 4, represents one artist group working in this vein.

In *Pollination*, Postcommodity (2015) presents dark viewing booths that museum audiences can enter and deposit a token to observe a garden scene through a window (see Figure 7.1). Enclosed by walls of mirrors and accentuated by artificial light (Joyce, 2015), the garden is positioned as a cultural fantasy—something to be seen, enjoyed, and exploited. Because this setup mimics the ways in which male voyeurs have surveyed female bodies

Table 7.1. Some Curricular Applications of Themes of Cultural Desires, Identity Stories, and Accountability

Big Ideas	Grade Levels	Ecopedagogical Goals	Key Concepts	Discussion/Reflection Prompts	Possible Artistic Responses
Cultural Desires	10–12	Identifying the role desire plays in consumer behavior Redirecting cultural longings toward more relational, sustainable modes of being	Some economic systems are more sustainable than others. Economic systems influence culture, including cultural values, dreams, and desires. Art can help people perceive the ways culture and cultural desires operate in sustainable and unsustainable ways.	How do economic systems influence culture? How does capitalism relate to consumer culture? How does a desire to accumulate capital show up in our lives? How sustainable are these patterns? What other dreams do people have that do not involve accumulating capital? If these dreams were realized, what would the social and environmental impact be?	Create a public sculpture or installation that exposes cultural excess. Construct a social experience or interactive event that engages the public in acting out a relational desire or narrative.

Identity Stories	6–12	Identifying the role cultural narratives (surrounding identity) play in justifying environmentally harmful behaviors	Human actions have social and environmental consequences. Artists can show how people's ideas about themselves (and society) do not always match with reality.	What kinds of characters do you tend to see in stories (e.g., heroine, villain, victim)? With which characters do people tend to identify? Have you ever read a story where the character type was not as obvious (e.g., a villain unaware they were causing harm or a character unaware they were being hurt)? How can art show people a part of the story they might be missing (particularly in relation to the environment)?	In a public location, display text and imagery that reframes cultural or human life. Use guerilla communications (e.g., memes or t-shirt designs) to empower people as agents of environmental change.
Accountability	7–12	Reflecting on the role industry and policy play in ecological destruction Holding environmentally harmful actors accountable	Accountability protects from abuses of power. Art can function as a citizen-driven accountability practice. Art can inspire policy change.	What is accountability? How are people and groups with power held accountable? To whom are they held accountable? If citizens feel certain powerful actors are not being held accountable, what actions might they take? What actions might artists take?	Engage in subvertising/culture jamming/brandalism to challenge corporate power, greed, or environmental irresponsibility.

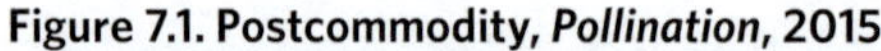
Figure 7.1. Postcommodity, *Pollination*, 2015

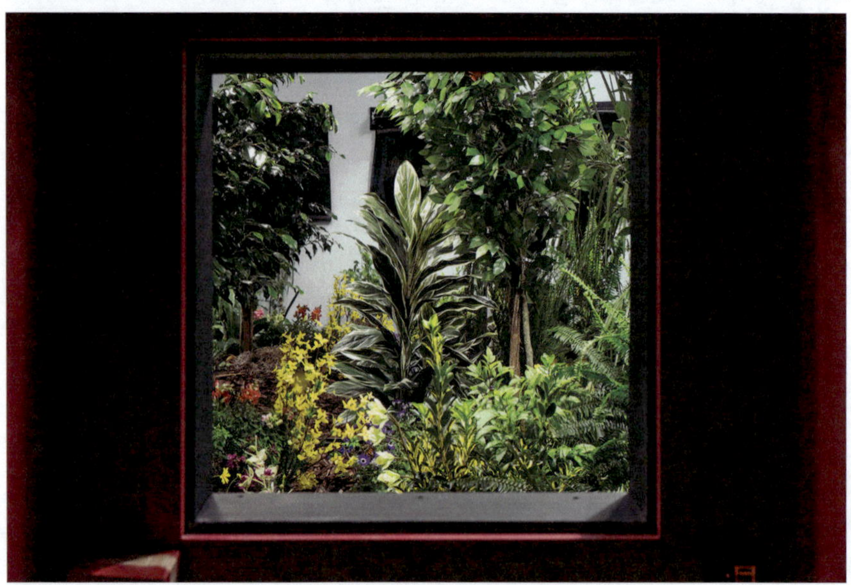

through peep shows, it draws attention to the ways in which both nonhuman nature and women have been objectified and "fetishized as powerless objects of desire" (Postcommodity, 2015, para. 2). Thus, this work draws upon ecofeminist philosophy in linking the male gaze to the anthropocentric gaze and underscoring power relations. (If presented to students in a manner similar to that described above, this work should be appropriate to include in most upper high school art curricula. However, additional images and online descriptions of this work contain more sexually explicit references. Thus, teachers should exercise their professional judgment when determining whether to present this work to students.)

Analyzing *Pollination*, Joyce (2015) describes how the "'pay-to-play' model brings in capitalism's role in the devastation of the natural world, global market systems, land development, and the exploitation of natural resources, all of which suggest Western colonial endeavors" (para. 5). As viewers pay to view the garden and can see their faces reflected in the mirror images, their complicity in these systems is reinforced.

In *The Night Is Filled with the Harmonics of Suburban Dreams*, Postcommodity (2011) inserted an aboveground pool into a gallery space with pool pipes sprawling in all directions (see Figure 7.2). Producing a continual oscillating noise, two pool-pump motors circulate water through the pipe's geometric configurations. Postcommodity (2011) explained, "The work recreates the sonic environment of suburban backyards where ubiquitous pool pumps sing through summer nights" (para. 2). Often an integral

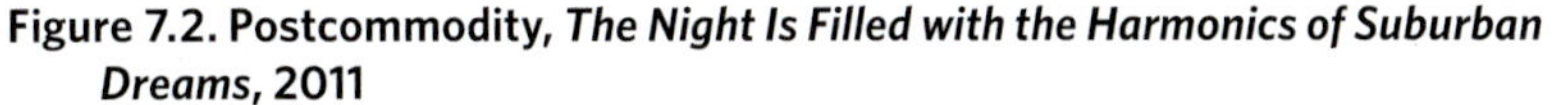

Figure 7.2. Postcommodity, *The Night Is Filled with the Harmonics of Suburban Dreams*, 2011

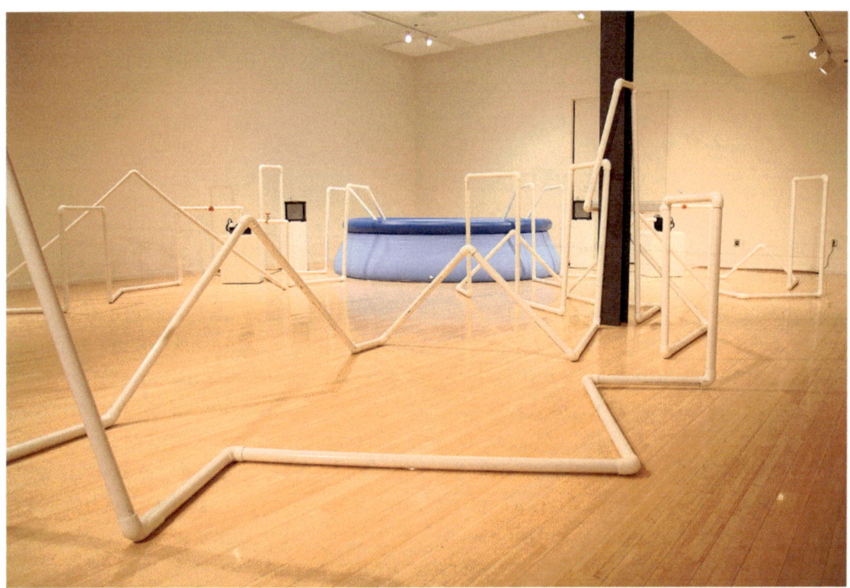

part of the suburban landscape, pools can function as suburban status symbols. As such, they reference middle-class freedom, escape, and economic growth under capitalism. Yet, as the pool's sanitized surfaces and unceasing motor hum have replaced the rich organic substances and animal vocalizations one might experience in more rural environments, we are reminded that this industrialized "prosperity" takes an ecological and social toll.

Curriculum Acknowledging and Redirecting Desire

Various reflective exercises can support students in identifying and interrogating cultural ambitions and fantasies (refer to Table 7.1). Students may journal, listing their own aspirations as well as those of their neighbors, friends, and family members. Next, they can engage in a coding activity, grouping their dreams and desires into categories. Through class discussions and visual-journal entries, students can reflect upon the ecological impacts of these wishes and explore the power artists have in exposing these cultural inclinations. Students could work in groups to explore one of the cultural-desire themes they identified through artmaking. Not all of the themes students investigate need be negative: while some desires have ecosocial consequences that could be exposed, such as the ones Postcommodity explored, other longings, like a yearning for a sense of community, could spur more positive outcomes. Thus, some student groups' art may fulfill an exposing function, much like

Postcommodity's installations, while others may highlight more constructive tendencies. For instance, students may set up the conditions for relational encounters between humans and more-than-humans to unfold, revealing our need for such connections. These types of approaches are explored further in Chapter 10.

REWRITING IDENTITY STORIES

Humans constantly construct narratives. As evolutionary biologist E. O. Wilson (2005) explained, "The mind is a narrative machine . . . The narratives and artifacts that prove most innately satisfying spread and become culture" (p. ix). As the stories we tell about ourselves have strong ecosocial implications, both individual and cultural narratives are important to examine.

One fundamental problem is the way these imaginaries validate and even urge environmental subjugation and other exploitations. Consider cultural stories and metaphors that position humans as possessors of the Earth, who are licensed to use the Earth at leisure; or as members of stable, technologically advanced societies, unlikely to be scathed by climate change. Also, consider the multitude of more specific, individual narratives that fit within these large cultural narratives: the heroic business executives creating jobs by razing grasslands for industrial development; the upper-middle-class family shielded from climate change because they have an emergency fund and live inland; and the high school student who absolves his environmental responsibilities by recycling his plastic water bottle each day at lunch. Despite all the irreparable environmental brutalities we inflict, we tend to see ourselves more as protagonists and rationally acting agents than desecrators and villains in our own accounts. Artists can play an important role in disrupting the flow of these story lines, reframing them, and making space for more ecologically sustainable narratives to emerge.

Artists Reframing Identity Narratives

The artworks presented in this section play different roles in reframing and rewriting the individual and collective stories we tell about ourselves. These various reshapings are important as varied ecologically unhealthy master narratives arise, to include settler colonial societies as innocent and uninvolved in perpetrating environmental degradations, human bodies as untouched by environmental atrocities, and concerned citizens as powerless in the face of large social, political, and economic forces. Reaching beyond art galleries and museums, the artists in this section situate their works in the contexts that will best assist them in this reframing process.

To confront the public's cognitive dissonance surrounding climate change, New York City–based artist Justin Brice Guariglia (2019) created a series of public art installations (see Figure 7.3). For *We Are the Asteroid II* and *We Are the Asteroid III*, Guariglia worked with ecotheorist Timothy Morton to develop various aphorisms, or "eco-haikus" (Guariglia & Morton, 2018–2019, 2019–2020; YBCA, n.d., para. 1), which he then brandished on solar-powered, electronic highway signs. In one installation, a sign displays the glowing text "WE ARE THE ASTEROID." As the sign rests in a grassy landscape with trees in the distance, the installation provides viewers with a site to visualize a meteor striking the Earth and serves as a visual reminder of the habitats at risk. The work's message is markedly explicit: just as a meteor sealed the fate of the dinosaurs, so dominant human society is catalyzing a new period of mass extinction. Through rebranding messages like "NEANDERTHALS 'R' US" and planetary warnings like "TRIASSIC WEATHER AHEAD" (YBCA, n.d.), this series situates our modern societal actions in broader geological and evolutionary frameworks. In so doing, it disrupts prevailing narratives that assume future planetary stability and absolve dominant human society of ecological responsibility.

Similar to Guariglia and Morton's (2019–2020) messages like "WARNING: HURRICANE HUMAN," artists have worked to counter

Figure 7.3. Justin Brice Guariglia and Timothy Morton, *We Are the Asteroid II*, 2018

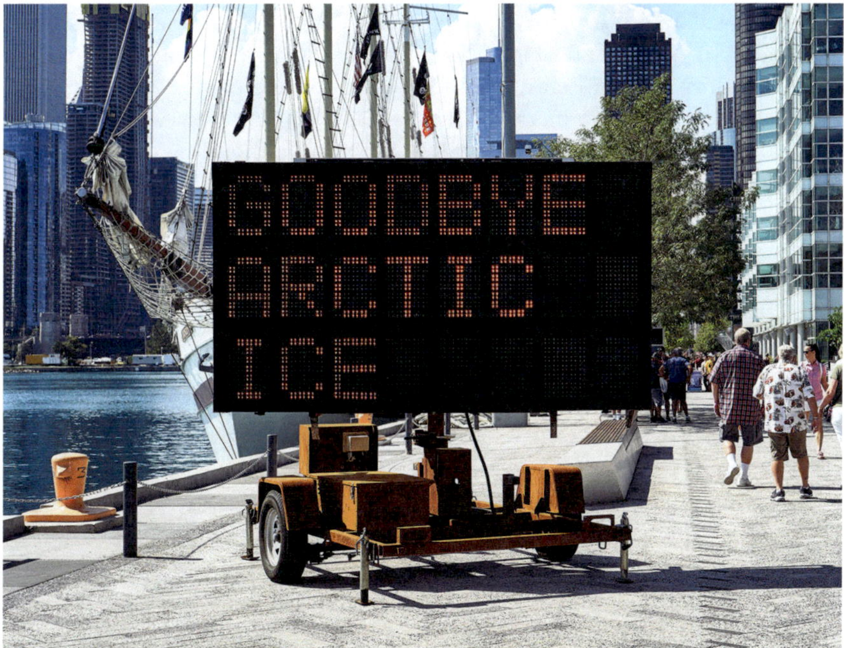

prevailing presumptions surrounding human invulnerability to the effects of climate change. At the conclusion of a dissatisfying United Nations Climate Change Conference in Madrid, Spanish design collective Luzinterruptus (2019b) installed the guerilla artwork *Death by Plastic* (Wang, 2020; see Figure 7.4). This protest art featured glowing, body-like sculptures—translucent body casings, stuffed with the plastic packaging waste from local retailers (Luzinterruptus, 2019a). Like a massive crime scene, the bodies sprawled along a street in Madrid, their silhouettes traced on the pavement with chalk. As the title suggests, they are victims of modern societies' excessive reliance on plastic, and the fossil fuels used to produce these materials—a narrative inadequately informing corporate and consumer actions.

So far, the art installations in this section have operated as unsettling cultural criticism, but not all works tackling dominant social narratives need be wholly negative. More positive, empowering messages can also function in countercultural ways. For instance, Chip Thomas's works often defy disempowering, fatalistic narratives that perpetuate compliance and inaction. By acknowledging the harsh realities of our current ecological condition but emphasizing agency, allyship, and acts of resistance, Thomas's works might be seen as advancing the cultural work these other artists had begun.

As a family physician and activist living and working on the Navajo Nation over 3 decades (Guzmán, 2018), Thomas often incorporates a holistic concern for the health of the Navajo peoples (Diné) and their land in his artworks. For *I Am the Change*, Thomas, or "Jetsonorama" (2015), responded to Navajo and Hopi Nation concern surrounding a ski resort's plans to spray artificial snow from recycled sewage on the San Francisco Peaks, a sacred mountain range (Justseeds, n.d.). For this work, Raechel Running, Stephanie Jackson, and Rey Cantil collaborated with Thomas, writing and painting on their faces. In *I Am the Change* (see Figure 7.5),

Figure 7.4. Luzinterruptus, *Death by Plastic*, 2019b

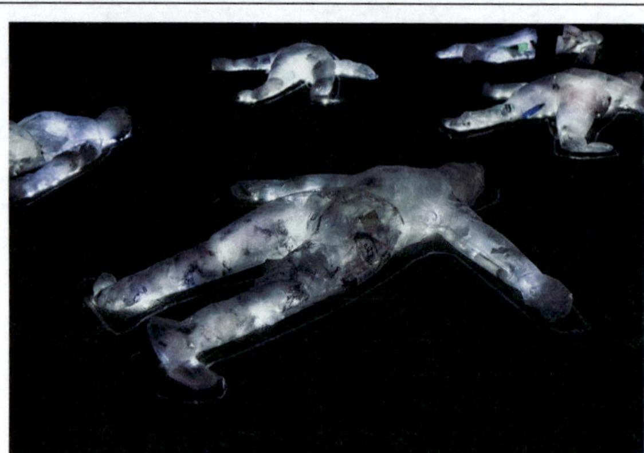

Figure 7.5. Chip Thomas, *I Am the Change*, 2015

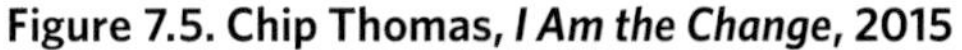

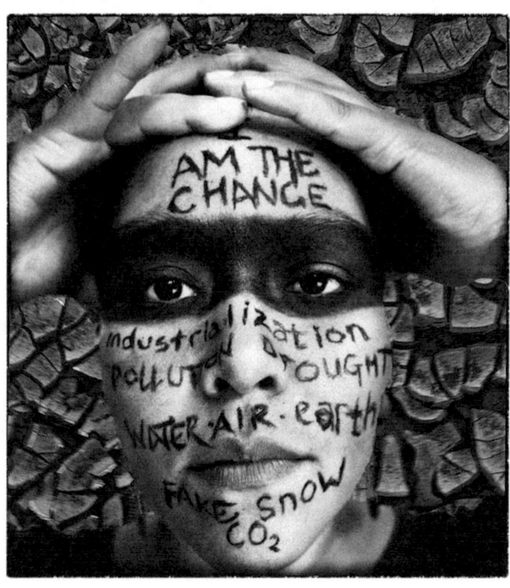

a woman's face fills the image. Words below a black strip of paint around her eyes allude to environmental concerns: "industrialization," "pollution," "drought," "water," "air," "earth" "fake snow," and "CO_2." Yet, significantly, the emboldening words "I AM THE CHANGE" are inscribed on her forehead. Despite the immensity of the environmental challenges the woman noted, she has chosen to position herself as an agent of change. As negative discourse can easily lead to cynicism and inaction, artworks like these that reframe individual and group identity in empowering terms may be especially critical.

Curriculum Resituating Identity

To engage students in reframing narratives surrounding identity (refer to Table 7.1), art teachers could begin by presenting artworks that allude to societal narratives both conducive and unconducive to ecological outcomes—thus, those narratives more in alignment with Western, individualist, and capitalist narratives and those that emerge from more relational paradigms. By analyzing and interpreting these works, students can gain proficiency in identifying such master narratives. By reflecting as a class on the significance of such discourses, particularly when these reflections are coupled with short readings of environmental texts, students can begin to understand the ways in which cultural scripts can impact environmental and political behaviors. Then, building upon these understandings, students could identify an ecologically healthy narrative surrounding identity to highlight or a more harmful narrative to dismantle through an artwork. By allowing students to address these dominant discourses publicly, in the contexts in which they tend to unfold, public art installations and performances are particularly poignant ways for students to take eco-activist, artistic action.

DEMANDING ACCOUNTABILITY

As students become more cognizant of the ways in which dominant cultural stories function, they may also become more aware of the ways prominent individuals, social and political organizations, and corporations manufacture and enact these narratives to the detriment of the ecosphere. From an environmental justice standpoint, major environmental offenders and their enablers need to be held accountable. Given the extent to which industry is wreaking ecological destruction and governmental policies permit these actions, individual concerned citizens' lone attendance to their own personal lifestyle choices (e.g., using reusable grocery bags, eliminating meat from their diets, and skipping showers), while commendable, is inadequate. Systemic change is needed, including stringent restrictions on the fossil fuel industry and other major polluters. As most corporations have shown they prefer "greenwashing" campaigns (e.g., lofty statements, inspiring advertisements, and insubstantial commitments) to measurable progress, the public can find ways to amplify sociopolitical pressures. Artists, as cultural actors, can play a key role in inspiring such cultures of aggressive engagement.

Artists Holding Environmental Offenders Accountable

Art activist practices, such as those associated with graffiti and street art; "subvertising," a blend of the words "subverting" and "advertising" (Dekeyser, 2021, p. 309); and culture jamming offer creative modes of directing public attention toward environmentally egregious industries, corporations, and products. These artistic practices are often subversive, reacting against asymmetrical power relations inherent to corporations' communications with the public (Carducci, 2006). As urban spaces are replete with corporate messaging, these spaces are particularly ripe for transgressive artistic engagement.

Graffiti and street art are image-making practices in urban spaces. While graffiti is typically unsolicited and illegal, focused on producing text, such as tags and pseudonyms, and created with spray paint, street art is a newer and broader practice that includes illicit and commissioned works, text- and image-based works, and a range of media (Avramidis & Tsilimpounidi, 2016). The public nature, political leanings, and provocative imagery of street art make it a particularly effective means of creatively countering dominant discourses that absolve those in power from environmental responsibility. For instance, one anonymous street-art piece ("The Earth Isn't Dying," n.d.) features a stencil-painted rabbit on a graffitied city wall. The animal holds a sign with the stenciled words: "THE EARTH ISN'T DYING/ IT'S BEING KILLED/ AND THOSE WHO ARE KILLING IT/ HAVE NAMES AND ADDRESSES," a quote commonly attributed to labor organizer, activist, and folksinger Utah Phillips.

Pointing out one of these wrongdoers, in response to the United States' withdrawal from the 2015 Paris Climate Agreement, a street artist, thought to be Pink Bear, painted Donald Trump standing next to the text "CLIMATE CHANGE THREATENS OUR PLANET" ("Climate Change Threatens," n.d.). With a red paintbrush in hand, the former U.S. president appeared to have crossed out the word "PLANET" and replaced it with "PROFIT." While many street art messages assign blame more generally, with rallying cries like "system change not climate change," art practices that sabotage and play off existing public imagery tend to go further in condemning specific offenders. These sorts of critiques may feel jarring initially, but given the scale of the atrocities being committed, these denunciations might be seen as relatively mild and hardly proportional.

As advertisements serve as the communicative landscapes of corporations and commonly perpetuate unsustainable consumerism, they can serve as powerful sites for critique. "Subvertising" is one means of countering slick corporate advertisements that obscure harmful environmental impacts. Common strategies include removing, supplementing, or replacing advertising images and text, particularly those advertising images located in outdoor urban environments, such as billboards, bus stops, and digital signage (Dekeyser, 2021; see Figure 7.6). These alterations are meant to transgress, contest, subvert, and profane these communications, to desecrate any ideas of their invulnerability and reclaim citizen ownership of public space. A form of subvertising—culture jamming—often works not only to critique advertising in general as it perpetuates consumerism, but to impugn specific advertising claims and denounce the corporations themselves, thereby holding these companies publicly accountable.

In concurrence with the 2015 United Nations Climate Change Conference, the anti-advertising activist group Brandalism installed a series of advertisement spoofs throughout Paris (Ecowatch, 2015). Visually appearing much like any other automobile advertisement, one Volkswagen poster (Brandalism, 2015) featured a car on a white background with the Volkswagen logo in the corner. Yet the advertisement's text was clearly altered. The words "We're sorry/that we got caught" hover above the car with smaller text at the bottom of the poster: "Now that we've been caught,/we're trying to make you think about the environment./ But we're not the only ones./#redlines #D12 #ClimateGames." As these satirical advertisements were placed in traditional advertisement displays, they likely surprised the

Figure 7.6. Artwork: Noel Douglas, Photo of work and installation: Brandalism *[Burn Now . . . Pay Later]*, 2021

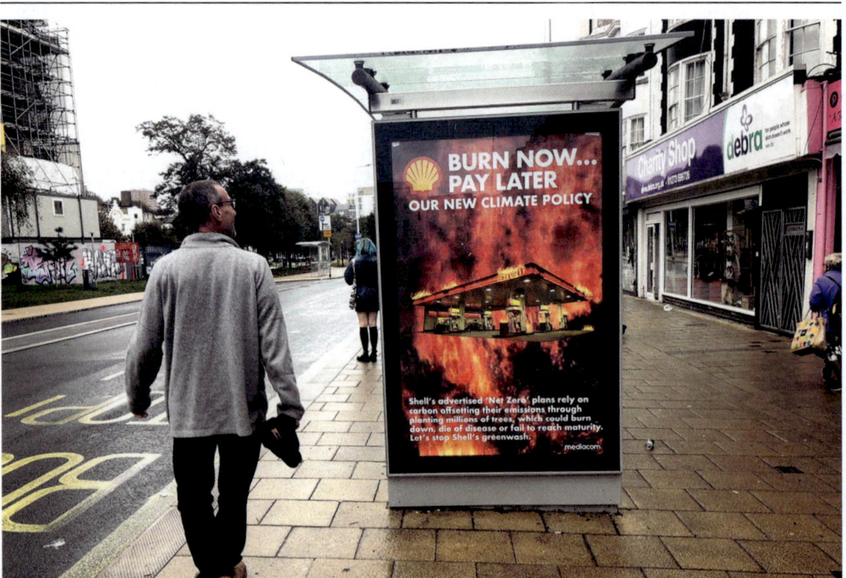

public and, in so doing, renewed public dialogues surrounding corporate responsibility (and irresponsibility).

Curriculum Seeking Environmental Justice

In working toward environmental justice, students could engage in various material interventions around the school building and campus (refer to Table 7.1). Less permanent forms of street art and subvertising (i.e., not spray paint–based) likely would be more attractive to school administrators and custodial staff and more likely be officially approved. Options might include reverse graffiti projects, where students wipe phrases and imagery onto grimy surfaces (Randazzo & Lajevic, 2013), and subvertisements, where students digitally alter and collage text and imagery onto advertisements (Chung & Kirby, 2009) and display them around the school. As a former middle school art teacher, I have found that with instruction, most 7th- and 8th-grade students are able to alter advertising text and imagery ironically and often enjoy exercising their wit in this way. The most egregious industries, companies, and products (e.g., high-carbon industries, fossil fuel corporations, and superfluous products) and zealous advertising messages are typically the easiest to critique. Students in earlier grades or students still developing an understanding of irony could be steered toward these easy consumerist targets.

CONCLUSION

Recognizing the hegemony of the Capitalocene, the curriculum introduced in this chapter is intended to help students move from passive acceptance. Students can perceive the Capitalocene's workings and, empowered as cultural producers, actively work to reconfigure dominant cultural narratives and practices. These actions are important at ideological and cultural levels. The next few chapters explore how students could build upon these cultural productions to envision and affect material change.

QUESTIONS FOR EDUCATOR REFLECTION

1. How does consumerism inform your own daily life choices? What does your home's material culture reveal about you as a consumer? What ideas, desires, and stories inform the way you think about products and their relationship to your life?
2. What stories and messages encourage you to take environmental action? Which messages are less impactful?
3. What are some of the ways the Capitalocene is visible in your own community? Which actors (e.g., prominent individuals, social and political organizations, corporations, and government agencies) perpetuate the Capitalocene, particularly the Capitalocene conditions you see playing out locally?
4. Walk through your school building and campus. What sites seem ripe for art interventions? How could art interventions at these sites gain widespread attention while also respecting the school building and those responsible for maintaining it?

CHAPTER 8

Envisioning Alternate States and Ways of Being

With Jonathan Purtill

Have you ever wondered about the future of humanity—considered the adaptations necessary for humans to survive and thrive in hostile environments, interstellar space, or digital worlds? Given the world's centuries of colonial/capitalist exploitation and now rapidly changing conditions, to include climate change, can thinking about possible futures, with or without humans, provide avenues to perceive and address these injustices? This chapter positions the imagination as a means to break with our current states of being to construct new realities.

Suvin (1979) defined science fiction as a literature of "cognitive estrangement" (p. 4), in which a novel invention, idea, or circumstance—"a novum" (p. 63)—provokes a revolutionary or emancipatory way of thinking. Cognitive estrangement could be contrasted with simpler expressions of futurity, unreality, or magic—"the marvelous" (Todorov, 1975, p. 25)—often found within genres like space opera, supernatural romance, or dystopian young adult adventures. In cases of cognitive estrangement, the trappings of science fiction or fantasy exist as a system of explicable world-building contingencies. For example, the lunar anarchist of Le Guin's *The Dispossessed* (1975), upon first encountering colonial capitalist nation-states, provides a new framework through which to view the functions of contemporary politics and economics. A counterexample, an example of the marvelous, might be seen in the original *Star Wars* (e.g., Lucas, 1977) films, in which futuristic or magico-religious technologies exist mainly to provide an opportunity for cinematic special effects; the existence of a lightsaber does not provide any reason to reconsider reasons for or methods of warfare, like the shields or stillsuits of *Dune* (Herbert, 1965), but rather provides a flashy visual update to the preexisting cinematic spectacle of a sword fight. Rather than apolitical spectacle, only concerned with innovative storytelling or imaginative world-building, cognitive estrangement puts forth future visions intrinsically bound up, especially when they appear not to be, with social, political, and cultural ideology. Thus, rather than promulgating superficial wish fulfillment, escapism, and other fantasies that reproduce existing social hierarchies and exploitations, works of cognitive estrangement can engage social consciousness and inspire movements toward action.

Due to this revolutionary power of cognitive estrangement, speculative fiction, art, and exercises can have important ecopedagogical roles to play. David Rousell et al. (2017) explained how speculative fiction can open space for students to dwell upon climate change, or other contemporary environmental issues, without being restricted by the anthropocentric thinking, discourses, and practices that currently prevail. In so doing, speculative fiction can equip students to resist present conditions and approach possible futures with a sense of urgency, social and environmental responsibility, and hope. In this chapter, we present works of art and design that, like speculative fiction, allow students to explore the implications of the Anthropocene/Capitalocene and radically reimagine alternative modes of thinking and living. Additionally, we propose curriculum to support students in such speculative endeavors (see Table 8.1).

Artists Alexis Rockman and Meydan Levy and architecture firm XTU examined the future of human relationships with the more-than-human world in the form of genetically engineered animals; three-dimensional, printed artificial "fruits"; and designs for fantastical buildings that float above a polluted future Earth. Wanuri Kahiu, Wilfred Ukpong, and Alexis Rockman focused on the future of humanity, or lack thereof, within the context of geological/climate change through a film of civilization in a water-scarce environment, mystical images of human rituals in the Niger Delta, and naturalistic paintings of a future without humanity. Many of these works operate at the nexus of utopia and dystopia, where one person's or being's utopia is another's dystopia. Astonishing or disconcerting viewers, they unsettle the ordinary, often showing us the "logical" conclusions to current trajectories. Additionally, many envision the extent to which we will have to adapt to survive under such unfriendly conditions. Finally, some put forth narratives of hope, achieved through desperate ecological action, that might act as seeds for social, racial, or environmental justice.

ENVISIONING THE FUTURE OF HUMAN AND NONHUMAN NATURE RELATIONS

The field of futures studies is based upon the premise that by envisioning potential futures, we can more effectually direct our lives; we can work toward attractive futures and avoid unfavorable ones (Masini, 2006). Moreover, futures studies involves efforts to understand the evolving relationship between humans, society, and the environment. This analysis can

Table 8.1. Some Curricular Applications of Themes of Nature and Posthuman

Big Ideas	Grade Levels	Ecopedagogical Goals	Key Concepts	Discussion/Reflection Prompts	Possible Artistic Responses
Nature	7–12	Understanding humans as part of nature. Recognizing unbalanced human actions can have consequences. Realizing more ethical ways of being are possible	Humans are a part of nature. Unbalanced human actions have social and environmental consequences. Artists and designers can envision future states. They can help society see where current trends might lead, to see possibilities and better ways of living.	What is nature? Are humans a part of nature? Sometimes humans act as if they are separate. What kinds of consequences could that idea produce? How are dominant human groups' actions impacting the environment? If these trends continue, how will they impact the future? How can artists/designers explore future possibilities? What works of art, design, or fiction explore futures? What works put forth new visions?	Illustrate the adaptations a species will need to survive changing conditions. Revise a human practice to meet the social or environmental demands of the future. Design architecture for a future in which civilization is more integrated into natural systems.
Posthuman	8–12	Understanding how cultural philosophies have real-world impacts Speculating social and ecological futures within broader contexts	Our cultural philosophies impact the way we perceive and live in the world. Philosophies (whether explicit or implicit) inform art. Artists can transcend disciplinary boundaries to accomplish their goals (e.g., transdisciplinary inquiry and collaborations).	How do people's ideas about life inform the way they live? How do those ideas shape art? What role can artists play in introducing new ideas/philosophies? Given rapidly changing global conditions, people have suggested ideas about humanity need to adjust. What are some ideas about humanity that might change? What ideas about our relationship to the Earth/land/other species might change? What impact might these ideas have on the ways we live? How can artists explore ideas that intersect with other subject areas?	Communicate a deep-time regional narrative of the future through a class mural. Create a graphic short story detailing a future being's experiences of the world, including how they navigate the challenges of their times.

occur from an ecological standpoint, whereby one explores the futures of human–environment relations—following current societal trends, extrapolating to where these trends might lead socially and ecologically, and evaluating the desirability of these ends. Such processes can yield valuable insights and defamiliarize existing practices. As dominant human groups position themselves as distinct from nature and tend to treat nonhuman nature as a resource to be exploited, the outcomes of these social tendencies can be envisioned.

Artists Theorizing the Future of the "Natural" World

In Margaret Atwood's (2003) novel *Oryx and Crake*, a culture of genetic experimentation leads to designer animals, plants, and microorganisms created to fulfill aesthetic and economic roles. Pigoons, pigs bred to grow redundant human organs for sale and transplant; Rakunks, racoon/skunk hybrids kept as pets; and ChickieNobs, brainless chicken bodies grown for "ethical" meat consumption, populate a technocratic semi-dystopia of corporate biological arms races. Similarly, the artists featured in this section depict human interventions with nature based on capitalistic, environmental, and social contingency. Neither idly speculative nor didactically utopian or dystopian, Alexis Rockman, Meydan Levy, and XTU Architects instead explore the *novum* of technological, genetic, and artistic manipulation of the more-than-human world.

The paintings of Rockman's (2000–2012) *Wonderful World* series combine the early American pastoral tradition of Grant Wood and Thomas Hart Benton with 1970s-era pulp sci-fi illustration in order to produce images of the future that are subversively slick; technological and biological innovation depicted with technical mastery contribute to a boringly sublime vision of the future, a "spectacular mediocrity" (Searle, 2004, para. 10), in which genetically modified plants and animals exist within the friendly American banality of Norman Rockwell. *The Farm* (2000) shows "optimized" animal modifications under industrialized agriculture that predict some of Atwood's hybrid creations—grotesque featherless chickens with multiple flightless wings, giant hogs overstuffed with meat and redundant organs, and cows deformed into a square shape for more efficient packing. *Pet Store* (2004) likewise presents genetically altered hybrid animals, this time in the context of a high-end retail display (see Figure 8.1). Real-world examples of dog breeds that are so genetically tailored that natural biological processes like breathing (e.g., pugs) or childbirth (e.g., English bulldogs) become difficult or impossible provide a starting point for Rockman's menagerie. Aesthetically altered, although assumedly living, pets—such as a red-and white-striped miniature saber-toothed tiger, a Janus-like beta fish, and a stylized gryphon—share an elaborate pedestal with more uncanny grotesqueries—a terrier, sans legs, modified into a handbag, and a fluffy pillow with

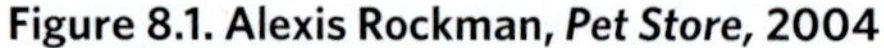

Figure 8.1. Alexis Rockman, *Pet Store,* 2004

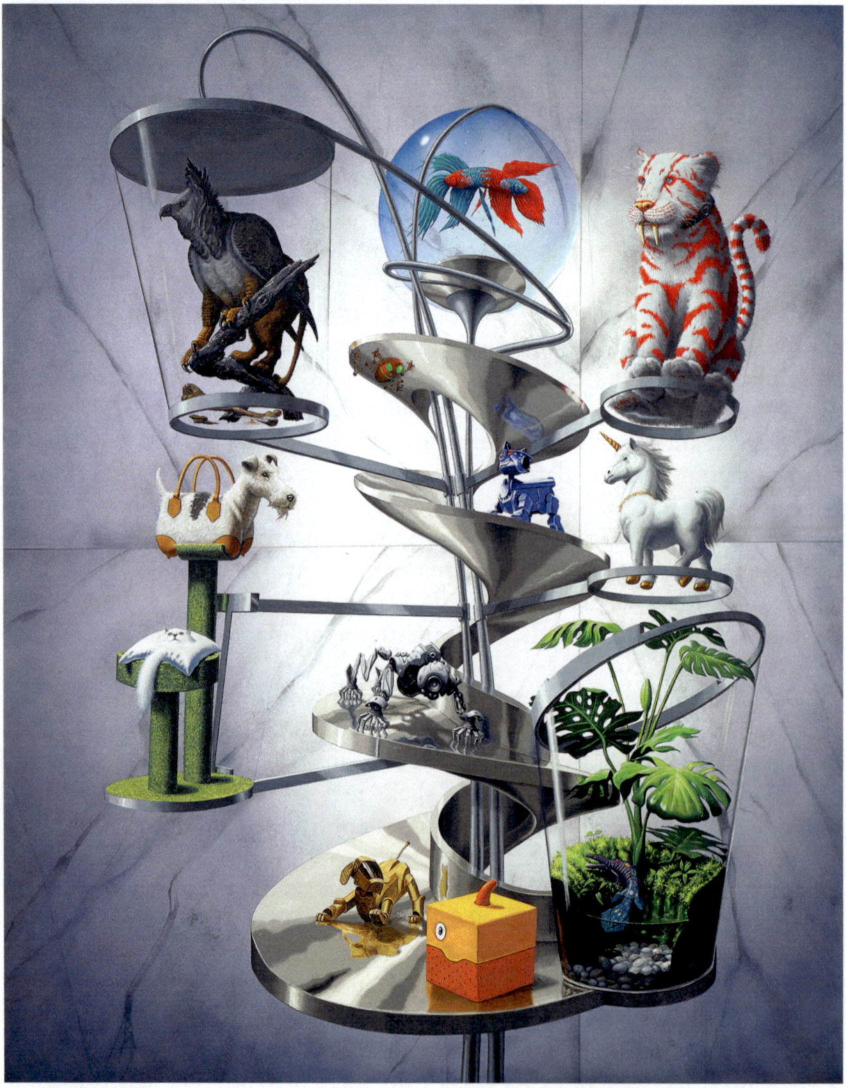

the face and tail of a kitten. This eerie collection of designer pets interrogates the culture of pet ownership and breed-as-commodity fetishism. *Sea World* (2001–2004) envisions the future of the animal entertainment industry as a carnival-cum-genetics experiment, with both existing and extinct deep-sea creatures frolicking alongside altered aquatic life; a Plesiosaur, ridden by a performer, shares a performance space with a bouncing polar bear ball. The juxtaposition of the setting of a zoo, an ecologically and ethically controversial industry, with overtly grotesque sideshow imagery problematizes even ostensibly humanitarian preservation endeavors.

Focusing on plants rather than animals, Meydan Levy's (n.d.-a) three-dimensionally printed *Neo Fruits* present a similarly ambiguous future for agriculture under mechanized production and fetishistic "maker" culture. *Neo Fruits* are a "speculative technological design project" (Levy, n.d.-b, para. 1) that consist of cellulose printed into flat shapes, to aid storage and shipping, which are later injected with a nutritious flavored liquid, created collaboratively with molecular gastronomists, which begins the shelf life of the "fruit." These objects are alien in appearance and function—somewhere between David Cronenberg's (1988) biomechanical tools in *Dead Ringers* and the neon industrialism of Syd Mead in *Blade Runner* (Scott, 1982). The "fruits" retain visual and haptic traces of preexisting foodstuffs: one must be scraped with the teeth like an artichoke, another contains colors and textures reminiscent of the insides of a dragon fruit. The final objects, though, are slightly uncanny with their industrial cellulose skin contrasting with the too-biological contents, such as tiny veins to aid in the distribution of a red liquid.

The effect of this work is complicated by the ambiguity of its purpose. *Neo Fruits* are ostensibly utopian in design and function, created to combat consumer waste and the ecological footprint of shipping fresh produce. Levy (n.d.-b) himself stated that this project "does not wish to critique, but to present an aspiration" (para. 12). This version of utopianism, though, is strictly technocratic and mechanized and provides a launching point for discussion regarding the optimization of the natural world: What capitalistic interventions into biological processes are we willing to accept once natural cycles (e.g., germination, pollination, and fruiting) become too inefficient to be profitable or unsustainable human habits disrupt them (e.g., bee colony collapse and coral bleaching)?

XTU Architects' approach to future living represents a slightly more affirming and utopian, or pseudo-utopian, approach to human interventions by embracing more natural processes. The French firm's conceptual designs imagine a post–climate change Earth where notions of cities, transportation, and sustainability must be reconsidered. *X Cloud* (XTU Architects, 2019), installed in the Mori Art Museum's *Future and the Arts: AI, Robotics, Cities, Life—How Humanity Will Live Tomorrow* exhibition (2019–2020), is a design for a city in a future where pollution and unpredictable weather have forced humanity to flee to the sky (see Figure 8.2). While motile cities have appeared elsewhere in science fiction and fantasy (e.g., Miéville, 2002; Miyazaki, 1986; Stephenson, 1992), XTU Architects emphasize the built-in sustainability necessary for the city to survive in a postcollapse future. *X Cloud* drew inspiration from classic science fiction, specifically the prevalence of airships and zeppelins in late 19th- and early 20th-century literature, to depict a system of helium-filled floating cities that rely on "plankton greenhouses, moisture

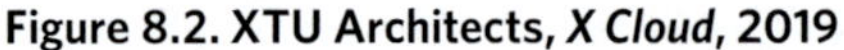
Figure 8.2. XTU Architects, *X Cloud*, 2019

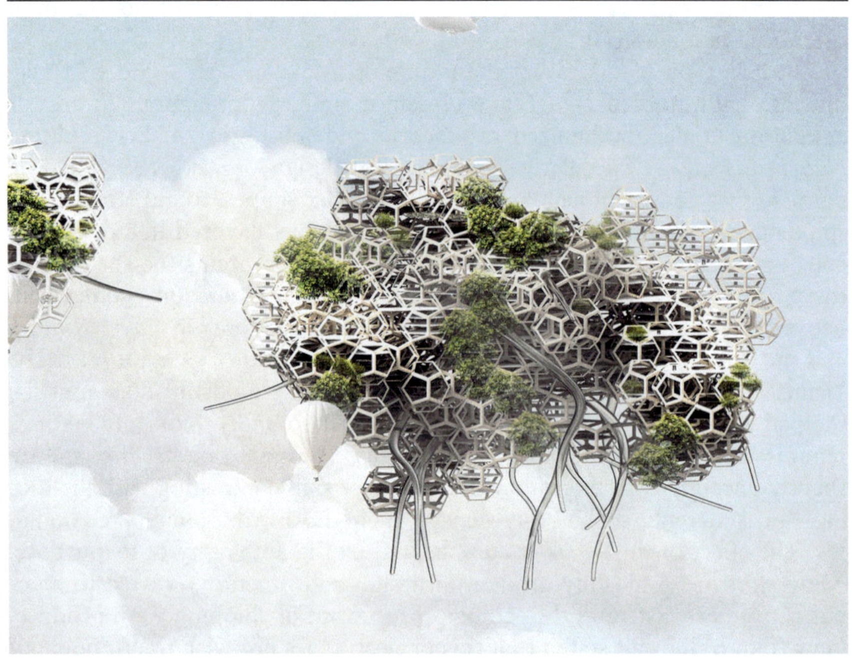

© XTU Architects

sensors, and epiphyte forests" for food, water, and greenery (XTU Architects & Myer, 2020, para. 3). The cities appear as a minimalist design activated by biological activity; inflatable geometric lattices that support trailing greenery are reminiscent of the Tillandsia air plants sold in gift shops and garden centers, and independent pods are meant to congregate like amoeba, sometimes drifting together, sometimes splitting apart, according to necessity.

Although the design for *X Cloud* was envisioned as a self-sufficient safe haven for humans, it should be noted that the optimism of the project is tempered by the knowledge that these utopian floating cities were only designed in response to a ruined world. Other concepts by XTU Architects are based on similar ideas. *Flohara* (n.d.-a), a hivelike structure that extends above and below sand, was intended to provide shelter and a sustainable microclimate in the face of desertification and drought. *Rigs City* (n.d.-b) is a design for a rehabilitated oil rig that uses weather cycles and ocean flora to make life possible in a future without land. The thread of survivability in the face of collapse that unites these projects suggests that, rather than an endless expansion of frontiers (e.g., Elon Musk on Mars and James Cameron [1989] in the abysmal depths), the future of humanity's relationship with the rest of nature might best be found in a retreat toward sustainable earthly living.

Curriculum Envisioning Human–Nonhuman Futures

Through exposure to speculative art and design, such as those works described above, students can begin to grasp the ways in which artists can play important speculative roles in society—imparting societal possibilities and, ultimately, drawing attention to the workings that would make these futures a reality (refer to Table 8.1). Provocative and insightful works of speculative fiction might be drawn upon to reinforce these understandings. While time tends to be limited in art classes and does not allow for extended reading of fiction, short excerpts might be read, film trailers might be played, students' prior knowledge of these stories might be activated, or collaborations might be initiated with English language arts teachers.

When engaging students in creating speculative art, particularly art exploring human relationships with the more-than-human world, teachers can focus the class on exploring one particular issue or encourage students to select issues of personal interest. With earlier grades, the class might focus on one particular issue, as students may be developing an understanding of these types of issues and would need the support that a whole-class investigation could provide.

Environmental issues could be explored, which might include climate change and the associated issues, like rising temperatures and sea levels, social upheaval, and mass migration; water, air, and land pollution; water scarcity; soil degradation; deforestation; acid rain; nuclear waste; ocean acidification; and overpopulation. Additionally, human responses to environmental issues, like renewable energy and ecosocialism, can be investigated. Other topics, often addressed in futures discussions, include artificial intelligence, memory alteration, body modification, mass surveillance, totalitarianism, and pandemics, to name a few. As students study a particular issue, they could be guided to consider the beings likely to be affected and the human practices impacted.

Conversely, rather than starting with an issue, teachers could have students commence with something more tangible. For instance, students can start with a particular species, especially one that is particularly meaningful to them, and consider the issues likely to impact it in the future. Students might study the adaptations that allow certain species to survive in the harsh environments humans have produced. For instance, epaulette sharks already walk on land to escape the warming waters associated with climate change (Heinrich et al., 2016). Or students could explore the ways humans directly impact species, much like Alexis Rockman (e.g., 2000, 2004) explored genetic modification (refer to Figure 8.1). Thus, students could speculate a future for one of these species and illustrate that future. Another approach could be to begin with a human practice, like the handling of waste materials or food production, and imagine how that practice or set of practices might evolve in response to rapidly changing environmental conditions.

For students struggling to formulate ideas, teachers could develop a list of issues, human practices, and organisms from which students might select, and then explore the potential future relationships between each selection in the future. Moreover, various divergent thinking or speculative exercises, coupled with exposure to speculative fiction, could support such practices. Through these exercises and experiences, teachers can encourage students to foresee the array of possible consequences to human actions and then conceive a range of responses.

ENVISAGING THE POSTHUMAN

In the face of global pandemics, climate change, and biosphere collapse, the future of humanity can feel precarious. Including both the relentlessly bleak "realism" of Cormac McCarthy's (2006) *The Road* and high-octane blockbusters like *Mad Max: Fury Road* (Miller, 2015), popular films and novels treat environmental apocalypse and sociopolitical dystopia as an inevitable consequence of human progress. In the face of such cultural leanings, imagining a utopian, or simply tolerable, outcome seems not just naïve, but a narrative impossibility. Moreover, as Jameson (1994) noted, "it seems to be easier for us today to imagine the thorough deterioration of the earth and of nature than the breakdown of late capitalism" (p. xii). Although apocalyptic narratives are popular, lingering on the kind of fatalism they present can provoke a kind of learned helplessness or nihilism. According to Julie Doyle (2020), "fear-laden imagery and negative narratives can generate feelings of disempowerment and disengagement" (p. 2752). Further, end-of-the-world scenarios are never ideologically neutral—the grim realities of the zombie apocalypse in *The Walking Dead* (Darabont, 2010–2022) and *World War Z* (Forster, 2013) mask a ruthlessly libertarian worldview: Rugged individualists prepared for an evil world survive, and trusting optimists and weaklings are indiscriminately culled. Thus, dystopian discourses in the classroom should be approached judiciously.

Artists Imagining the Posthuman

The word "posthuman" in this section fulfills a dual function: it references both the state of humanity within possible futures, adapting, either socially or biologically, to catastrophe, and the state of the world without humans. The posthuman artworks examined here avoid the dystopian/apocalyptic trap by maintaining a kind of narrative ambiguity. Similar to the artists in the prior section, Wanuri Kahiu, Wilfred Ukpong, and Alexis Rockman offer no clear didacticism nor fatalistic narratives. Although it would be inaccurate to call the futures examined by these artists optimistic, as they all deal with ecological or social collapse in one way or another, a thread of hope and wonder runs through their respective *novums*.

Whereas the paintings of Alexis Rockman (2000, 2001–2004, 2004) discussed earlier in this chapter referenced the agrarian idealism of early American landscape painting, Rockman's *The Great Lakes Cycle* (2015–2017) reaches further back in history to the Romanticism of the Hudson River School and the gothic sublime of Caspar David Friedrich. Presented as a series of panoramic landscapes, these paintings show the industrial wreckage of a posthuman world populated by real and imagined hybrid animals frolicking, feeding, and reproducing. The paintings are thematic rather than geographic, focusing not on individual sites within the Great Lakes region, but on imagined future consequences of human industry, tourism, and consumption within the aquatic environment (Voon, 2018). *Watershed* (2015) shows an oxbow split in two, half a pristine landscape of American romantic tradition, and half a ruined canal corrupted by industrial runoff. Mutated hybrid sea creatures swim through water made opaque by pollution (the GMO chicken, pig, and cow from *Farm* made cameo appearances, suggesting that this is the eventual future of Rockman's *Wonderful World* series). *Spheres of Influence* (2017b) shows the fragility of ecosystems in the midst of globalized tourism and industry, contrasting the remnants of air and water travel (i.e., planes and ships from different eras) with native and invasive avian species. Rockman highlighted the indirect effects of human interference with native ecosystems: Claire Voon (2018) observed, "algae blooms are responsible for avian botulism as toxins move through the food chain, consumed by invasive zebra mussels and round gobies" (para. 8).

Most apocalyptic is *Forces of Change* (2017a), which shows an enormous *E. coli* bacteria emerging kraken-like from a pool surrounding an abandoned factory (see Figure 8.3). The focal point of this painting is shared by the exaggerated germ and an unassuming tree of heaven, an invasive tree in North America brought by European settlers from China, suggesting that the threat of innocuous invasive species is akin to that of a monstrous mutant beast. The inclusion of this plant adds some complexity to Rockman's treatment of the posthuman landscape: the future of nature without future human interference may not be an idyllic paradise, but an oppressive monoculture. There is some tendency to imbue nature, especially nature sans humanity, with a kind of Romantic purity. Rockman's *The Great Lakes Cycle*, however, hypothesizes that although we have certainly damaged our natural landscape, the absence of human interference, at this point, is not a viable solution. Without the careful stewardship of conscientious gardening and tending, given the forces we have unleashed, the future of the landscape might belong to tree of heaven, English ivy, and privet.

Wanuri Kahiu's (2009) short film *Pumzi*, which "imagine(s) a black feminist future through ecological imagery" (Rico, 2017, p. 81), offers a similarly ambiguous view of humanity's postcollapse sociopolitical structure and relationship with nature (see Figure 8.4). In the film, Asha, the protagonist, works as a curator at the "Virtual Museum of Natural History" within a

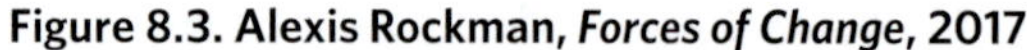

Figure 8.3. Alexis Rockman, *Forces of Change*, 2017

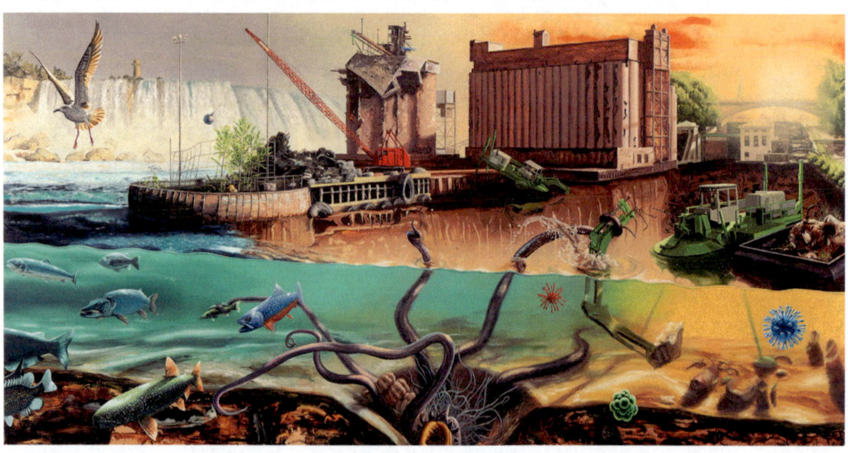

Figure 8.4. Wanuri Kahiu, *Pumzi*, 2009

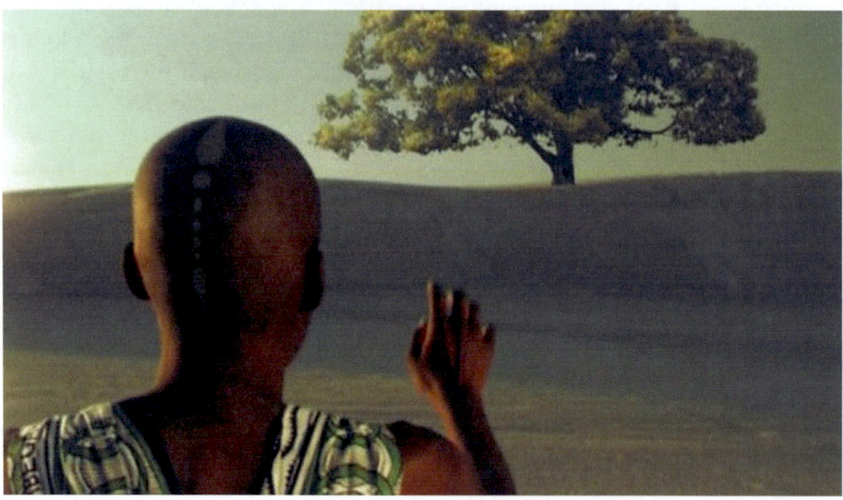

future in which water is exceedingly rare, and the landscape outside the city is an irradiated wasteland that will not support plant life. Kahiu's treatment of the city hesitates between utopian progress and dystopian control. The city is a preservation habitat, and all the energy produced therein is sustainable/renewable, yet the citizens take mandated medication to suppress dreams, and the renewable energy is produced by enforced manual labor. Asha and others throughout the film recycle their sweat and urine into potable water, like the Fremen of *Dune* (Herbert, 1965). After receiving a sample of water-rich soil that germinates seeds, Asha has visions of finding the soil's source and an enormous tree that grows from the desert. Then Asha is punished by the city's council, forced to labor on energy-producing machines, until she escapes into the desert, where she uses her body's water to plant and nourish the seed.

The *novums* that Kahiu explored in this film do not come from simple narrative convenience, but from a profound connection with contemporary geographical and social issues. James Wachira (2020) observed that *Pumzi* "engages in a remediation of African history by connecting futuristic imagery with contemporary African problems. History in *Pumzi* is re-envisioned through notions of futurity that show ways out of the current tendencies of environmental exploitation" (p. 332). The growing trend of online education finds its natural endpoint in the idea of a virtual museum, with nature forever preserved, accessible but untouchable (Ali & Kahiu, 2020). The practice of tree planting as remediation for drought and desertification, specifically in Africa, has roots in Wangari Maathi's Green Belt Movement (Wachira, 2020). In *Pumzi*, Kahiu avoids a purely pessimistic depiction of a social/environmental dystopia by positing the hope that individual action can make a profound difference, even in the face of utilitarian "perfection."

Working with similar concepts, though with a more mysterious narrative and surreal imagery, Wilfred Ukpong's (2010–ongoing) Afrofuturist *Blazing Century* series includes photographs, short films, and sound/sculptural installations produced collaboratively with members of regions affected by environmental crises. *Blazing Century 1* (2010–2020) focuses on the Niger Delta, an oil-rich but historically impoverished region in southern Nigeria (Banks, 2022). These works, which are produced via workshops and relational performances with local community members, depict oblique mystical rituals enacted by figures covered in red or black pigment. Ukpong (quoted in Aikulola, 2020) claimed that the predominant red and black reference violence, blood, and oil, while the minimal yellow in the works symbolizes hope. As Ukpong came from a family of ExxonMobil managers and engineers but rejected this path himself (Nonino, 2021), these colors might also allude to the company's corporate branding, among other possible references. In *BC1: Mediating Object #1 Dream Chasers (Boys) on a Time Capsule* (Ukpong, 2017), four figures, their bodies and clothes painted carbon black, ride a red industrial tank in the surf (see Figure 8.5). In *BC1-ND-FC: Alas, My Thirst Lumbers to the Sea for Our Saline Zone is Barren With Crude #2* (n.d.), a similarly pigmented figure kneels on a rocky beach, either drinking red liquid from, or vomiting it into, a tidal pool. The focus here does not seem to be on narrative consistency, as we cannot discriminate whether these actions are everyday activities, moments in a story, or magical rituals. Rather, the dreamlike figures, objects, and scenes, which draw upon site-specific symbolism, local myth and legend, and ecological history (Banks, 2022), construct a highly developed world with transformative potential. It opens a third space

Figure 8.5. Wilfred Ukpong, *BC1: Mediating Object #1 Dream Chasers (Boys) on a Time Capsule* (c 2017)

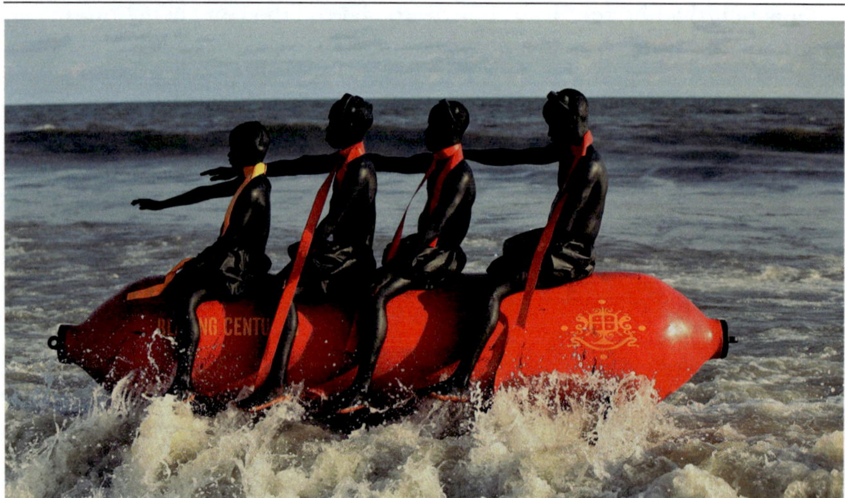

Produced courtesy of Wilfred Ukpong and Blazing Century Studios, Nigeria, France, and the USA

(Bhabha, 2009) to critically recognize contemporary regional conditions, reframe deficit narratives surrounding the region, and re-envision social and ecological justice with new hope (Aikulola, 2020).

Curriculum Engaging With the Posthuman

While the notion of posthuman is complex and has been interpreted in a myriad of ways, students may begin to grapple with the concept by considering how humanity might exist in futurity (refer to Table 8.1). As posthumanism collapses anthropocentric hierarchies that locate humans above other species (Wolfe, 2018), notions of the posthuman subject will emphasize human ecological embeddedness rather than the transcendence over earthliness and mortality sometimes seen in transhuman and "posthuman" science fiction. To emphasize ecological relationality and interdependence further, the focus might shift from humans to the land. One project prompt could ask students to study a locality and the forces that currently impact it (e.g., geological, ecological, social, and political) and speculate on how those forces might extend into the future. In such cases, students could construct an artwork (e.g., mural, film, or performance) that tells a deep-time future narrative of the region. On a more micro scale, students could be asked to tell a graphic story detailing one future person or nonhuman animal's experience of the world, including how they navigate future challenges. Such approaches could be dystopian, pointing toward adverse future impacts and, perhaps, calling attention to especially destructive current actors and practices likely to cause such crises; utopian, offering fresh, imaginative templates for reshaping society; or some quasi-utopian/dystopian blend, emphasizing the complexities of just and sustainable living.

CONCLUSION

Within an ecopedagogical curriculum, speculative art and fiction can open nonthreatening, imaginative spaces for students to engage with societal thinking and patterns, and to conceive of and critically reflect upon future developments from a safe standpoint (Leavenworth & Manni, 2021). A growing body of literature (Doyle, 2020; Leavenworth & Manni, 2021) suggests that play may be a key ingredient in students' co-creating stories about the future. While speculative fiction and art are inherently creative and playful, teachers can intentionally work to set the conditions for such play to flourish. For instance, Julie Doyle (2020) suggests that an emphasis on collective participation, learning outside the classroom, and immersive "play events" (p. 2767) can promote this type of play and, ultimately, bold, imaginative engagement. While this chapter focused on how students may dynamically envision futures, the next two chapters address how students could enact their visions within the contexts of their schools and broader communities.

QUESTIONS FOR EDUCATOR REFLECTION

1. Cognitive estrangement can provide commentary or offer insight into contemporary society. When have you experienced this phenomena in literature or film? How did it impact you? Which *novum* (i.e., a novel invention, idea, or circumstance) was particularly meaningful?
2. Speculative art and literary genres/subgenres are diverse and can include science fiction, climate fiction or "cli-fi," Afrofuturism, magical realism, fantasy, alternate history, horror, superhero fiction, cyberpunk fiction, and steampunk fiction, to name a few. What ecopedagogical advantages and challenges might be associated with an emphasis on each of these genres/subgenres?
3. How could you encourage students to move beyond escapist, technoscientific fantasies (e.g., flying cars and time travel) to provide commentary on or insight into contemporary life?
4. What ecopedagogical role can dystopias play? What are the dangers of dwelling in dystopian speculation?
5. Which media and art forms lend themselves well to complex storytelling?

CHAPTER 9

Greening the School and Revitalizing School Culture

With Lauren Farkas

How could schools function as models for life beyond school? What would it mean to nurture school cultures of sustainability and well-being? How could educators not only encourage students' ecologically sustainable behaviors, but foster school cultures where those activities are intrinsically motivating, communally supported, and responsive to local contexts? Culture as a concept is multifaceted and intimately tied to history, place, people, and actions. This chapter will look at how art education, through an ecopedagogical lens, can revitalize school cultures and senses of school as a place toward the goals of enhancing student well-being and engendering genuine, actionable care for the Earth.

To begin, we want to acknowledge non-place (Augé, 2008) as a phenomenon to disrupt or re-envision. Marc Augé (2008) described non-places as uniform sites built for efficiency without a clear sense of identity, history, or connection to other localities (e.g., hospital waiting rooms and airport terminals). Given this definition, many schools might be seen as operating at some levels as non-place (Bertling, 2018). First, the built environments of schools can feel rigid, institutional, and sterile. Gregory (2009) described how generic school architecture can reinforce non-place relations: the hallways produce a "labyrinth of fractal repetition," the floor polish generates a "shimmering mirage of confusion both in front and behind," and the hard floor and locker surfaces project sound, "creating a background soup of continuous murmur" (p. 33). Beyond architectural and design issues, not to mention the ecological devastation often present in these settings, Gregory argued that modern schooling reinforces individuality over community connection: "every attempt has been made for the students to feel like individuals rather than students of a particular school" (p. 42). Thus, modes of bringing students together, like songs, chants, marches, and uniforms, are increasingly absent. Gregory described how such conditions, ensuring that students progress through interior space as individuals, can foster "distraction," "passivity," and "insecurity" (p. 41), which negatively impact students' well-being.

To counter these trends, meaningful placemaking and community-building activities can infuse school life. Such efforts not only have impacts on student well-being, but schools emphasizing place and community will be better positioned to model and promote ecological sustainability. Research suggests the fundamental interconnectedness of psychosocial wellness and pro-environmental behaviors: sustainable actions can contribute to enhanced well-being (Brown & Kasser, 2005; Vatovec & Ferrer, 2019; Xiao & Li, 2011), and enhanced well-being can predict sustainable behaviors (Nguyen et al., 2022). Thus, in schools, each can benefit from investment in the other. This chapter will explore how educators and students can work together to transform schools into places prioritizing community, well-being, and sustainability (see Table 9.1).

The focus of the chapter is twofold—placemaking in indoor spaces and in outdoor spaces. In each main section we will introduce artists whose works aim to cultivate place. Their emplacing practices invite human and, often, more-than-human community members into communion and employ diverse methods, including interpersonal organizing, ritual, permaculture design, and guerrilla gardening tactics. Along with these works, each section includes ideas for engaging students in transdisciplinary school placemaking initiatives that prioritize ecologically sustainable community living.

Placemaking initiatives aim to enhance the cultural value of public spaces. Encompassing murals, parks, pop-up social events, concert series, playgrounds, and art installations, these interventions aim to foster relationships between people and the spaces they inhabit. Such projects are inherently participatory and asset-based; they facilitate "creative patterns of use, paying particular attention to the physical, cultural, and social identities that define a place and support its ongoing evolution" ("What Is Placemaking?" 2007, para. 1). Artists who engage in creative placemaking efforts seek to leverage the unique assets and creative potential of places and support community-led change. Moreover, in settler colonial contexts, placemaking can acknowledge space as storied and political earth, work to project futures that forefront Indigenous presence, take steps toward truth and reconciliation, and, in all contexts, care for the Earth and its more-than human inhabitants.

The placemaking works discussed in this chapter range widely in approach and scale, from a few square meters to multiple hectares. The common thread through these installations, structures, and earth-based projects is a commitment to enhancing community involvement and collective well-being, as artists, gardeners, designers, and community members work to intervene meaningfully in spaces. The corresponding curricular ideas may act as inspiration for sustainable placemaking in schools, although we recommend that any undertakings respond to the unique needs and assets of local communities.

Table 9.1. Some Curricular Applications of the Theme of Place

Big Idea	Grade Levels	Ecopedagogical Goals	Key Concepts	Discussion/Reflection Prompts	Possible Artistic Responses
Place	K–12*	Engaging in sustainable placemaking Perceiving ecological degradation associated with built environments and recognizing the ecosocial opportunities inherent in these spaces	Places are meaningful locations. Art and design can play important roles in producing place. Creative placemaking can enhance the cultural and ecological value of public spaces. Artists can play important roles in implementing and modeling ecologically sustainable practices.	What is your favorite place? What makes it feel special? What is your favorite part of the school? Why? How can built environments promote a sense of place? How can they promote community? How might ecology impact our sense of place? How might thriving ecosystems impact our sense of place? How might communities engage in placemaking with the goal of ecologically sustainable living?	Conduct a needs assessment on campus and design material interventions, which could include • Installing gardens (e.g., butterfly, rain, herb, or container garden) • Creating an urban farm • Decorating and installing recycling bins, rain barrels, bicycle racks, and signage promoting other sustainable behaviors • Building chicken coops and goat playgrounds

*The wording of key concepts and prompts will likely need to be modified for use with elementary students.

PLACEMAKING IN INDOOR SPACES

This section is focused primarily on relational transformations of interior space. Each work imaginatively invites social interaction; they emphasize place by intentionally designing sites that facilitate beneficial experiences for the people who use these spaces. Additionally, as each work is made from locally sourced, sustainable materials, they allude to local ecology. As research shows that students consistently prefer, report higher attention levels, and experience higher well-being in classrooms with biophilic elements, like potted plants (van den Bogerd et al., 2020), school buildings and campuses could benefit from attendance to these elements. While not all schools have outdoor areas that can support substantial school gardens or outdoor classrooms, all schools have interior spaces that might be reconfigured to cultivate a stronger sense of place. The works presented below can inspire meaningful engagements with place to support shifts in school culture toward community and sustainability.

Artists Constructing Place Indoors

Fritz Haeg, a U.S. artist, has presented a series of participatory installations, or domestic performances, in cities across North America and Europe. Each *Domestic Integrities* (2012–2014) installation unfolded over time as participants engaged with the work, typically involving a large, communally crocheted rug and collective presentation (see Figure 9.1). To begin each piece, local volunteers would bring excess textiles and then collectively crochet the strips (Haeg, n.d.). Each rug then became the stage where various rituals might be enacted. While some enactments included lengthy plant processions culminating at the rug (Walker Art Center, 2013), other versions engaged community members in ritually approaching the space with an attitude of offering; participants brought and presented their bounty–things they found, harvested, or made in their domestic spaces (Haeg, n.d.). Over time, as these collections began to languish or fade, they would be ritually restocked. Visitors were invited to take off their shoes, sit, and engage their senses in interacting with the objects and plants there. Haeg described how the work went beyond simple interactions as it operated as a charged site "for testing, performing, and presenting how we want to live" (para. 5). Additionally, this work shows how simple materials, when orchestrated with intention to honor people and material environments over time, can enliven place in profoundly meaningful ways. From an educational perspective, as the work shares some resemblance to elementary circle time, it might inspire classes to re-envision relationality in these spaces.

Whereas Haeg's (2012–2014) installation transforms ground-level space, much as could occur on an elementary classroom floor, this next, more structural work stretches organic limbs into the ceiling rafters, and provides a simple example of how generic built environments could be imaginatively

Figure 9.1. Fritz Haeg, *Domestic Integrities*, 2012

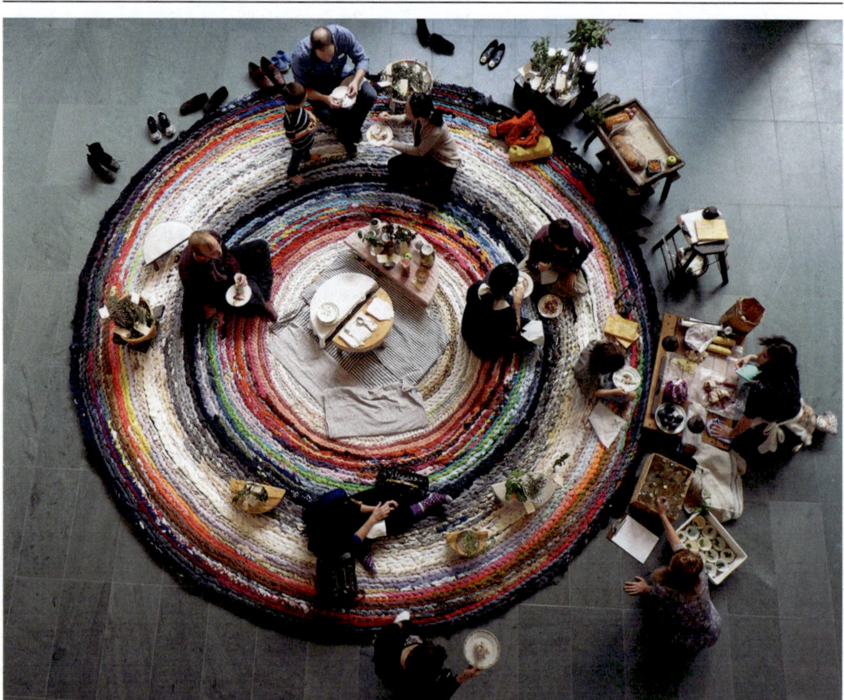

disrupted. In *The Storyteller's Tree*, Denmark-based recycling art activist Thomas Dambo (2019a) created an enlivening atmosphere using ecologically sustainable materials (see Figure 9.2). This structure, made out of recycled pallet wood, "grows" in the open-use area of the main library in Esbjerg (Dambo, 2019b). The sprawling forms invite physical engagement; community members can rest on its roots, climb into its cavelike center to read, meet under its boughs, and read aloud from its circular stage.

Curriculum Constructing Place Indoors

Entry-level placemaking engagements with students can focus on the spatial experience of the school and how to enhance that experience for students. An indoor/outdoor seating project, *Pop-Up Furniture* (Nabolagshager et al., 2019), in Oslo, Norway, demonstrates how strategic placemaking can rejuvenate school settings and involve students. As part of a participatory research project, high school students, under the direction of a mentor, conducted a school needs assessment, identifying the need for moveable seating, visual interest, and greenery in their schoolyard to promote community interaction (Reich, 2019). Consequently, these students, with support from

Figure 9.2. Thomas Dambo, *The Storytellers' Tree*, 2019

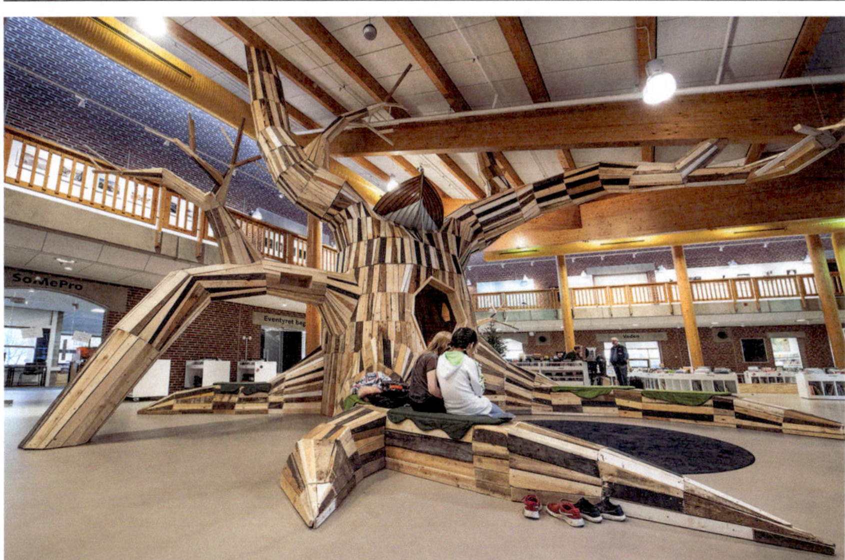

www.thomasdambo.com

several organizations and volunteers, worked to design and build six mobile furniture modules, complete with stratified seats, lined planters, berry bushes, and flowers. Through this process, students learned basic carpentry, gardening, and urban agricultural methods. Even more importantly, they were empowered to lead their own placemaking initiatives, to create sustainable, relational environments where people want to meet and interact.

Much like the Oslo youth, students can be positioned as researchers, conducting needs assessments of their school environments and recommending modifications. With limited time and resources, even small-scale modifications can be helpful, such as opening blinds; displaying student work; bringing in plants; and finding or fashioning rugs, lamps, curtains, and soft seating. Note that organic interior interventions, like Haeg's textile work (2012–2014; refer to Figure 9.1) and Dambo's wooden work (2019a; refer to Figure 9.2), have the potential to increase sound absorption in schools, an invisible environmental factor that contributes to spatial experience. Diverse rituals, as seen in Haeg's work, could be adopted to promote community in these spaces. Additionally, traditional arts projects could infuse the material culture of the school: a gallery space near the school entry, an art installation in the commons, a sculpture garden in the school courtyard, or a striking theater set. In all these cases, students can employ sustainable materials and processes.

While these entry-level approaches are socially beneficial, to go further ecologically, efforts toward sustainable living could infuse interior spaces.

For instance, students could install composting stations in the cafeteria or recycling bins in each classroom and hallway accompanied by student-produced visual instructions, or students could audit the school's energy usage, formulate solutions, and use arts-based approaches to enact those solutions and mobilize student body participation. Such ecologically oriented placemaking projects could naturally extend outside the school building to the surrounding campus, efforts that will be explored in the next section.

PLACEMAKING IN OUTDOOR SPACES

Outdoor works approach placemaking through a stronger ecological orientation. Importantly, these works encourage people to rethink space—how it is used by humans and how it might be transformed to support local communities and ecosystems. While each of the works described below emerges from the particularities of certain locales, they employ methods that could be adapted to other contexts.

Artists Constructing Place Outdoors

At New York University, artist and engineer Natalie Jeremijenko directed the x-Design Environmental Health Clinic (xClinic), a clinic committed to addressing the planets' infirmities through urban public experiments. For the *No Park* project, Jeremijenko and the xClinic (n.d.) targeted no parking zones, rarely used paved spaces near fire hydrants, around New York City. By removing the asphalt and placing low-clearance plants in these spaces, they transformed the pavement into mini-parks that beautify the streetscape, strategically attract butterflies, and intercept and cleanse storm-water runoff (Schaffer, 2008). Given the low growth of these mosses and grasses, the spaces can still be accessed by emergency vehicles, since even after being flattened, the plants will generate (Jeremijenko, 2014, 7:50–9:50). As many schoolyards are overpaved, this work provides a model for how school communities could begin to recognize these ecologically unproductive spaces and others like them, and approach them as ecosocial opportunities.

Artists and community organizers Jordan Weber (2021) and Ron Finley (2020) have demonstrated how gardening can play a critical role in mobilizing and transforming communities. By intentionally cultivating gardens in unforeseen, often neglected urban spaces, both artists conspicuously widen senses of urban community to include more-than-human life. Moreover, as their work is centered in neighborhoods impacted by environmental racism, to include proximity to superfund sites (Weber, 2022) and limited access to fresh produce (Ron Finley Project, 2022a), both artists' works foreground environmental justice.

Along with architects, neighbors, and Black and Indigenous community leaders in North Minneapolis, Weber partnered with Youth Farm, a nonprofit that uses education and service to empower young people to grow and distribute produce (Joyce, 2020, para. 5). His public rain garden and urban farm, *Prototype for Poetry vs Rhetoric (Deep Roots)*, supported 36 plant species, almost all of which are edible, and include native grasses and other pollution-mitigating flora (Weber, 2022; see Figure 9.3). The raised beds were fashioned in the shape of a basketball court, reflecting the artist's aim to welcome local youth into the garden space.

Ron Finley's "Gangsta' gardening" movement operated with similar foci to empower city-dwellers to "transform food deserts into food sanctuaries" (Ron Finley Project, 2022b, para. 2). In 2010, Finley fought against the city for the right to cultivate food plants in the neglected strips of soil alongside South Central Los Angeles streets (Ron Finley Project, 2022a). His victory pioneered a path for Los Angeles residents to become food sovereign—to define and control their food systems—and his foundation continues to invest in the community by supporting guerilla gardening efforts. In speaking about his gardening as art, Finley (2013) explained:

> Just like a graffiti artist, where they beautify walls, me, I beautify lawns, parkways. I use the garden, the soil, like it's a piece of cloth, and the plants and the

Figure 9.3. Jordan Weber, *Prototype for Poetry vs Rhetoric (Deep Roots)*, 2021

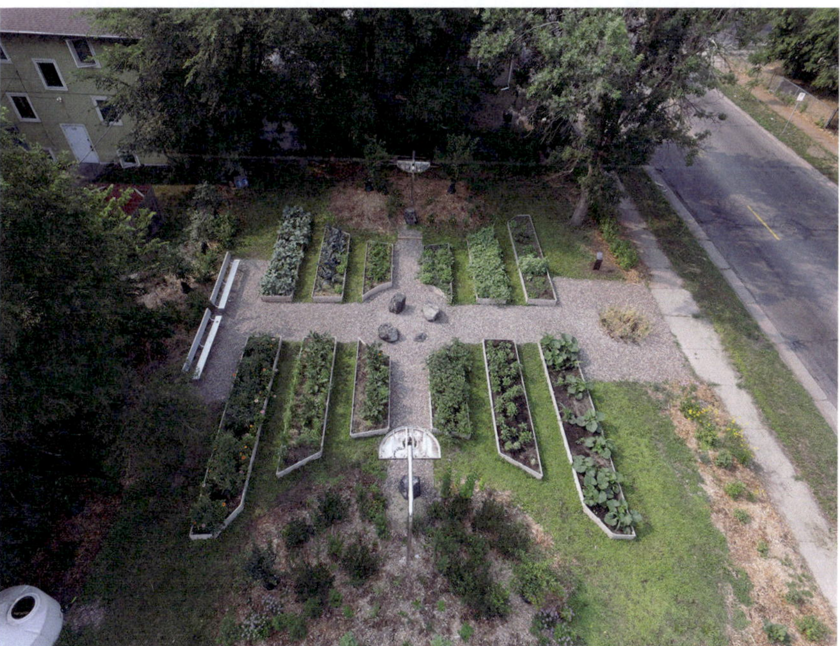

Photographer: Teddy Grimes

trees, that's my embellishment for that cloth. You'd be surprised what the soil could do if you let it be your canvas. (4:45–5:20)

In another approach to urban agriculture and sustainable living, Indigenous artist T'uy't'tanat Cease Wyss (2022), of Skwxwú7mesh (Squamish), Stó:lō, Hawaiian, and Swiss descent, employed permaculture design to re-envision a formerly neglected urban space in Vancouver, British Columbia (Rajme, 2020). Permaculture, a portmanteau of "permanent" and "agriculture" or "culture," is based on a set of principles aimed at creating harmonious, diverse, and resilient ecological places ("Permaculture Design Principles," n.d.; see Figure 9.4).

Figure 9.4. David Holmgren, graphic by Darren Roberts, *The Ethics and Domains From Permaculture Principles & Pathways*, 2019

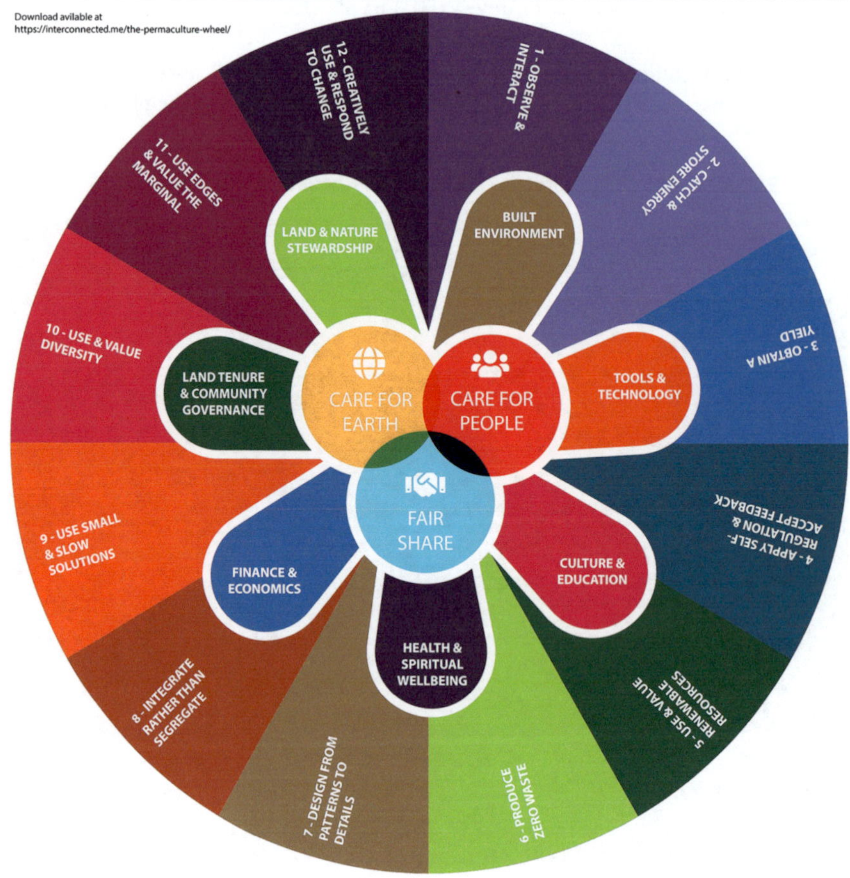

https://www.interconnected.me/the-permaculture-wheel/

Embracing these kinds of concepts, Wyss's (2019–ongoing) permaculture space *x̱aw̓s shew̓áy̓ New Growth* 《新生林》 revitalized the land tucked between buildings on unceded lands of the Squamish, Musqueam, and Tsleil-Waututh Nations (Semi-Public, n.d.; see Figure 9.5). The dynamic space, structured by traditional Coast Salish design elements, was designed for community use to include community programming led by the artist and Mudgirls Collective (Rajme, 2020). The design was intentionally relational and decolonial; Rajme (2020) explained, "All parts of the garden are grounded in a dialogue with a history of land art and decolonization of the land" (para. 4). The permaculture principles Wyss adopted frame a relational approach to the Earth that honors Indigenous presence in flora, fauna, and human life. While permaculture principles are intended primarily to inform agricultural and ecological activities, they are also highly relevant to the practice of teaching as educators work to create harmonious, diverse, and resilient classroom cultures.

One hallmark of permaculture design is that it takes time to do well. Artist Jackie Brookner (2010–ongoing) approached *The Fargo Project* with

Figure 9.5. T'uy't'tanat-Cease Wyss, *x̱aw̓s shew̓áy̓ New Growth* 《新生林》, 2021

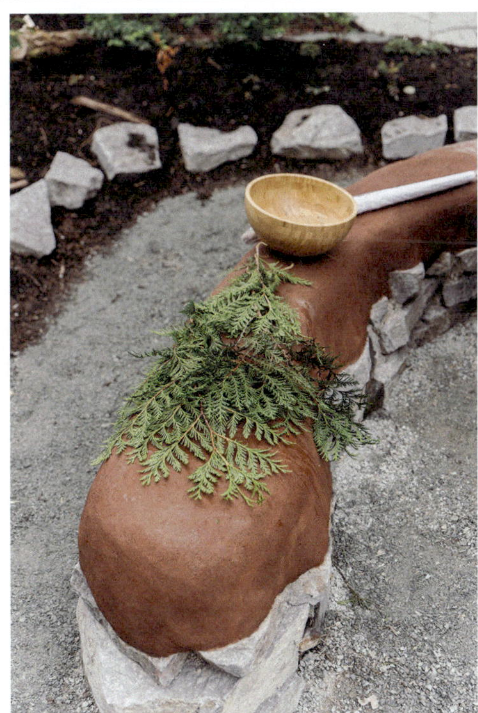

Photographer: Damaris Riedinger

similarly slow-guiding principles: "let the water lead, learn from the natural environment, involve the community, and experience nature and ecology" (Fargo Project, n.d., para. 9). Over the span of several years, Brookner, working with the city of Fargo, coalesced the community, including over 100 local institutions, community groups, and Indigenous and immigrant communities, to transform a 7-hectare drainage basin into a place that invited social interaction, supported local wildlife, and treated storm water (see Figure 9.6). The planning itself took multiple years of highly involved multidisciplinary exercises and outreach, and Brookner intentionally set the stage for continued engagement (Fargo Project, n.d.). Brookner explained that the goal was to develop "a positive relationship between citizens and with the watersheds they live in" (National Endowment for the Arts, n.d., para. 5).

Curriculum Engaging Place Outdoors

Outdoor settings can serve as vital sites for exploring and enacting ethical relationality (refer to Table 9.1). In schools that have outdoor space, even if small (e.g., parking lot islands, sidewalk strips, and window ledges),

Figure 9.6. Jackie Brookner, The Listening Garden, a feature of the World Garden Commons, the pilot site for *The Fargo Project*, in Fargo, ND, 2010–ongoing

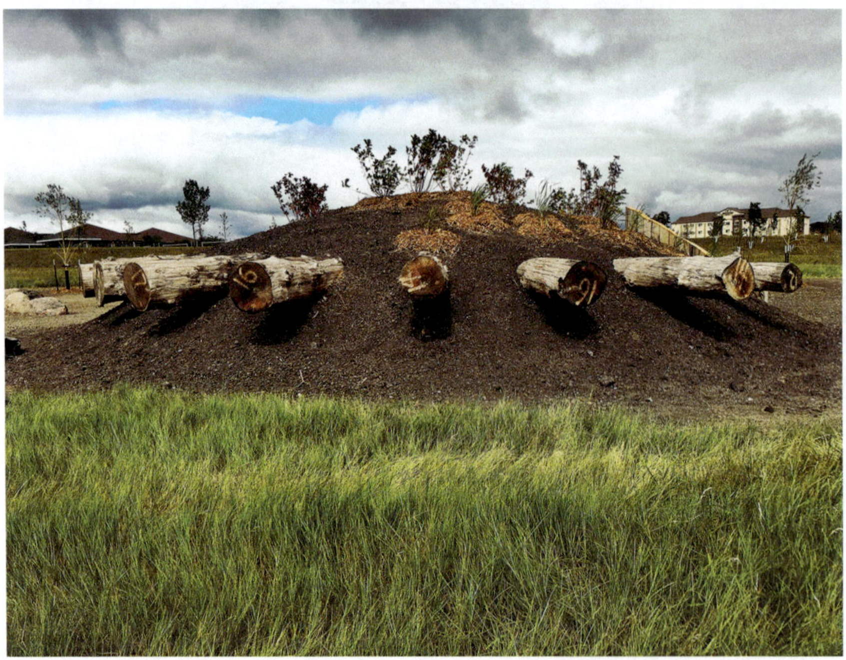

Photographer: Rachel Asleson

art education can engage students in outdoor placemaking. In such cases, students can plan, introduce, test, and revise possibilities for place in conjunction with local communities. Permaculture understandings or other sustainable design principles can be applied to gardens, urban farms, and earth installation projects on the school campus. Beyond the value of students experiencing these sites on campus, students' active involvement in creative placemaking processes presents valuable opportunities for community-building and implementing sustainable practices that students could eventually enact outside the bounds of the school campus.

Because creative placemaking inevitably involves creative problem-solving, design thinking could play a central role in such endeavors. Design thinking represents collaborative, empathetic, iterative processes of developing solutions to real-world problems (Graham, 2021). While design thinking processes have been defined in multiple ways, they tend to progress from students' understanding and exploring a problem to materializing and refining solutions. One prominent model articulates five, not necessarily sequential, phases of engagement: empathize, define, ideate, prototype, and test (Dam, 2022).

While such design processes are commonly associated with neoliberal aims like preparing students for participation in a "capitalist designer economy" (Graham, 2021, p. 780) where creativity and innovation are in demand (Kalin, 2019), more recently, scholars (e.g., Graham, 2020) have begun emphasizing its potential for critical social engagement. Specifically, design could function as social practice and critically reinvent prevailing conditions. When such critical, socially oriented design processes are applied to school environments, they offer a means of restoring social and ecological possibilities. Thus, by plotting out a space for a vegetable garden, channeling rainwater in rain gardens and rain barrels, weaving ropes to support walking "buses," designing chicken coops, constructing "idle-free zone" signs for the car line, creating sculptures that act as secure bicycle parking, planning the optimal layout of solar panels, or constructing an outdoor classroom, students are introducing new possibilities for schooling and new ways of being in the world.

CONCLUSION

As creative placemaking initiatives are instituted in schools, the material environment undergoes sustainable transformations: a formerly austere chain-link fence supports a vertical garden of used beverage containers now planters strapped to the fence, a small courtyard hosts a worm farm, once-bare computer lab walls display student-produced visual instructions for reducing energy usage, and school entryways feature colorful bicycle helmet lockers. The school's materiality reflects the day-to-day behaviors that occur in such schools—the social practices embedded in school cultural systems. As culture is not fixed or static, school cultural transformation can be produced and co-created through the engagement of multiple stakeholders over time. Movements addressing both the social and physical components of school life hold strong promise for fostering self-sustaining school cultures of ecological sustainability, ultimately contributing to more safe, just, and sustainable societies.

QUESTIONS FOR EDUCATOR REFLECTION

1. Which aspects of your school contribute to a sense of community? Which facets contribute to a sense of place?
    a. Which spaces stand out as particularly attractive, meaningful, historical, unique, or otherwise significant?
    b. Which spaces could use some attention or re-envisioning?
2. How does the material culture of your classroom contribute to a sense of place?
3. How does your school currently address ecological sustainability?
4. How could your school go further to adopt and model sustainable practices? How could art and design play a central role in these efforts?

CHAPTER 10

Restoring Ecosystems and Empowering Communities

Though the frequency and scale of ecological destruction can feel overwhelming, it is important that we do not succumb to apathy and despair. The field of restoration ecology offers one avenue for individuals and communities to take physical action to counteract such trends while still recognizing that larger policy change is needed to sustain these efforts. Ecological restoration is the practice of aiding ecosystems that have been damaged or destroyed—effectively setting up the conditions to allow microorganisms, plants, and other animals to carry on the work (Society for Ecological Restoration, 2020). It is a set of practices that various Indigenous groups have carried on for hundreds of years, and sometimes millennia, by maintaining traditional land management practices as well as restoring overexploited land or land degraded by outsiders (Reyes-García et al., 2019). Ecological restoration practices tend to support degenerated ecosystems in returning to their undisturbed states, typically before humans inflicted harm (Holl, 2020). However, in many cases, such a return is impossible (e.g., due to species extinction or irreversible soil changes [van Andel & Grootjans, 2006]), and thus, ecological restoration aims more to achieve a functioning system within an acceptable range rather than returning to a historical condition (Palmer et al., 2006). Restoration efforts can vary from repairing a whole ecosystem to reestablishing one species in the ecosystem (van Andel & Grootjans, 2006). Definitions of restoration ecology are "broad and variable" (Holl, 2020, p. 7) and include a range of efforts to restore ecosystems. Some examples of restoration efforts follow:

- *Revegetation*—reestablishing native plant life, particularly to control erosion and improve water quality.
- *Reforestation*—planting trees on previously forested lands.
- *Habitat enhancement*—improving a site's ability to support specific species.
- *Remediation*—improving or creating an ecosystem where one had been damaged or destroyed previously (Holl, 2020; Vaughn et al., 2010).

Due to the complexity and scope of this work, ecological restoration crosses disciplinary boundaries, often merging perspectives of ecology, other life sciences, social sciences, the arts, and humanities (Gillson et al., 2022). Gold et al. (2006) explained, "Successful restoration requires interdisciplinary participation from land managers, policy-makers, scientists, and educators" (para. 2). Artists working in the area of restoration ecology often do so collaboratively and, sometimes, playfully—artfully intervening in local ecosystems and enlisting the public in these projects.

This chapter introduces contemporary artists who have collaborated with communities to mobilize ecological restoration at various levels and proposes some modes of engaging students in such projects. I present both small- and large-scale community efforts, led or supported by artists and designers, to remediate local ecologies. When introduced in art curricula, these projects can stir students to act, either on a small scale, collaborating within their classrooms, or on a larger scale, inspiring or joining community ecologically restorative initiatives, much as contemporary artists and designers have done in recent years. Curricular themes that might be explored include restoration, coalitions, and multispecies assemblages. See Table 10.1 for an outline of possible approaches to engaging with these themes in the classroom.

RESTORING SPECIES AND ECOSYSTEM PROCESSES

While large, well-funded projects involving multidisciplinary teams and community members are ideal for supporting ecological restoration, these types of community projects are not always available locally and, even if occurring, might not be accessible during the school day due to transportation or scheduling issues. In such cases, students might still engage in ecological restoration, albeit on a smaller scale: more modest restoration practices can be initiated independently in art class and integrated into existing schooling structures and practices. Smaller efforts conducted wholly or primarily by students may not be able to restore whole ecosystems, but they may be able to rescue or reintroduce a specific species or assist an ecosystem process. The following contemporary artists and designers model how smaller ecological restoration projects might be conducted in evocative ways that draw in the public and, in so doing, point toward the necessary and evolving role of art in the Anthropocene.

Artists Acting to Support Ecosystems

The artworks described in this section linger in the spaces between scientific project and symbolic action. While these works do not necessarily employ the most expedient, utilitarian methods to maximize ecological impact, such as those employed by scientists, their value lies more in drawing visibility to local

Table 10.1. Some Curricular Applications of Themes of Restoration and Coalitions

Big Ideas	Grade Levels	Ecopedagogical Goals	Key Concepts	Discussion/Reflection Prompts	Possible Artistic Responses
Restoration	K–8*	Acting to support diverse biological communities and enhance ecosystem services	Art can have many different purposes, including affecting social and ecological change. Art can involve interventions in local ecologies (particularly when ecosystems have been disrupted).	Can art make a physical difference in the world? In local ecologies? What places do you know that have experienced ecological harm due to human activities (indirectly or directly)? How might art play a role in beginning to remedy those harms? What role can science and traditional ecological knowledge play in artistic processes (involving ecological restoration)?	Design and install homes for nonhuman animals (e.g., birdhouses, bat houses, ladybug houses, or bee hotels). Craft and launch indigenous seed bombs. Install artful erosion barriers using biodegradable materials. Remove invasive vines and create sculptures from the materials.
Coalitions and Multispecies Assemblages	6–12	Forming and sustaining diverse coalitions for ecological and political change Embracing diverse human and nonhuman lifeways when restoring multispecies landscapes	To realize artistic (and ecological) visions, artists often collaborate with diverse groups. Other species have agency and ways of being that should be honored. Politics allow us to build consensus for change.	What are some ways artists collaborate with other people, organizations, and species? Can an artistic vision be co-constructed and shared? How can collaboration help realize an artistic (and ecological) vision? How can other species and matter play a role in realizing an artistic vision? How do politics infuse our daily lives? How do politics play a role in art? How can art be political?	Design plans for a local ecological restoration project and present it to potential partners. Join with and assist in a local ecological restoration initiative (e.g., planning, implementing, maintaining, and/or monitoring).

*The wording of key concepts and prompts will likely need to be modified for use with elementary students.

ecological degradations and the possibility of restorative practice. By conspicuously acting in memorable ways, they can incite ecosocial transformation.

A number of artists have engaged in animal habitat restoration through sculptural installations. Colorado-based artist Lynne Hull is a pioneer in this field, having engaged in "trans-species [art]" (quoted in Preece, 2011, para. 5) or "eco-atonement" (quoted in Preece, 2011, para. 27) since the 1970s. In creating sculptures for her "clients," which have included butterflies, frogs, newts, turtles, salmon, ducks, swallows, and raptors, she consulted biologists to understand specific species' needs while also weighing various aesthetic factors (Preece, 2011, para. 2). Her works are typically constructed from found biotic and abiotic materials: wooden perches for migratory birds, carved sandstone water basins for desert animals, and moss-laden islands for amphibians (Vierling, 2003).

In fashioning habitats for nonhuman animals, some artists have seized the opportunity to explore human associations and relationships with particular species. In 2010, San Francisco's famed Presidio park became a site for a number of well-known artists' animal habitat installations (Finkel, 2010). Mark Dion with Nitin Jayaswal (2010) erected a small house on a pole for Mexican free-tailed bats (see Figure 10.1). Constructed from building materials salvaged from the park, the bat house mimicked the Presidio's stark military architecture (For-Site Foundation, n.d.). This military defense theme was reinforced through the title, *Winged Defense*, and the emblem on the side (see Figure 10.2), perhaps alluding to the way these bats function as a kind of protector of humans and other animals through their mosquito consumption (ArtDaily, n.d.).

Likewise alluding to human and nonhuman animal relations, celebrated Chinese artist Ai Weiwei (2010) created *Owl House* (see Figure 10.3). No ordinary utilitarian owl habitat, a number of these patterned blue and white porcelain vessels were tethered high in the Presidio's cypress trees. The classical Ming Dynasty design evokes a host of associations, including those related to the area's trade and cultural histories (*Ai Weiwei*, n.d.). One critic mentioned the vessels' resemblance to traditional funerary urns, which might allude to the owl species' local decline prior to the work (Northern Lights, 2011). Unfortunately, the vessels' level of success in housing western screech owls is unknown.

In addition to producing animal habitats, some artists have designed interventions to target specific environmental problems, like soil erosion. Erosion—greatly accelerated by human activities—degrades land, reduces vegetation, and, ultimately, contributes to climate change (Sulaeman & Westhoff, 2020). Leslie Birch's (2015a) sculptural intervention *#StormWater Snakes* aimed to mitigate this process by physically slowing storm water and monitoring its changes (see Figure 10.4). Birch (2015b) stitched together burlap bags containing natural materials like rocks, coconut fiber, and wood chips to withstand rushing water. Resembling snakes, these compostable, soil-enriching sculptures were placed in strategic locations, like eroding hillsides

Figure 10.1. Mark Dion With Nitin Jayaswal, *Winged Defense*, 2010

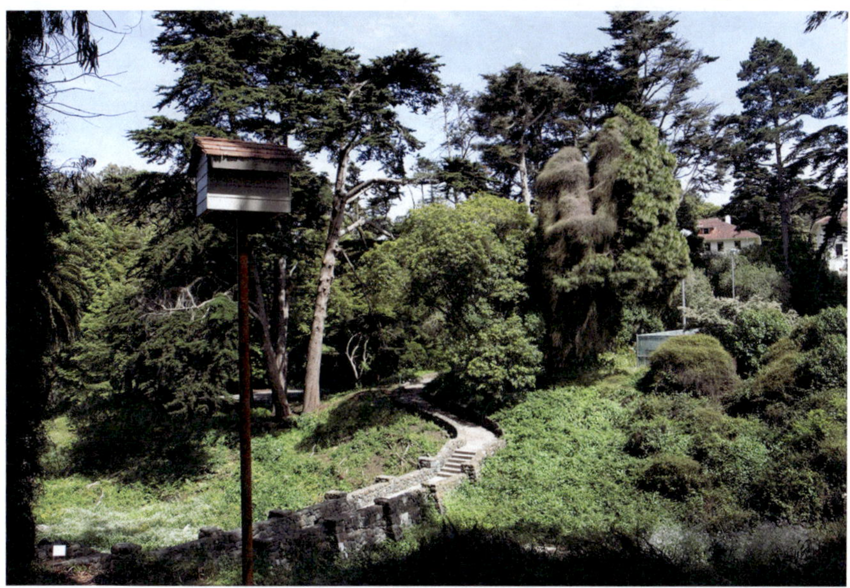

Courtesy of FOR-SITE Foundation, Photo by Monique Deschaines

Figure 10.2. Mark Dion With Nitin Jayaswal, *Winged Defense* [close-up view], 2010

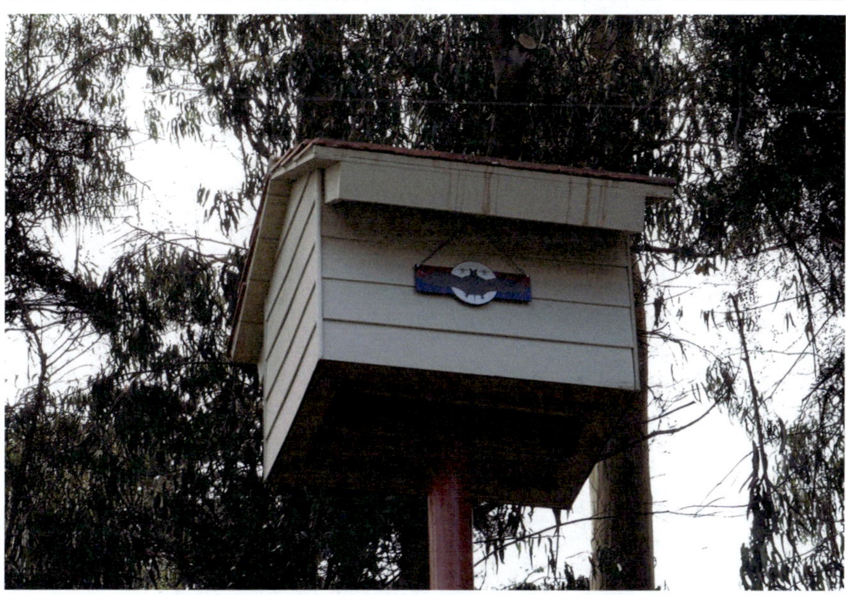

Courtesy of FOR-SITE Foundation, Photo by Monique Deschaines

Figure 10.3. Ai Weiwei, *Owl House*, 2010

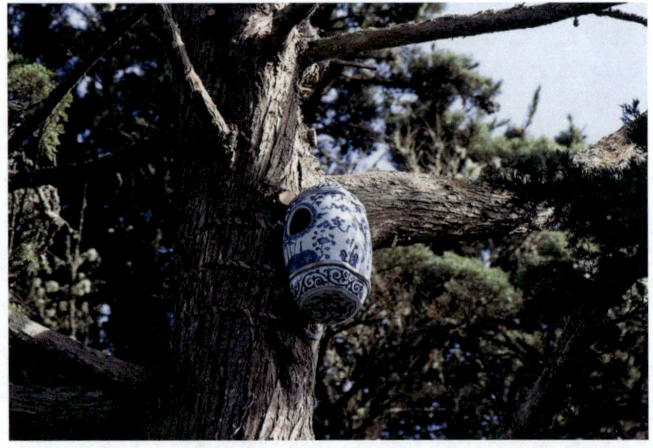

Courtesy of Ai Weiwei Studio and FOR-SITE Foundation, photo by Monique Deschaines

Figure 10.4. Leslie Birch, *#StormWater Snakes*, 2015a

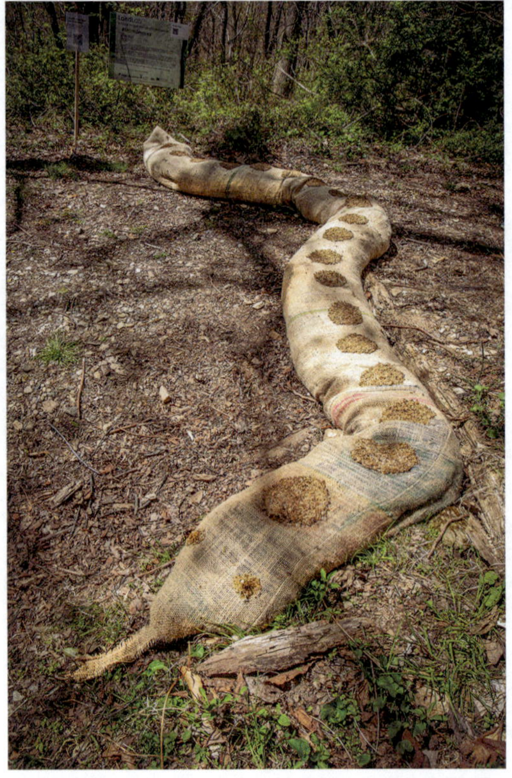

Photo by R. W. Gretzinger

along water channels (Birch, 2014). They were accompanied by water monitoring devices and solar power units to monitor changes in water depth and temperature, among other factors (Birch, 2015b). Bringing together art, technology, and citizen science, *#StormWater Snakes* models how citizens might get involved fairly easily in supporting local ecology.

Curriculum of Active Restoration

Projects similar to the ones described above could be undertaken by K–12 art students (refer to Table 10.1). Animal habitat construction seems especially well-suited for elementary and early middle grades students, who are often capable of fabricating these types of items with minimal support (e.g., constructing clay vessels, stitching burlap, and attaching wood scraps under supervision). As these kinds of projects blend art and science, interdisciplinary collaborations within the school could facilitate this restorative work. Teachers and students could research the target species and, ideally, consult with local ecological knowledge-holders.

This research would be important, as ecosystems are complex and interfering with them can produce unintended consequences. Consider Bradford pear trees in the southeastern United States. These flowering trees and their hybrids displace native plants and, with their thick growth, create ecological "dead zones" (Tran, 2021, para. 18) beneath their canopies. Planting these trees would contribute to more biodiversity loss. A more ecological alternative might be to uproot these species. Beyond concerns of invasiveness, other factors associated with ecological restoration, like impacts on human allergies, might not be readily apparent without some initial research. For instance, urban reforestation projects prioritizing male pollen-producing trees have been shown to increase pollen exposure and allergy suffering (Nowak & Ogren, 2021). Despite these types of concerns, due to the extensive damage humans have already inflicted in many places (e.g., monoculture lawns), thoughtful interventions with native species at these sites can be expected to be more ecologically and socially beneficial than harmful.

ESTABLISHING COALITIONS AND MULTISPECIES ASSEMBLAGES

The small-scale ecological restoration efforts described above can be implemented with minimal adjustments to schooling as usual, but to affect significant change, larger-scale projects might be attempted and whole ecosystems targeted. These types of ambitious projects require extensive resources and community input, and thus necessitate alliances with groups and initiatives beyond the school. Collaborators might include local nonprofit organizations, corporations, government agencies, Indigenous nations, community leaders, landholders, professionals in these fields, and concerned citizens. Moreover, from a multispecies lens (Aisher & Damodaran, 2016), native species are critical collaborators and vital change agents in ecological restoration processes.

Artists and Communities Working for Ecological Change

Artists can play varying roles in halting and reversing human acts of environmental degradation at a large scale. Jessica Fain (2011) described four ways in which artists tend to be involved:

> 1. "Artist-led remediation"—artists independently envision and lead the enactment of a large-scale intervention (usually with some support from others to realize the project).
> 2. "Post-facto artistic engagement"—artists become involved later in the remediation process.
> 3. "Artists as activators"—artists initiate and design the project before remediation occurs (and then delegate the project for other groups to realize).
> 4. "Integrated models"—artists integrally collaborate with other professionals and stakeholders throughout the process. (pp. 12–13)

In this section I describe two ecological restoration projects that could be classified as "integrated model" environmental remediation, as artists were involved since the early stages, collaborating with other groups and stakeholders throughout the design and realization process.

In the first example, interdisciplinary artists Mary O'Brien and Daniel McCormick (2014) joined the Nature Conservancy and The Nevada Museum of Art on the *Nevada Rivers Project*. For *River Fork Ranch Flood Plain*, one of five works created as part of this project, this team sought to restore a damaged floodplain in Nevada's Carson Valley (Hill, 2018). O'Brien explained their motivation:

> As a civilization, we have inherited a great deal of environmental loss. Growing up, whether we know it or not, we have all witnessed the degradation of our environment. And each generation inherits what we don't preserve, or what we damage. (quoted in Gavenus & O'Brien, 2017, para. 3)

For this project, their aim was multifold: to control erosion, enhance water quality, and develop habitats (Hill, 2018). The work was truly a community project. Over 400 volunteers from corporations, art groups, and schools assisted in planning and creating the work (Vagner, 2015). To reestablish the riparian forest and native animal species that had previously inhabited the river, the artists and volunteers gathered materials exclusively from the local watershed (Hill, 2018) and bundled them into long, sinuous thickets. They situated these 110-meter-long living sculptures, interspersed with 750 live-staked, native willows, on the parched floodplain in the hopes that they would redirect floodwaters and become homes for insects, birds, turtles, and other animals (Billman, 2015; O'Brien & McCormick, 2014; see Figures 10.5 & 10.6).

As with all of O'Brien and McCormick's works, the project was meant to extend well beyond the sculpture's installation. As the sculptures "grow into silt traps, erosion control implements, fish habitat, and other ecological enhancements" (Fox, 2017, quoted in Gavenus & O'Brien, 2017, para. 12), they are reclaimed by the environment. The local, engaged citizen volunteers, including students, who were involved in the installation stages of these projects became the works' stewards as the sculptures evolved to become part of the land and water (Gavenus & O'Brien, 2017). While O'Brien and McCormick have monitored their projects annually and conducted major assessments every 5 and 10 years, local citizens are the ones who have taken ownership (Gavenus & O'Brien, 2017; Whittaker, 2016). So far, these works have experienced multiple seasonal floods and continue to enhance local ecology (Gavenus & O'Brien, 2017).

Another example of the artist-integrated model of environmental remediation, surprisingly, occurred at a new sewage treatment plant in Sonoma County, California. *Ellis Creek Water Recycling Facility/Wildlife Sanctuary* represents a major site of extensive ecological restoration. Environmental artist Patricia Johanson (1999–2009) co-designed the facility and its

Figure 10.5. Floodplain Wall, Studio of Watershed Sculpture, 2014. A habitat restoration installation on the Brockliss Slough of the West Carson River (Minden, Nevada) at The Nature Conservancy's River Fork Ranch.

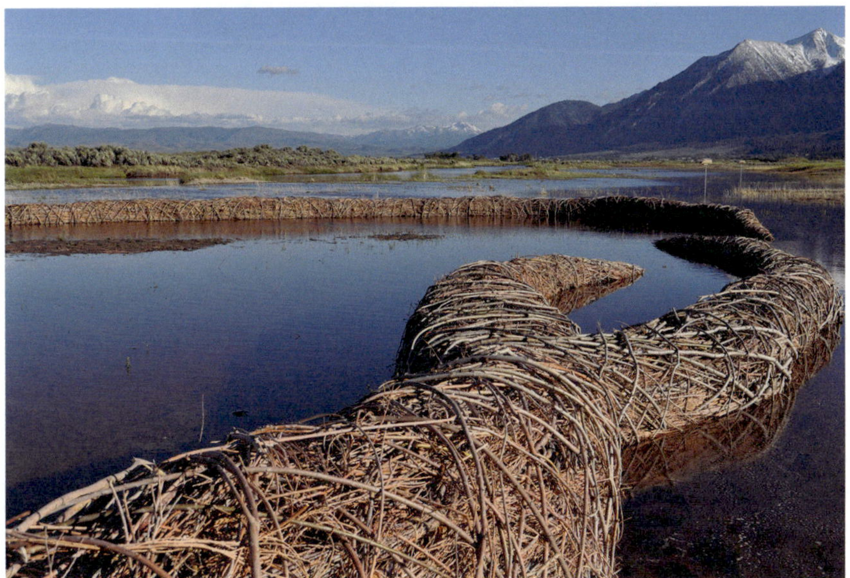

Figure 10.6. Floodplain Wall Detail, Studio of Watershed Sculpture, 2014. Daniel McCormick and Mary O'Brien, Nevada in partnership with the Nature Conservancy of Nevada and the Center for Art + Environment, Nevada Museum of Art, Reno, Nevada.

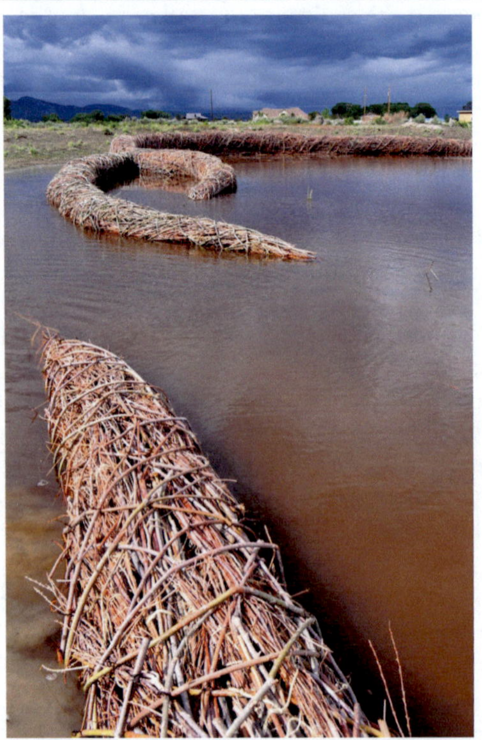

Photographer: Mary O'Brien

surrounding "wetland garden" (Slater, 2016, p. 8) with a team of engineers. Writing of the 600-acre site, Slater (2016) claimed that the project "boldly pairs wetland wastewater treatment with economic development, wildlife habitat, and public access to a public park with more than four miles of trails, while producing a saleable product: recycled water" (p. 9). Johanson considered local plant and animal imagery in site design, arranging water reservoirs, trails, and other structures in the shape of the salt marsh harvest mouse and a morning glory flower (Negley, 2015; see Figure 10.7).

Embracing innovative water treatment technologies, the facility set the conditions for natural processes to play key roles in water purification, for algae and bacteria to break down waste, and for wetlands to remove heavy metals (Water Technology, n.d.). Beyond water purification, the facility was designed to support diverse vegetation and animal habitats. For instance, open-air pond islands functionally direct water but also accommodate nesting birds (Slater, 2016; see Figure 10.8). By demonstrating how human and

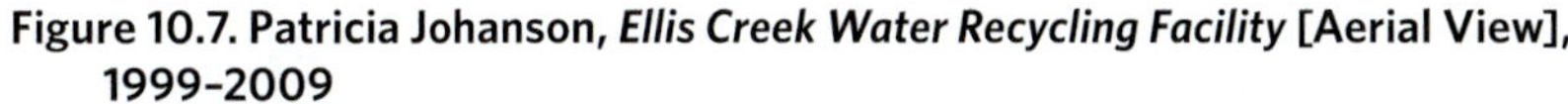

Figure 10.7. Patricia Johanson, *Ellis Creek Water Recycling Facility* [Aerial View], 1999–2009

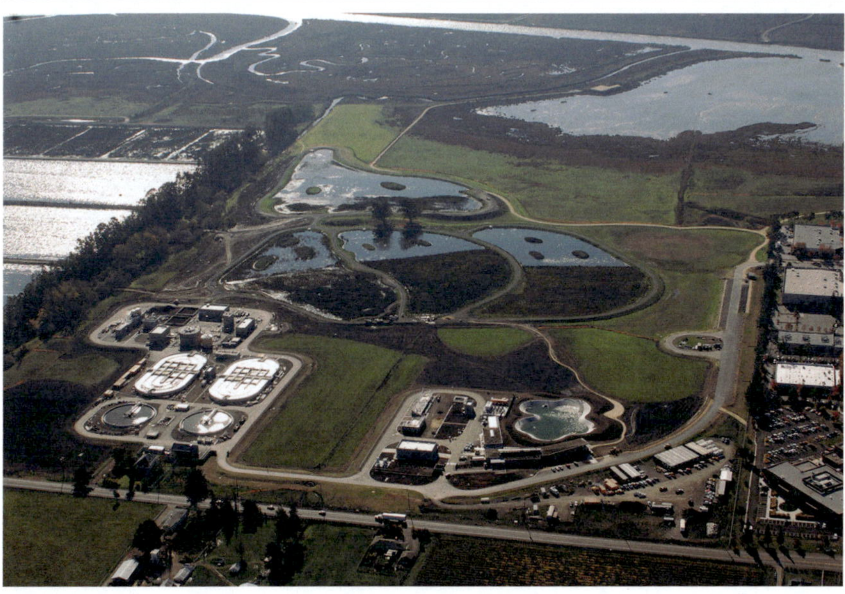

© Patricia Johanson

more-than-human needs might be met concurrently, the project publicly showcases a multispecies assemblage with the potential to inspire other new, multispecies modes of living and communing.

Curriculum for Collective Restorative Action

Like many of the other artworks discussed in this book, works of ecological restoration can play an important role in expanding students' ideas about the nature and potential of art (refer to Table 10.1). The relational works described in this chapter and others should be weighed not only with regard to aesthetic concerns, but also with respect to social and ecological practice. These forms of engagement are increasingly common components of contemporary art. Evaluative criteria could include the manner and extent to which restorative projects engage human and more-than-human community members, contribute to local ecology, and appear likely to inspire future change. As these criteria differ significantly from those used to assess traditional artworks, they can incite valuable classroom dialogues and inspire students' own more relational "artmaking" practices.

In terms of artistic involvement, local conditions and resources will inevitably shape the projects in which students engage. Where ecological restoration projects already abound, partnerships may be formed so that art

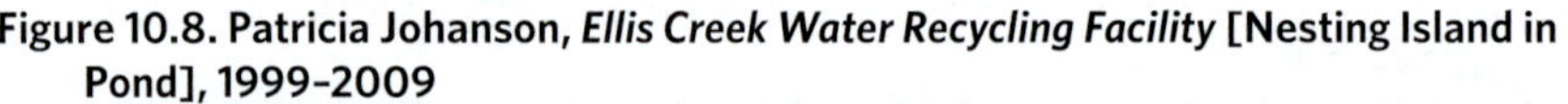

Figure 10.8. Patricia Johanson, *Ellis Creek Water Recycling Facility* [Nesting Island in Pond], 1999–2009

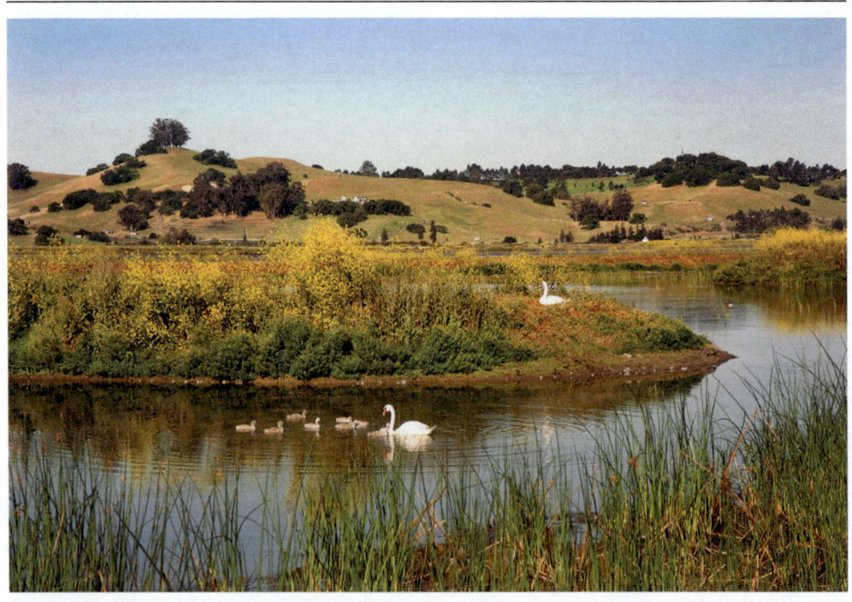

classes can join with such initiatives and directly contribute to ecological renewal. While challenges, like transportation, will inevitably arise, teachers can seek out projects within walking distance or consider ways any material components could be crafted on campus rather than on-site. Where such undertakings are scarce or nonexistent, students may perform the role of "artists as activators" (Fain, 2011, p. 12), planning and inspiring communities to engage in remediative works. In selecting areas to remediate, classes can employ an environmental justice lens. Given that communities of color and economically disadvantaged groups are more likely to experience environmental inequities, like reduced tree canopy cover and increased pollution exposure (Zhou & Kim, 2013), these areas can be prioritized in restoration efforts, in close consultation with local community members.

Student designs may be presented formally to local businesses, nonprofits, or city councils. Additionally, grant funding can be explored. While such actions exceed typical teacher planning responsibilities and can be time-consuming, the social and ecological outcomes are likely to be well worth the effort.

CONCLUSION

Affecting ecological change directly can be deeply rewarding and personally and ecologically transformational. Yet, when such efforts take place, teachers should take care to ensure that these restorative efforts are not positioned as easy fixes for late capitalist ecocide or as substitutes for political action. Students need to recognize that ecosystems are much easier to destroy than repair and that full restoration is not guaranteed, regardless of the human efforts expended (Holl, 2020, p. 13). Overconsumption and overdevelopment have long-lasting and often permanent consequences. Additionally, students need to grasp the anthropogenic forces at work that negatively impact ecosystems across the globe, resulting in escalating temperatures, shifting precipitation patterns, and rising sea levels. These forces can significantly hinder restoration efforts or undo their progress. Holl (2020) summarized this challenge: "Whereas restoration may mitigate some anthropogenic impacts on the natural world, restoration is a useless exercise unless it is part of an effort to reduce the drivers of habitat conversion, which are complex and vary across the globe (Geist et al., 2006)" (pp. 5–6). Moreover, active restoration efforts have been found to be less effective than simply removing the disruptors negatively impacting the system and allowing ecosystems to passively recover (Jones et al., 2018). Given this science, restoration ecology on its own is not the pinnacle of ecopedagogy. To affect more lasting change, political action must intermingle with these efforts. Through art education, students can exert their political imaginations to envision and realize political futures where ecological restoration is bolstered by policy and unobstructed by unsustainable human acts.

QUESTIONS FOR EDUCATOR REFLECTION

1. Which native species are threatened in your area? What factors have led to their population declines? What can be done to minimize those threats?
2. What invasive species contribute to biodiversity loss and monocultures in your area? How can those species be detected and removed without introducing new disruptors, like pesticides, to ecosystems?
3. What other factors disrupt ecosystems locally? How could these disruptors be mitigated through art interventions/ecological restoration projects?
4. What ecological restoration projects are happening in your area? Which organizations are involved? What role could art students play in supporting these efforts?
5. If no ecological restoration projects are occurring locally, what areas nearby need restoration? What types of projects could be possible here? How could students inspire and mobilize community groups toward these ends?

Conclusion

> Utopia is the process of making a better world, the name for one path history can take, a dynamic, tumultuous, agonizing process with no end. Struggle forever. (Robinson, 1990/2013, p. 95)

As a *utopian* pedagogical project (Antunes & Gadotti, 2006), ecopedagogy strives for a more just and sustainable planet. It moves beyond wishful thinking to full engagement with the world and its realities. In so doing, it acknowledges that this change cannot occur by following dominant society's trajectories: notions of progress must change. As Ursula K. Le Guin (1989/1997) stated, "I don't think we're ever going to get to utopia again by going forward, but only roundabout or sideways" (p. 98).

As with any utopian movement, the concept of hope is frequently discussed in ecopedagogy. Various theorists have expounded upon the role hope might play in such movements. Paulo Freire (1998), for instance, argued strongly for hope, identifying it as central to human agency and crucial in confronting social injustice.

In the case of climate change and related issues, hope feels more complicated. First, a form of hope, or "'false' hope" (Snyder et al., 2002, p. 1003), manifesting as climate denial, has contributed to the crisis. This illusory hope is based upon flagrant distortions of reality that perpetuate inaction (Ojala, 2012). Second, hope is complicated by the gravity of situational realities. Given climate change's scale, complexity, acceleration, and existential risks, in many ways, it represents the ultimate wicked problem. Further exacerbating the problem, unchecked, hastening global disruptive forces now reinforce feedback loops, or climate "dominoes" (Wunderling et al., 2021, p. 603), that contribute to increased temperatures across the planet. For instance, warming permafrost releases methane, a potent greenhouse gas (Xu et al., 2022), further impacting temperatures (Xu et al., 2022). Likewise, climate-change-induced drought and diminished agricultural yields can contribute to societal destabilization (e.g., migration and wars), which, in turn, can produce environmental stresses (Kelly et al., 2017) that bolster climate change.

Given the enormity of these kinds of challenges and the incredible losses already experienced, absolute hope for a pristine outcome feels implausible.

Countless species have gone extinct (Román-Palacios & Wiens, 2020). Millions of people globally have died prematurely from exposure to air pollution (Burnett et al., 2018). Innumerable ecosystems have been lost and, even with active intervention, are unlikely to recover fully (Jones et al., 2018). Understandably, these circumstances can elicit a host of negative emotions, including stress, anger, fear, regret, hopelessness, and helplessness—often described as "climate change worry," "eco-anxiety," or "climate grief" (Ojala et al., 2021, p. 35). Children and young people around the world are already experiencing these feelings (Hickman et al., 2022). From a psychological perspective, these negative responses are normal, yet, if experienced apart from more positive emotions like hope, can be counterproductive (Ojala, 2005; Ojala et al., 2021).

Contemporary thinkers and actors have argued for various agentic responses to such dire, knotty conditions. For instance, ecofeminist scholar Donna Haraway (2016) cautioned against the hope and despair often associated with futuristic thinking and, instead, encouraged more present-oriented, gritty forms of engagement—"staying with the trouble" (p. 4). She posited a new form of, or alternative to, hope, in the form of "viral response-ability" (p. 114), which involves the recognition of a multitude of accountabilities and works toward the utopia of "multispecies flourishing in the face of terrible histories" (p. 116). Influenced by Haraway's work, S. Eben Kirksey et al. (2013) poetically described the relationship hope played in their multispecies activist art project as "hopes moving like oil in water" and identified multispecies alliances as generating "openings for more audacious hopes" (p. 250). This metaphor of hopes of oil in water can be generative in emphasizing the fluid yet sustained nature of such work, where bursts of hope may be coming and going, spurring energies, carrying us, and allowing us to persevere through desperate realities, rather than burning brightly and extinguishing quickly (i.e., acting on unrealistic hope and then succumbing to despair and cynicism). In such cases, hope might involve our acknowledgment of the realities and constraints within which we will have to maneuver until greater change occurs. Given the power of emotional states and perspectives in the face of such sizeable obstacles, educators might co-reflect upon the stances and metaphors that resonate with them and their communities in this work.

Despite the nuances surrounding how hope might manifest, research surrounding climate-change responses clearly points to the value of hope for children and young people, albeit hope not founded in denial. Maria Ojala (2012), researching the relationship between hope and pro-environmental behavior, claimed that hope was critical for youth's environmental engagement. She explained how positive emotions like hope are useful in "providing momentary respite from the harsh reality and giving people the strength needed to face the threat at hand and search for solutions" (p. 636). She also pointed to trust in environmental organizations and anger as potentially useful. Moreover, Ojala (2012) claimed that hope had a unique positive influence on pro-environmental behaviors that could not be replaced by, for instance, teaching environmental values.

Given the critical significance of hope, how could we cultivate this posture for ourselves and with our students? Research points to several broad approaches that could be integrated into teaching for positive outcomes:

- *Bypass discourses of fear.* While some forms of worry can be motivating, excessive fear can be debilitating (Whitmarsh, 2011). Fear-based messages are effective in motivating people to act proactively in relation to the environment only under special circumstances (Stern, 2012). These messages are most effective when they are accompanied by recommendations for specific actions that might be taken; otherwise, they can be detrimental (Whitmarsh, 2011). For instance, research (Stern, 2012; Whitmarsh, 2011) shows that when climate deniers are faced with fear-inducing information and do not have opportunities or guidance to take positive action to mitigate the problems, they are likely to try to reduce their fear by denying the science or discrediting the source. The situation is further complicated by the similarities between communications aimed at environmental awareness, which can be beneficial (Trott, 2020), and messages conjuring fear, as they both tend to communicate environmental realities but have different effects. In spite of these complexities, a general guideline might be for educators to not dwell in particularly fearful territory and to accompany any distressing environmental information with opportunities for students to act proactively. Although Chapters 5 through 8 in this book address some topics that might induce fear, engagement with these subjects should be carefully framed to emphasize awareness and imaginative action over chaos and calamity.
- *Encourage trust in pro-environmental actors.* Youth with strong trust in environmental actions undertaken by other individuals and groups like environmental organizations are more likely to exhibit hope (Ojala, 2012). Rather than leading students to shirk responsibilities by placing environmental responsibility solely on others, this trust can serve as a motivating force (Ojala, 2012). This trust may even extend to their classmates and other collaborators on eco-art projects that they will fulfill their roles and that their collective actions will have an impact. Participation in many of the activities described in Chapters 4, 9, and 10, which emphasize community and collective acts, can play a role in helping students build this trust.

- *Support taking action and exercising resistance.* Young people need opportunities to transform their environmental worries into action. Ojala (2012) claimed that hope can be embodied through such actions. As Ojala (2017) explained, "By demonstrating that other ways of being are possible, a sense of agency and hope are evoked" (p. 80). The Part II chapters in this book, particularly Chapter 10, outlined ways students can physically and proactively respond to the atrocities they are witnessing.
- *Intentionally cultivate a sense of agency.* Students need to feel like they have some control or impact on their circumstances: they need to trust their own ability to affect change (Ojala, 2012). When students take constructive actions to mitigate environmental concerns, they can develop a sense of agency, particularly when they experience tangible success early in the process and can witness the fruits of their labors firsthand (Trott, 2020). Educators can be strategic in strengthening students' agency. For instance, rather than simply displaying their art, classes could organize opening receptions so they can experience audiences' positive responses. Additionally, teachers might prioritize the earliest-grade students in creating a garden, as these students will be on campus and able to observe the impact of their labors for years to come. In terms of policy, teachers and students might seek out easy local "wins" at first, like applying to the school board for a crossing guard to support students in walking to school safely. Moreover, nearly all ecopedagogical endeavors could work to ensure student ownership and choice (Bertling, 2015).
- *Prompt new ways of thinking.* Cognitive reappraisals are ways in which people transform their thinking related to specific issues and situations, such as climate change and its impacts, which, in turn, allows them to regulate their emotions (Panno et al., 2020), and, in many cases, positions them to take constructive action (Ojala, 2012). For instance, students can be prompted to reframe climate change as something they are capable of addressing and acting toward collectively and joyfully. In schools, teachers and students can co-create empowering, hopeful stories and discourses at the "positive nexus of risk and hope" about the global future (Reid et al., 2010, p. 433). Additionally, Vanessa Apaolaza et al. (2022) suggest that mindfulness training could be helpful in spurring students' regular positive reappraisals of environmental issues to prompt positive acts.

When hope feels elusive, these strategies can be drawn upon to rematerialize a sense of possibility. As art is commonly known for rousing hope and bringing seeds of change, many of the works described in this text may have key roles to play in this ecopedagogical, hope-inducing process.

Finally, in seeking hope and models of resilience, we might look beneath us to the earth—to fungi. Forming vast, symbiotic networks with other fungi and plants, fungi demonstrate the strength of connection, collaboration, and interdependence. Engaging multiple organisms in complex interactions (Deveau et al., 2018), fungi demonstrate comfort with the intricacies inherent to diverse collaborations. As these networks are dynamic and continuously adapting, repairing themselves and nourishing damaged environments (Boswell et al., 2006; Deveau et al., 2018), they reveal the power of attunement and responsiveness for life in damaged terrains. Growing in irregular, entangled, boundary-crossing configurations, they model how abundant life can unfold in the spaces in between or outside of traditional categories (Flanagan, 2021). And by hastening decomposition, making and "unmak[ing] pieces of life" (Sheldrake, 2020, p. 224), they can serve as a reminder of the always-present possibility of renewal and remaking, of finding new ways to exist on and in the Earth/earth.

In this environmentally troubling era, we do not have the luxury of time. We cannot wait until we are perfectly prepared and positioned before we act. For art educators, that may mean moving forward with ecopedagogy without any formal coursework or professional development in ecology, environmental science, or environmental education. It may also mean moving forward with smaller initiatives until larger ones can be set in place. It may mean making use of the resources at our disposal right now. Just as fungi are rooted communally in the rich messiness of the soil, we can make our way, embracing the inherent challenges, complexities, and moments of "just not getting it right," while continually pushing roundabout, sideways . . . anything but in the direction of the social oppressions and environmental exploitations so commonly associated with linear, Euro-Western progress. Please do not delay. Please do not discount your abilities. Please do not underestimate your influence. Reach deeply for strength, embrace any sources of joy along the way, and trust that your fellow art educators are exerting their spheres of influence in educational spaces all across the globe, and that together we can make a profound difference.

Artists and Their Websites

Websites of Artists Discussed in this Text*

Artist Name	Website
Timo Aho	http://www.timoaho.org/
Leslie Birch	https://www.lesleybirchartist.com/
Yolanda Bonnell	https://www.yolandabonnell.com/
Justin Brice Guariglia	https://www.justinbrice.com/
Jackie Brookner	http://www.jackiebrookner.net/
Rogan Brown	https://roganbrown.com/home.html
Kaitlin Bryson	http://www.kaitlinbryson.com/
Krista Caballero & Frank Ekeberg	https://www.birdingthefuture.net/
T'uy't'tanat Cease Wyss	https://tuyttanatceasewyss.ca/
Amanda Cotton	http://www.amandacotton.co.uk/
Thomas Dambo	https://thomasdambo.com/
Agnes Denes	http://www.agnesdenesstudio.com/
Torkwase Dyson	https://www.torkwasedyson.com/
Ron Finley	https://ronfinley.com/
Mellissa Fisher	https://www.mellissafisher.com/home**
Fritz Haeg	http://www.fritzhaeg.com/studio.html
HeHe	http://www.hehe.org/
Allison Janae Hamilton	http://www.allisonjanaehamilton.com/
Nitin Jayaswal	https://www.nitinjayaswal.com/
Min Jeong Seo	http://www.seo-minjeong.de/index.html
Patricia Johanson	https://patriciajohanson.com/
Wanuri Kahiu	http://www.wanurikahiu.com/
Emma Kisiel	http://www.emmakisiel.com/
Adam Kuby	https://www.adamkuby.com/

Artist Name	Website
Athena LaTocha	https://athenalatocha.com/home.html
Heikki Leis	http://heikkileis.com/en**
Luzinterruptus	https://www.luzinterruptus.com/
Azuma Makoto	https://azumamakoto.com/
Dillon Marsh	http://dillonmarsh.com/
Cristóbal Martínez	https://cristobalmartinez.net/
Pekka Niittyvirta	https://niittyvirta.com/
Mary O'Brien & Daniel McCormick	https://watershedsculpture.blogspot.com/
Jill Pelto	https://www.jillpelto.com/
Postcommodity	http://postcommodity.com/**
Alexis Rockman	http://alexisrockman.net/
Joshua Pablo Rosenstock	https://www.joshuarosenstock.com/
Kathleen Ryan	https://www.kathleen-ryan.com/
Semiconductor	https://semiconductorfilms.com/
Chip Thomas	https://jetsonorama.net/
Elin Thomas	https://www.elinthomas.com/
Wildred Ukpong/Blazing Century Studios	https://www.blazingcentury.net/
Jordan Weber	http://jordanjweber.com/
Ai Weiwei	https://www.aiweiwei.com/
XTU Architects	https://www.xtuarchitects.com/

Websites of Additional Artists Who Have Produced Some Form of Eco-Art*

Artist Name	Website
Deru Anding	https://www.deruanding.com/
Siri Austeen	http://humannatureshow.com/artist/siri-austeen/
Ana Teresa Barboza	https://www.anateresabarboza.com/**
Mandy Barker	https://www.mandy-barker.com/
Nicholas Blowers	http://www.nicholasblowers.com/
David Brooks	http://davidbrooksstudio.com/
Carolina Caycedo	http://carolinacaycedo.com/
Mel Chin	https://melchin.org/oeuvre/mel-chin/**
Xavier Cortada	https://cortada.com/art2022/underwater/underwater-hoa/

Artist Name	Website
Jason deCaires Taylor	https://www.underwatersculpture.com/
Morel Doucet	https://www.moreldoucet.com/
Alejandro Durán	https://alejandroduran.com/
Dudley Edmondson	https://dudleyedmondson.com/
Paige Emery	https://paigeemery.com/**
Robert Flach	https://www.robertflach.com/
LaToya Ruby Frazier	https://latoyarubyfrazier.com/
Alexandra Daisy Ginsberg	https://www.daisyginsberg.com/
Cannupa Hanska Luger	http://www.cannupahanska.com/
Alma Heikkilä	https://www.almaheikkila.net/
Chris Jordan	https://www.beautyemerging.com/
Reena Saini Kallat	https://reenakallat.com/
Oliver Kellhammer	http://oliverk.org/
Jenny Kendler	https://jennykendler.com/home.html
Rebecca Louise Law	https://www.rebeccalouiselaw.com/
Courtney M. Leonard	https://courtneymleonard.com/home.html
Maya Lin	https://www.mayalinstudio.com/
Elin Mar Øyen Vister	https://elinmar.com/
Mary Mattingly	https://marymattingly.com/
Courtney Mattison	https://courtneymattison.com/
Elise Morin	http://elise-morin.com/
Klaus Pichler	https://klauspichler.net/**
Kaitlin Pomerantz	http://www.kaitlinpomerantz.com/
Queer Ecology Hanky Project	https://hankyexhibit.bigcartel.com/about-us**
Carlo Ratti	https://carloratti.com/
Pedro Reyes	http://pedroreyes.net/index.php
Jae Rhim Lee	https://creative-capital.org/projects/infinity-burial-project/
Cara Romero	https://www.cararomerophotography.com/**
John Sabraw	https://www.johnsabraw.com/
SCAPE	https://www.scapestudio.com/
Tiffany Shaw-Collinge	http://www.tiffanyshawcollinge.com/
Jean Shin	https://jeanshin.com/

Artist Name	Website
Studio Klarenbeek and Dros	https://www.ericklarenbeek.com/
Studio Tomas Saraceno	https://studiotomassaraceno.org/
Esther Traugot	https://esthertraugot.com/home.html
W-LAB	https://www.wds-lab.com/
Mitchell Whitelaw	https://mtchl.net/

*These websites are presented as sites teachers might explore to identify new instructional content.

**Due to some site content (e.g., nudity or sexual references), this site may not be appropriate for K–12 students to view.

Inclusion of Nature in Self Scale*

Please circle the picture that best describes your relationship with the natural environment. How interconnected are you with nature?

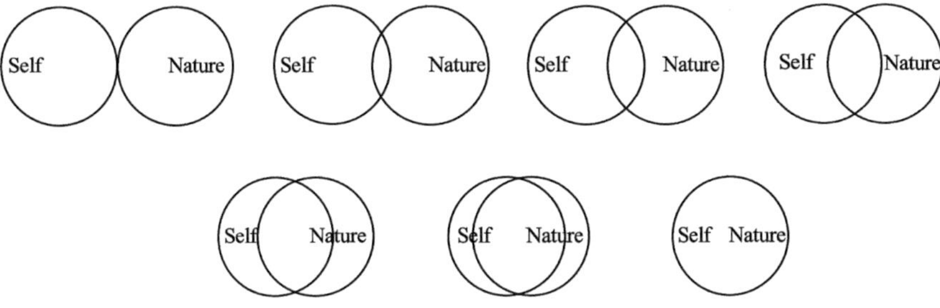

*Format may not match the original tool (Schultz, 2002).

Environmental Identity Scale*

Please indicate the extent to which each of the following statements describes you by using the appropriate number from the scale below.

1	2	3	4	5	6	7
Not at all true of me			Neither true nor untrue			Completely true of me

______ 1. I spend a lot of time in natural settings (woods, mountains, deserts, lakes, ocean).
______ 2. I think of myself as a part of nature, not separate from it.
______ 3. If I had enough time or money, I would certainly devote some of it to working to protect the environment.
______ 4. When I am upset or stressed, I can feel better by spending some time outdoors communing with nature.
______ 5. I feel that I have a lot in common with other species.
______ 6. Behaving responsibly toward the Earth—living a sustainable lifestyle—is part of my moral code.
______ 7. Learning about the natural world should be an important part of everyone's upbringing.
______ 8. I would rather live in a small room or house with a nice view than a bigger room or house with a view of other buildings.
______ 9. I would feel that an important part of my life was missing if I were not able to get out and enjoy nature from time to time.
______ 10. I have never seen a work of art that is as beautiful as a work of nature, like a sunset or a mountain.
______ 11. I feel that I receive spiritual sustenance from experiences with nature.

*Format may not match the original tool (Clayton, 2003).

Glossary of Terms

Abiotic: referring to matter that is nonliving

Agar art (microbial art): art created from colorful microbes, cultured in agar dishes to form images or designs

Animism: a relational worldview that assumes the world and the natural objects and phenomena within it, like rocks, trees, birds, and wind, are spiritual beings and worthy of respect

Anthropocene: one proposed term to define our current geological epoch, defined by human geoengineering of the Earth; a cultural term encapsulating the array of environmental degradations occurring, recognizing the scale and rapidity with which they are occurring, and placing this change within a historical context

Anthropocentric: a human-centered orientation; a belief that humans are separate from nature and superior to other life forms

Biophyllia: the idea that humans have an innate tendency or need to connect with other life forms

Biophysical world: biotic and abiotic surroundings; can vary in scale from microscopic to global

Biotic: referring to living organisms and their byproducts

Black feminist geographies: Black women's complex, critical, intersectional thought regarding geographic space; often resisting binaries and redefining oversimplified, limiting categories like Blackness, gender, and sexuality

Capitalocene: an alternative to the term *Anthropocene* that foregrounds rampant capitalism's role in global ecological destruction

Critical place-based education: a critically oriented form of education that situates educational experiences within local geographic and sociocultural environments; focused on social change and environmental responsibility

Critical posthumanism: theory that reconceives humanity within complex webs of relations

Deep ecology: an environmental philosophy and social movement that emphasizes the value of all life (decenters humans and their needs) and calls for deep societal change for more ethical, relational living.

Eco-art: a contemporary art genre, encompassing diverse artistic practices, that works at social and ecological levels to promote ecological health and integrity.

Eco-visualization: visual representations of ecological data for the purposes of encouraging more sustainable attitudes and behaviors

Ecocide: severe harm to ecosystems on a large scale

Ecofeminism: activist movement and form of intellectual critique; focuses on the interconnected system of oppression that sustains a range of dualisms and subordinates various groups including women and nonhuman species

Ecojustice: a contraction of the term "ecological justice" emphasizing how environmental issues and social issues intersect and seeking justice in both arenas

Ecopedagogy: a utopian educational movement that ultimately seeks planetary sustainability

Ecopoetry: poetry addressing ecological or environmental topics that has the ability to transform the way people think and live in relation in the world; more contemporary ecopoetry adopts a more critical approach in acknowledging environmental degradations and questioning humanity's relationship with the Earth

Ecoracism (or environmental racism): policies and practices that place environmental burdens disproportionately on communities of color

Ecosphere: the totality of the Earth's ecosystems, from below ground to the atmosphere, with an emphasis on biotic and abiotic relations.

Ecowomanism: a spiritual approach to environmental justice influenced by African cosmologies and deeply rooted in African and African American women's histories, presences, and practices

Environmental art: a broad term for art engaging with environmental content; can range from historical art to more contemporary art forms

Environmental colonialism: the ways in which colonial practices have intentionally or unintentionally altered ecosystems and exploited the land to the detriment of Indigenous communities

Gaia: the idea that biotic and abiotic systems on Earth act as one unit, and, through complex interactions, establish a balanced, harmonious system capable of sustaining life

Human exceptionalism and exemptionalism: the dominant view that humans are unique among other organisms and do not need to conform to natural limits (i.e., can alter and exploit the environment without limits)

Indigenous onto-epistemologies: relational worldviews blending sacred and secular elements and emphasizing interdependence and interconnection of everything within the universe

Indigenous peoples: diverse communities, clans, tribes, and nations that tend to historically connect with pre-settler societies; have deep connections to the land; have distinct linguistic, social, cultural, economic, and/or political characteristics; represent nondominant social groups; and commit to preserving their distinctive ways of life and rights to traditional lands (United Nations Permanent Forum on Indigenous Issues, 2006)

Inquiry-based learning: an approach to active learning that engages students in posing questions and actively constructing knowledge surrounding those questions

Intersectional analysis: the critical examination of how various social identities, often based on factors such as race, class, gender, sexual orientation, and religion, intersect and overlap to perpetuate oppression or privilege

Land art (or earth art or earthworks): an art movement of the 1960s and 1970s where art was made in or from the landscape; the practice of making art by shaping the land or using materials foraged from the land to construct sculptures

Master narratives: recurring ideological scripts that are deeply embedded in society, shape public perceptions and sense of identity, and serve those in power; can be disrupted by counternarratives

Monoculture: an area where biodiversity is extremely limited, often due to human impacts (e.g., agricultural crop specialization and traditional lawn maintenance) and/or invasive species

More-than-human world: an alternative to the term "nature" that includes humans but surpasses them to include other earthly organisms and environments

Multispecies interactions: exchanges between more than one species

Mycoremediation: the use of fungi to neutralize or remove environmental pollutants from contaminated sites

Nature: a contested term traditionally referencing organisms and environments not including or impacted by humans (i.e., nonhuman nature); a more ecocentric use of the term would include humans and their cultural productions

Onto-epistemologies: ways of knowing and being; how we perceive and understand the world

Outdoor education: a form of experiential education and, typically, environmental education, where students engage firsthand, and primarily outdoors, with the biophysical environment

Place-based education: an educational approach dedicated to instilling place consciousness and, correspondingly, pro-ecological attitudes and behaviors, by rooting education within the local environment

Placemaking: the process of transforming public spaces to strengthen connections between communities and place; often a participatory process with significant input and assistance from diverse stakeholders and communities

Posthuman: a transdisciplinary field, critiquing humanism and anthropocentricism and, in the process, dramatically transforming the notion of human, to include positioning humans as embedded, only one life form among many (Braidotti & Hlavajova, 2018); can also reference life in which humanist and anthropocentric notions of rational human progress and domination over "nature" are no longer possible because of global, often dystopian, developments (e.g., pandemics and environmental destruction on a mass scale) that emphasize human vulnerability and technoscientific fallibility

Praxis: the combination of critical reflection and action in order to transform societal structures

Queer ecology: a blend of ecological criticism and queer theory; diversifies ecological discourse and reframes reductive, heteronormative assumptions, particularly regarding sexuality and nature

Radical relationality: deep recognition of one's embeddedness in webs of relation, embrace of reciprocal multispecies co-dwelling, and attribution of personhood to more-than-human kin; often rooted in Indigenous onto-epistemologies

Restoration ecology: the scientific study of practices aimed at restoring ecosystems disturbed by direct or indirect human actions

Settler colonialism: a type of colonialism where invasive settler societies displace Indigenous peoples by various harmful means and claim the land for themselves, eventually forming new identities and governments there

Slow pedagogy: an educational approach that seeks to establish healthy affective bonds between people and environments by staging opportunities for students to slow down and linger in place

Speciesism: the notion that one species, typically humans, is superior to other organisms and should have more rights; often coupled with exploitation of nonhuman animals

Technocentrism: faith in scientific technologies to control the environment and solve environmental problems caused by humans

Traditional ecological knowledge (TEK): Indigenous peoples' and local communities' evolving, accumulating bodies of knowledge, practices, and beliefs, developed through firsthand experience with the land and accumulated over centuries or millennia, passed down to subsequent generations through oral traditions and other forms of cultural transmission

Transdisciplinary: surpassing the boundaries of one particular discipline

Visual culture: all tangible or visual expressions of a society, encompassing forms and practices associated with everyday life, popular culture, and high art

Visual journal: a form of journal or sketchbook where imagery and text together can be used to explore and communicate meaning

Wicked problems: large, complex, real-world problems that defy single and risk-free solutions

References

Aagerstoun, M. J. (2021, August 18). Ecological art and Black Americans' relationships to the land. *Ecoartspace*. https://ecoartspace.org/Blog/10939674

Abram, D. (1996). *The spell of the sensuous: Perception and language in a more-than-human world*. Pantheon.

Abram, D., & Jardine, D. (2000). All knowledge is carnal knowledge: A correspondence. *Canadian Journal of Environmental Education, 5*(1), 167–177. https://cjee.lakeheadu.ca/article/view/307/232

Affifi, R., & Christie, B. (2019). Facing loss: Pedagogy of death. *Environmental Education Research, 25*(8), 1143–1157. https://doi.org/10.1080/13504622.2018.1446511

Aho, T., & Niittyvirta, P. (2018). *Lines (57° 59′N, 7° 16′ W)* [Installation]. http://www.niittyvirta.com/lines-57-59-n-7-16w/

Aho, T., Niityvirta, P., & Google Arts and Culture. (2020). *Coastline paradox* [Online climate data experiment]. https://experiments.withgoogle.com/coastline-paradox

Ai Weiwei. (n.d.). Haines. https://hainesgallery.com/ai-weiwei-12882

Aikulola, S. (2020, January 26). Changing Niger Delta narrative through arts. *The Guardian*. https://guardian.ng/art/visual-arts/changing-niger-delta-narrative-through-arts/

Aisher, A., & Damodaran, V. (2016). Introduction: Human-nature interactions through a multispecies lens. *Conservation & Society, 14*(4), 293–304. https://www.jstor.org/stable/26393253

Ali, S., & Kahiu, W. (2020). Pumzi [Interview transcript]. *e-flux Video & Film*. https://www.e-flux.com/video/334045/pumzi/

Amsen, E. (2019, November 20). Bacteria becomes art tools in annual agar art competition. *Forbes*. https://www.forbes.com/sites/evaamsen/2019/11/20/bacteria-become-art-tools-in-annual-agar-art-competition/

Anderson, T., & Suominen Guyas, A. S. (2012). E*arth* education, interbeing, and deep ecology. *Studies in Art Education, 53*(3), 223–245. https://doi.org/10.1080/00393541.2012.11518865

Antunes, A., & Gadotti, M. (2006). Ecopedagogy as the appropriate pedagogy to the Earth Charter process. In P. Blaze, M. Vilela, & A. Roerink (Eds.), *The Earth Charter in action: Toward a sustainable development* (pp. 135–137). Kit Publisher.

Apaolaza, V., Paredes, M. R., Hartmann, P., Barrutia, J. M., & Echebarria, C. (2022). How does mindfulness relate to proenvironmental behavior? The mediating influence of cognitive reappraisal and climate change awareness. *Journal of Cleaner Production, 357*(131914), 7. https://doi.org/10.1016/j.jclepro.2022.13194

Arndt, J., Solomon, S., Kasser, T., & Sheldon, K. M. (2004). The urge to splurge: A terror management account of materialism and consumer behavior. *Journal of Consumer Psychology, 14*(3), 198–212. https://doi.org/10.1207/s15327663jcp1403_2/

ArtDaily. (n.d.). *Presidio habitats: A year long exhibition in the landscape.* https://artdaily.cc/news/38785/Presidio-Habitats—A-Year-Long-Exhibition-in-the-Landscape#.YqEP9y-B1ZE

Atwood, M. (2003). *Oryx and crake*. Nan A. Talese.

Augé, M. (2008). *Non-places: An introduction to supermodernity* (2nd ed.). Verso. (Original work published 1995)

Avramidis, K., & Tsilimpounidi, M. (2016). *Graffiti and street art: Reading, writing and representing the city*. Routledge.

Banks, G. (2022, May 18). Interdisciplinary approaches in photography: Wilfred Ukpong. *Lenscratch*. http://lenscratch.com/2022/05/wilfred-ukpong/

Barbosa, A. (1991). Art education and environment. *Journal of Multicultural and Cross-Cultural Research in Art Education, 9,* 59–64.

Becker, E. (1973). *The denial of death*. Free Press.

Bell, A. (2014). *Relating Indigenous and settler identities: Identity studies in the social sciences*. Palgrave Macmillan.

Bequette, J. W. (2007). Traditional arts knowledge, traditional ecological lore: The intersection of art education and environmental education. *Studies in Art Education, 48*(4), 360–374. https://doi.org/10.1080/00393541.2007.11650114

Berger, H. (2011). *Caterpillage: Reflections on seventeenth century Dutch still life painting*. Fordham University Press.

Berk, S. (2016). Designing for the future of education requires design education. *Art Education, 69*(6), 16–20. https://doi.org/10.1080/00043125.2016.1224844

Bertling, C., & Bertling, E. (2020). [Ephemeral installation]. Knoxville, Tennessee.

Bertling, J. G. (2013). Exercising the ecological imagination: Representing the future of place. *Art Education, 66*(1), 33–39. https://doi.org/10.1080/00043125.2013.11519206

Bertling, J. G. (2015). The art of empathy: A mixed methods case study of a critical place-based art education program. *International Journal of Education & the Arts*, *16*(13), 1–26. https://www.ijea.org

Bertling, J. (2018). Non-place and the future of place-based education. *Environmental Education Research, 24*(11), 1627–1630. https://doi.org/10.1080/13504622.2018.1558439

Bertling, J. G. (2021). (Com)postmodernity: Artists cultivating a lust of mortality. *Art Education, 74*(4), 51–57. https://doi.org/10.1080/00043125.2021.1905435

Bertling, J. G., Hodge, L., & King, S. (2021). The case for data visualization in the art classroom. *Art Education, 74*(2). https://doi.org/10.1080/00043125.2020.1852381

Bertling, J. G., & Moore, T. C. (2021a). A portrait of environmental integration in United States K-12 art education. *Environmental Education Research, 27*(3), 382–401. https://doi.org/10.1080/13504622.2020.1865880

Bertling, J., & Moore, T. (2021b). The United States K–12 art education curricular landscape: A nationwide survey. *Studies in Art Education, 62*(1), 23–46. https://doi.org/10.1080/00393541.2020.1858007

Bertling, J. G., & Moore, T. C. (2022). Educational approaches within U.S. art teacher education: The status of ecological and environmental education. *International Journal of Education through Art, 18*(3), 359–376. https://doi.org/10.1386/eta_00106_1

Bhabha, H. K. (2009). In the cave of making: Thoughts on third space [Preface]. In K. Ikas & G. Wagner (Eds.), *Communicating in the third space* (pp. ix–xiv). Routledge.

Bidwell, N. J., & Winschiers-Theophilus, H. (2012). Audio pacemaker: Walking, talking Indigenous knowledge. In J. Kroeze & de Villiers, R. (Eds.), *SAICSIT '12 Proceedings of the South African Institute for Computer Scientists and Information Technologists Conference* (pp.149–158). ACM Digital Library. https://doi.org/10.1145/2389836.2389855

Billman, M. (2015, April). Innovative sculptures restoring Truckee River Bank. *KUNR*. https://www.kunr.org/energy-and-environment/2015-04-02/innovative-sculptures-restoring-truckee-river-bank

Binlot, A. (2021, February 17). Torkwase Dyson dives into the history of Black liberation with "Bird and Lava." *Document*. https://www.documentjournal.com/2021/02/torkwase-dyson-dives-into-the-history-of-black-liberation-with-bird-and-lava/

Biomimicry Institute. (2022). *Solutions to global challenges are all around us*. https://biomimicry.org/examples/#construction

Birch, L. (2014). *Introducing #StormSnakes—A LandLab project*. The Schuylkill Center. https://www.schuylkillcenter.org/news/introducing-stormsnakes-a-landlab-project/

Birch, L. (2015a). *#StormWater Snakes* [Sculptural installation]. https://lesliebirch.com/2015/08/26/stormsnakes-environmental-art-monitoring/

Birch, L. (2015b). *#StormWater Snakes*. Leslie Birch. https://lesliebirch.com/2015/08/26/stormsnakes-environmental-art-monitoring/

Blandy, D., & Bolin, P. (2018). *Learning things: Material culture in art education*. Teachers College Press.

Blandy, D., & Hoffman, E. (1993). Toward an art education of place. *Studies in Art Education, 35*(1), 22–33. https://doi.org/10.2307/1320835

Bolin, P., & Blandy, D. (2003). Beyond visual culture: Seven statements of support for material culture studies in art education. *Studies in Art Education, 44*(3), 246–233. https://doi.org/10.1080/00393541.2003.11651742

Bonnell, Y. (n.d.). *Bio*. https://www.yolandabonnell.com/

Bonta, M., Gosford, R., Eussen, D., Ferguson, N., Loveless, E., & Witwer, M. (2017). Intentional fire-spreading by "firehawk" raptors in Northern Australia. *Journal of Ethnobiology, 37*(4), 700–718. https://doi.org/10.2993/0278-0771-37.4.700

Boswell, G. A., Jacobs, H., Ritz, K., Gadd, G. M., & Davidson, F. A. (2006). The development of fungal networks in complex environments. *Bulletin of Mathematical Biology, 69*, 605–634. https://doi.org/10.1007/s11538-005-9056-6

Bourriaud, N. (2002). *Relational aesthetics*. Les presses du réel. (Original work published 1998)

Bowers, C. A. (2002). Toward an eco-justice pedagogy. *Environmental Education Research, 8*(1), 21–34. https://doi.org/10.1080/13504620120109628

Bowers, C. A. (2006). *Transforming environmental education: Making the renewal of the cultural and environmental commons the focus of educational reform* (revised ed.). Ecojustice Press. https://scholarsbank.uoregon.edu/xmlui/handle/1794/3070

Braidotti, R., & Hlavajova, M. (2018). Introduction. In R. Braidotti & M. Hlavajova, *Posthuman glossary* (pp. 1–14). Bloomsbury.

Branch, J. (2020, December 9). They're among the world's oldest living things. The climate crisis is killing them. *New York Times*. https://www.nytimes.com/interactive/2020/12/09/climate/redwood-sequoia-tree-fire.html

Brandalism. (2015). *[Subvertisement]*. https://www.ecowatch.com/wp-content/uploads/2021/10/1036135497-img.jpg

Braubach, M., & Fairburn, J. (2010). Social inequities in environmental risks associated with housing and residential location—a review of evidence. *European Journal of Public Health, 20*(1), 36–42. https://doi.org/10.1093/eurpub/ckp221

BRIC. (n.d.). *Athena LaTocha: In the wake of . . .* https://www.bricartsmedia.org/art-exhibitions/athena-latocha-wake

Brookner, J. (2010–ongoing). *The Fargo project* [Garden and community space]. https://www.thefargoproject.com/

Brown, K. W., & Kasser, T. (2005). Are psychological and ecological well-being compatible? The role of values, mindfulness, and lifestyle. *Social Indicators Research, 74*, 349–368. https://doi.org/10.1007/s11205-004-8207-8

Brown, R. (2014). *Outbreak* [Installation]. London. https://roganbrown.com/artwork/3543642-Outbreak.html/

Brown, S. L., Osborn, M., Blom, S., M., Brown, A., & Wijesinghe, T. (2020). Staying with the traces: Mapping-making posthuman and indigenist philosophy in environmental education research. *Australian Journal of Environmental Education, 36*(2), 105–128. https://doi.org/10.1017/aee.2020.31

Bryson, K. (n.d.-a). *Mycelium shoes for remediation.* http://www.kaitlinbryson.com/#/new-gallery-61/

Bryson, K. (n.d.-b). *As above, so below.* http://www.kaitlinbryson.com/#/884688365675/

Bryson, K. (2015). *As above, so below* [Installation]. http://www.kaitlinbryson.com/#/884688365675/

Bryson, K. (2017). *Mycelium shoes for remediation* [Mycoremediative project]. http://www.kaitlinbryson.com/—/new-gallery-61/

Burnett, R., Chen, H., Szyszkowicz, M., Fann, N., Hubbell, B., Pope III, A., Apte, J. S., Brauer, M., Cohen, A., Wichenthal, S., Coggins, J., Di, Q., Brunekreef, B., Frostad, J., Lim, S. S., Kan, H., Walker, K. D., Thurston, G. D., Hayes, R. B., Lim, C. C., . . . Spadaro, J. V. (2018). Global estimates of mortality associated with long-term exposure to outdoor fine particulate matter. *PNAS, 115*(38), 9592–9597. www.pnas.org/cgi/doi/10.1083/pnas.1803222115

Bush, C., & Richardson, J. (2021, October 1). U of G supports unique sound project with Indigenous perspective. *University of Guelph News*. https://news.uoguelph

.ca/2021/10/u-of-g-supports-unique-sound-project-with-indigenous-perspective/

Butterfield, D. (2017). *Millie fire* [Bronze sculpture]. Danes/Corey, New York, NY, United States. https://www.danesecorey.com/artists/deborah-butterfield

Caballero, K., & Ekeberg, F. (2013–2018). *Birding the future* [Installation series]. https://www.birdingthefuture.net/

Caballero, K., & Ekeberg, F. (2014). Birding the future. *Leonardo, 47*(5), 498–499. https://www.muse.jhu.edu/article/555686

Cameron, J. (Director). (1989). *The abyss* [Film]. Twentieth Century Fox.

Capps, A. (2019, February 26). More floods in the future? Knoxville's flood fits growing trend in rainfall totals. *Knoxville News Sentinel.* https://www.knoxnews.com/story/news/local/2019/02/26/knoxville-floods-rainfall-records-totals-part-growing-climate-trend/2992900002/

Carducci, V. (2006). Culture jamming: A sociological perspective. *Journal of Consumer Culture, 6*(1), 116–138. https://doi.org/10.1177/1469540506062722

Carpenter, B. S., & Tavin, K. M. (2010). Drawing (past, present, and future) together: A (graphic) look at the reconceptualization of art education. *Studies in Art Education, 51*(4), 327–352. https://doi.org/10.1080/00393541.2010.11518812

Carter, C. (2018). Blood in the soil: The racial, racist, and religious dimensions of environmentalism. In L. Hobgood & W. Bauman (Eds.), *The Bloomsbury handbook of religion and nature: The elements* (pp. 45–62). Bloomsbury Academic.

Chacon, R. (n.d.). *Contact*. Raven Chacon. http://spiderwebsinthesky.com/contact/

Cheng, J. C., & Monroe, M. C. (2012). Connection to nature: Children's affective attitude toward nature. *Environment and Behavior, 44*, 31–49. https://doi.org/10.1177/0013916510385082

Chisholm Hatfield, S., Marino, E., Whyte, K. P., Dello, K. D., & Mote, P. W. (2018). Indian time: Time, seasonality, and culture in Traditional Ecological Knowledge of climate change. *Ecological Processes, 7*, 25. https://doi.org/10.1186/s13717-018-0136-6

Chung, S. K., & Kirby, M. (2009). Media literacy art education: Logos, culture jamming, and activism. *Art Education, 62*(1), 34–39. https://doi.org/10.1080/00043125.2009.11519002

Clayton, S. (2003). Environmental identity: A conceptual and an operational definition. In S. Clayton & S. Opotow (Eds.), *Identity and the natural environment: The psychological significance of nature* (pp. 45–65). MIT Press.

Climate Change Threatens [Tweet]. (n.d.). Twitter. https://twitter.com/martin1smith2/status/877884112052166658?lang=cs

Coats, C. (2020). Embrace art education's indiscernibility. *Art Education, 73*(4), 44–47. https://doi.org/10.1080/00043125.2020.1717818

Cole, A. G. (2007). Expanding the field: Revisiting environmental education principles through multidisciplinary frameworks. *The Journal of Environmental Education, 38*(2), 35–45. https://doi.org/10.3200/JOEE.38.1.35-46

Cotton, A. (2012). *Ear wax necklace* [Necklace]. http://www.amandacotton.co.uk/ear-wax-necklace

Courtney, C. (2015, September). *2015* At first sight *exhibition review.* University of New Mexico Graduate Art Association. http://gaa.unm.edu/news.php

Cramer, M. (2021, June 22). The Great Barrier Reef has lost half its corals. *New York Times.* https://www.nytimes.com/2020/10/14/climate/great-barrier-reef-climate-change.html

Creel, M. S. (2005). *The endangered species sculpture garden: An interdisciplinary environmental art education curriculum for at-risk children* (AAT 3183052) [Doctoral dissertation, Florida State University]. ProQuest Dissertations and Theses.

Crenshaw, K. (1989). Demarginalizing the intersection of race and sex: A Black feminist critique of antidiscrimination doctrine, feminist theory and antiracist politics. *University of Chicago Legal Forum, 1*(8), 139–167. https://chicagounbound.uchicago.edu/uclf/vol1989/iss1/8

Cronenberg, D. (Director). (1988). *Dead ringers* [Film]. Twentieth Century Fox.

Crutzen, P. J., & Stoermer, E. F. (2000). The "Anthropocene." *IGBP Newsletter, 41*, 17–18. http://www.igbp.net/download/18.316f18321323470177580001401/1376383088452/NL41.pdf

Dam, R. F. (2022). *The five stages in the design thinking process.* Interaction Design Foundation. https://www.interaction-design.org/literature/article/5-stages-in-the-design-thinking-process

Dambo, T. (2019a). *The storytellers' tree* [Installation]. https://thomasdambo.com/works/storytellerstree/

Dambo, T. (2019b). *The storytellers' tree.* https://thomasdambo.com/works/storytellerstree/

Darabont, F. (Creator). (2010–2022). *The walking dead* [Television series]. AMC Networks.

Datta, R. (2015). A relational theoretical framework and meanings of land, nature, and sustainability for research with Indigenous communities. *Local Environment, 20*(1), 102–113. https://doi.org/10.1080/13549839.2013.818957

Dean, K., & Bertling, J. G. (2020). Eco-visualizations: Facilitating ecological relationships and raising environmental awareness. *Art Education, 73*(3), 54–61. https://doi.org/10.1080/00043125.2020.1717823

Dekeyser, T. (2021). Dismantling the advertising city: Subvertising and the urban commons to come. *Society and Space, 39*(2), 309–327. https://doi.org/10.1177/0263775820946755

Delacruz, E. M., & Dunn, P. C. (1996). DBAE: The next generation. *Art Education, 48*(6), 46–53. https://doi.org/10.2307/3193572

DeLuca, D. K. (2018). Biomimicry: Nature inspiring design. In R. Egenhoefer (Ed.), *Routledge handbook of sustainable design* (pp. 459–469). Routledge.

Denes, A. (1992). *Tree mountain—A living time capsule* [Land artwork]. Ylöjärvi, Finland. http://www.agnesdenesstudio.com/works4.html

Desai, D. (2020). Educating for social change through art: A personal reckoning. *Studies in Art Education, 61*(1), 10–23. https://doi.org./10.1080/00393541.2019.1699366

Deveau, A., Bonito, B., Uehling, J., Paoletti, M., Becker, M., Bindschedler, S., Hacquard, S., Hervé, V., Labbé, J., Lastovetsky, O. A., Mieszkin, S., Millet, L. J., Vajna, B., Junier, P., Bonfante, P., Krom, B. P., Olsson, S., van Elsas, J. D., & Wick, L. Y. (2018). Bacterial–fungal interactions: ecology, mechanisms and challenges. *FEMS Microbiology Reviews*, *42*(3), 335–352. https://doi.org/10.1093/femsre/fuy008

Dion, M., & Jayaswal, N. (2010). *Winged defense* [Sculptural installation]. San Francisco, United States. https://www.for-site.org/project/presidio-habitats-mark-dion-nitin-jayaswal-winged-defense/

Diver, S., Vaughn, M., Baker-Medard, M., & Lukacs, H. (2019). Recognizing "reciprocal relations" to restore community access to land and water. *International Journal of the Commons*, *13*(1), 400–429. https://doi.org/10.18352/ijc.881

Dobbs, S. M. (1992). *The DBAE handbook: An overview of discipline-based art education.* Getty Center for Education in the Arts. https://files.eric.ed.gov/fulltext/ED349253.pdf

Doughman, A. (2012, May). Groups discuss suburban sprawl's effects on Spartanburg County natural resources. *GoUpstate.* https://www.goupstate.com/news/20120530/groups-discuss-suburban-sprawls-effects-on-spartanburg-county-natural-resources

Douglas, K. M., & Jaquith, D. B. (2018). *Engaging learners through artmaking: Choice-based art education in the classroom (TAB)* (2nd ed.). Teachers College Press.

Douglas, N. (2021). *Burn now . . . pay later* [Subvertisement]. https://www.noeldouglas.net/banfossilads-2/

Doyle, J. (2020). Creative communication approaches to youth climate engagement: Using speculative fiction and participatory play to facilitate young people's multidimensional engagement with climate change. *International Journal of Communication, 14*, 2749–2772. http://ijoc.org

Dravenstadt, D. W. (2018). Learning to let go: Motivating students through fluid teaching in a choice-based found object assemblage unit. *Art Education, 71*(5), 8–13. https://doi.org/10.1080/00043125.2018.1482158

Drengson, A., Devall, B., & Schroll, M. A. (2011). The deep ecology movement: Origins, development, and future prospects (toward a transpersonal ecosophy). *International Journal of Transperson Studies, 30*(1–2), 101–117. https://dx.doi.org/10.24972/ijts.2011.30.1-2.101

Drew, J. A. (2005). Use of traditional ecological knowledge in marine conservation. *Conservation Biology, 19*(4), 1286–1293. https://doi.org/10.1111/j.1523-1739.2005.00158.x

Dunlap, R. E., Van Liere, K. D., Mertig, A. G., & Jones, R. E. (2000). Measuring endorsement of the new ecological paradigm: A revised NEP scale. *Journal of Social Issues, 56*(3), 425–442. https://doi.org/10.1111/0022-4537.00176

Duru, J. (2014). Rogan Brown's bizarre bacteria-inspired paper sculptures. *Maximilian Büsser & Friends.* Retrieved June 1, 2020 from https://www.mbandf.com/en/parallel-world/rogan-brown-s-bizarre-bacteria-inspired-paper-sculptures/

Earth Charter Commission. (1994–2000). *Earth charter.* https://earthcharter.org/wp-content/uploads/2020/03/echarter_english.pdf?x51102

The Earth isn't dying [Street art]. (n.d.). https://madeinpain.wordpress.com/2012/11/18/the-earth-isnt-dying/

Ecowatch. (2015, December 11). *VW: "We're sorry we got caught."* https://www.ecowatch.com/vw-were-sorry-we-got-caught-1882129392.html

Elbein, A. (2018, February 5). In Australia, arsonists may have wings. *New York Times*. https://www.nytimes.com/2018/02/05/science/australia-firehawks-aboriginal.html

Environmental Protection Agency. (n.d.). *Environmental justice*. https://www.epa.gov/environmentaljustice

Evans, H. (2008). *Nuage vert*. http://hehe.org.free.fr/hehe/texte/nv/

Fain, J. (2011). *Remediation by inspiration: Artist-driven models for environmental clean-up* [Master's thesis, Massachusetts Institute of Technology]. https://dspace.mit.edu/bitstream/handle/1721.1/67226/759095839-MIT.pdf?sequence=2&isAllowed=y

The Fargo project: Jackie Brookner & city of Fargo, ND. (n.d.). Municipal Artist Partnerships. https://municipal-artist.org/profiles/profiles/the-fargo-project/

Feitelberg, R. (2018, May). Mushroom-made fashion authority Aniela Hoitink talks global change-sparked innovation. *Los Angeles Times*. https://www.latimes.com/fashion/la-ig-wwd-aniela-hoitink-mushroom-fashion-20180529-story.html/

Finkel, J. (2010, May). The Presidio in San Francisco installs animal habitat art project. *Los Angeles Times*. https://www.latimes.com/entertainment/la-ca-presidio habitats-20100530-story.html

Finley, R. (2013). Ron Finley: A guerrilla gardener in South Central L.A. *TED*. https://www.ted.com/talks/ron_finley_a_guerrilla_gardener_in_south_central_la/transcript?language=en

Finley, R. (2020). *The Ron Finley project* [Guerrilla gardening project]. https://ronfinley.com/

Fisher, M. (2015). *Microbial me* [Agar sculptures]. The Eden Project, England. https://www.mellissafisher.com/microbial-me/

Flanagan, K. (2021, May 7). Climate resilience lessons from fungi. *Medium*. https://medium.com/climate-conscious/climate-resilience-lessons-from-fungi-9988ee3e0437

Fleerackers, A., & Brown, R. (2019, November 28). Creators—Rogan Brown. *Art the Science*. https://artthescience.com/blog/2019/11/28/creators-rogan-brown/

For-Site Foundation. (n.d.). *Presidio habitats: Mark Dion with Nitin Jayaswal: Winged defense*. https://www.for-site.org/project/presidio-habitats-mark-dion-nitin-jayaswal-winged-defense/

Forster, M. (Director). (2013). *World War Z* [Film]. Paramount Pictures.

Foster, R., Makela, J., & Martusewicz, R. A. (2019). *Art, ecojustice, and education: Intersecting theories and practices*. Routledge.

Freedman, K. (2019). Visual culture and visual literacy. In R. Hickman (Ed.), *The international encyclopedia of art and design education* (pp. 981–990). https://doi.org/10.1002/9781118978061.ead079

Freire, P. (1998). *Pedagogy of freedom*. Rowman & Littlefield.

Freire, P. (2014). *Pedagogy of the oppressed* (30th anniversary ed.). Bloomsbury. (Original work published 1968)

Fukaya, M. (2016). Perspectives on the body in early modern Japan. In S. S. Morishita (Ed.), *Materiality in religion and culture* (pp. 73–80). LIT.

Future and the arts: AI, robotics, cities, life—How humanity will live tomorrow. (2019–20). Mori Art Museum, Tokyo, Japan. https://www.xtuarchitects.com/x_cloud

Gablik, S. (1991). *The re-enchantment of art*. Thames and Hudson.

Gadotti, M. (2000). *Pedagogy of the Earth and culture of sustainability* (Eng. trans.). https://earthcharter.org/library/pedagogia-de-la-tierra-y-cultura-de-la-sustentabilidad-2000/

Gadotti, M., & Torres, C. A. (2009). Paulo Freire: Education for development. *Development and Change, 40*(6), 1255–1267. https://doi.org/10.1111/j.1467-7660.2009.01606.x

Garber, E. (2004). Social justice and art education. *Visual Arts Research, 30*(2), 4–22. https://www.jstor.org/stable/20715349

Gates, L. (2016). Rethinking art education practice one choice at a time. *Art Education, 69*(2), 14–19. https://doi.org/10.1080/00043125.2016.1141646

Gavenus, E., & O'Brien, M. (2017, March 30). Lending aesthetic weight to restoration. *MAHB*. https://mahb.stanford.edu/blog/lending-aesthetic-weight/

Gillson, L., Chirango, Y., & Julier, A. (2022). An interdisciplinary approach to restoration ecology in the Anthropocene. *Anthropocene*. https://www.sciencedirect.com/journal/anthropocene/special-issue/101MH8TJC3H

Gilman, C. P. (1998). *Herland* (Dover ed.). Dover Publications. (Original work published 1915)

Girak, S., Lummis, G. W., & Johnson, J. (2019). Creative reuse: The impact artmaking has on raising environmental consciousness. *International Journal of Education Through Art, 15*(3), 369–385. https://doi.org/10.1386/eta_00009_1

Gloshay, S. M. (2020). *Indigenous ways of knowing and its interpretation of the White Mountain Apache Holy Ground Spiritual Movement* (27957994) [Doctoral dissertation, New Mexico State University]. ProQuest Dissertations.

Golańska, D., & Kronenberg, A. K. (2020). Creative practice for sustainability: A new materialist perspective on artivist production of eco-sensitive knowledges. *International Journal of Education through Art, (16)*3, 303–318. https://doi.org/10.1386/eta_00035_1

Gold, W., Ewing, K., Banks, J., Groom, M., Hinckley, T., Secord, D., & Shebitz, D. (2006). Collaborative ecological restoration. *Science, 312*(5782), 1880–1881. https://doi.org/10.1126/science.1128088

Goldsworthy, A. (1987). Rowan leaves and hole [Photograph]. In *Beyond exhibition* (accessed January 10, 2022). https://beyondproject.weebly.com/rowan-leaves-and-hole.html

Goodalle, S. E. (2019, August 27). At the river's edge: Allison Janae Hamilton interviewed by Stephanie E. Goodalle. *BOMB*. https://bombmagazine.org/articles/at-the-rivers-edge-allison-janae-hamilton-interviewed/

Gradle, S. (2007). Ecology of place: Art education in a relational world. *Studies in Art Education, 48*(4), 392–411. https://doi.org/10.1080/00393541.2007.11650116

Graff, T. (1990). Art, art education and the ecological vision. *NSCAD Papers in Art Education, 5*(1), 79–96.

Graham, M. A. (2007). Art, ecology and art education: Locating art education in a critical place-based pedagogy. *Studies in Art Education, 48*(4), 375–391. https://doi.org/10.2307/25475843

Graham, M. A. (2020). Deconstructing the bright future of STEAM and design thinking. *Art Education, 73*(3), 6–12. https://doi.org/10.1080/00043125.2020.1717820

Graham, M. A. (2021). The disciplinary borderlands of education: Art and STEAM education. *Journal for the Study of Education and Development, 44*(4), 769–800. https://doi.org/10.1080/02103702.2021.1926163

Gray, T., & Birrell, C. (2015). "Touched by the Earth": A place-based outdoor learning programme incorporating the arts. *Journal of Adventure Education and Outdoor Learning, 15*(4), 330–349. https://doi.org/10.1080/14729679.2015.1035293

Green, C. (2022, March 2). Time signatures: Athena LaTocha interviewed by Christopher Green. *BOMB*. https://bombmagazine.org/articles/time-signatures-athena-latocha-interviewed/

Greene, M. (2000). *Releasing the imagination: Essays on education, the arts, and social change*. Josey-Bass. (Original work published 1995)

Greer, D. (1984). Discipline-based art education: Approaching art as a subject of study. *Studies in Art Education, 25*(4), 212–218. https://doi.org/10.2307/1320414

Gregory, T. (2009). *No alarms and no surprises; the rise of the domestic non-place* [Doctoral dissertation, University of New South Wales]. https://doi.org/10.26190/unsworks/19569

Gruenewald, D. A. (2003). The best of both worlds: A critical pedagogy of place. *Educational Researcher, 32*(4), 3–12. https://doi.org/10.3102/0013189x032004003

Gruenewald, D. A. (2004). A Foucauldian analysis of environmental education: Toward the socioecological challenge of the Earth Charter. *Curriculum Inquiry, 34*(1), 71–107. https://doi.org/10.1111/j.1467-873X.2004.00281.x

Gruenewald, D. A., & Smith, G. A. (2014). Introduction: Making room for the local. In D. Gruenewald & G. Smith (Eds.), *Place-based education in the global age: Local diversity* (pp. xiii–xxiii). Psychology.

Guariglia, J. B., & Morton, T. (2018–2019). *We are the asteroid II* [Public art installation]. https://www.justinbrice.com/wata-2

Guariglia, J. B., & Morton, T. (2019–2020). *We are the asteroid III* [Public art installation]. https://www.justinbrice.com/we-are-the-asteroid-iii

Gutierrez, F., & Prado, C. (2013). *Ecopedagogia e cicadania planetária* (4th ed.). Cortez. (Original work published 1999)

Guyotte, K. W., Sochacka, N. W., Costantino, T. E., Walther, J., & Kellam, N. N. (2014). STEAM as social practice: Cultivating creativity in transdisciplinary spaces. *Art Education, 67*(6), 12–19. https://doi.org/10.1080/00043125.2014.11519293

Guzmán, A. I. (2018, July 30). Jetsonorama: Messages for the future. *Southwest Contemporary*. https://southwestcontemporary.com/jetsonorama-messages-for-the-future/

Haeg, F. (n.d.). *Domestic integrities*. http://www.fritzhaeg.com/domestic-integrities/main.html

Haeg, F. (2012–14). *Domestic integrities* [Participatory installation]. http://www.fritzhaeg.com/domestic-integrities/main.html

Haley, D. (2021). A walk on the wild side: Steps toward an ecological arts pedagogy. *International Journal of Education Through Art, 17*(1), 135–152. https://doi.org/10.1386/eta_00054_1

Hamilton, A. J. (2019a). *Floridawater III* [Archival pigment print]. https://marianneboeskygallery.com/artists/60-allison-janae-hamilton/works/25285-allison-janae-hamilton-floridawater-iii-2019/

Hamilton, A. J. (2019b). *Three girls in sabal palm forest II* [Archival pigment print]. https://bombmagazine.org/articles/at-the-rivers-edge-allison-janae-hamilton-interviewed/

Hamilton, A. J. (2022). *Allison Janae Hamilton: About.* http://www.allisonjanaehamilton.com/biography

Hammerman, D. R., Hammerman, W. M., & Hammerman, E. L. (2001). *Teaching in the outdoors* (5th ed.). Interstate. (Original work published 1964)

Hanington, B. (2018). Empathy, values, and situated action: Sustaining people and planet through human centered design. In R. Engenhoefer (Ed.), *Routledge handbook of sustainable design* (pp. 193–206). Routledge.

Haraway, D. (1991). *Simians, cyborgs, and women: The reinvention of nature* [e-Book edition]. Routledge.

Haraway, D. (2015). Anthropocene, Capitalocene, Plantationocene, Chthulucene: Making king. *Environmental Humanities,* 6(1), 159–165. https://doi.org/10.1215/22011919-3615934

Haraway, D. (2016). *Staying with the trouble: Making kin in the Chthulucene.* Duke University Press.

Harrison, G. (2006). Romanticism, nature, and ecology. *Romantic Circles.* http://romantic-circles.org/pedagogies/commons/ecology/harrison/harrison.html

Harvey, G. (2019). Animism and ecology: Participating in the world community. *The Ecological Citizen, 3*(1), 79–84. www.ecologicalcitizen.net

HeHe. (2008). *Nuage vert* [Public installation]. http://hehe.org.free.fr/hehe/texte/nv/

Heinrich, D. D., Watson, S., Rummer, J. L., Brandl, S. J., Simpfendorfer, C. A., Heupel, M. R., & Munday, P. L. (2016). Foraging behaviour of the epaulette shark *Hemiscyllium ocellatum* is not affected by elevated CO_2. *ICES Journal of Marine Science, 73*(3), 633–640. https://doi.org/10.1093/icesjms/fsv085

Henao, L. A., & Torchia, C. (2019, August 27). Respiratory ailments hit in Amazon as Brazil spurns G-7 aid. *AP News.* https://apnews.com/article/31167541a4a742d59b61bf5e705b71a4

Herbert, F. (1965). *Dune.* Chilton Books.

Hess, C. (2018). *Choosing to change: Discipline based art education to choice based art education* (Publication No. 10841044) [Doctoral dissertation, Moore College of Art and Design]. ProQuest Dissertations.

Hickman, C., Marks, E., Pihkala, P., Clayton, S., Lewandowski, E., Mayall, E. E., Wray, B., Mellow, C., & van Susteren, L. (2022). Climate anxiety in children and young people and their beliefs about government responses to climate change: A global survey. *The Lancet Planetary Health, 5*(12), 863–873. https://doi.org/10.1016/S2542-5196(21)00278-3

Hicks, S. R. (1991, April). Global problems are too big for little kids. *Wall Street Journal, CCXVII*(4), 1. https://www.stephenhicks.org/wp-content/uploads/2009/02/globalproblems-wsjenglish.pdf

Hill, E. (2018, March 30). The artist duo whose land art is rejuvenating the environment. *Artsy.* https://www.artsy.net/article/artsy-editorial-artist-duo-land-art-rejuvenating-environment

Hilton, J. (1960). *Lost horizon* (William Morrow ed.). Pocket Books. (Original work published 1933).

Hofman, F. (2012). Slow slugs [Sculptural installation]. https://inhabitat.com/40000-plastic-bags-re-purposed-to-create-florentijn-hofmans-gigantic-slow-slug-sculptures/

Hofsess, B. A. (2020). Don't call this world adorable & other salvaged stories: A precarious stance. *The Journal of Social Theory in Art Education, 40*(1), 28–48.

Hoitink, A. (2016). *MycoTEX dress* [Dress]. https://neffa.nl/portfolio/mycotex/

Hokusai, K. (1832). *Thirty-six views of Mount Fuji* [Print series]. The Met, New York, NY, United States. https://www.metmuseum.org/art/collection/search/36492

Holl, K. D. (2020). *Primer of ecological restoration.* Island Press.

Holmes, T. (2009). *Eco-visualisation: Combining art and technology to reduce energy consumption* [Doctoral dissertation, University of Plymouth]. https://pearl.plymouth.ac.uk/handle/10026.1/2784

Holmgren, D., & Roberts, D. (2019). *The ethics and domains from permaculture principles & pathways* [Diagram]. https://www.interconnected.me/the-permaculture-wheel/

Holschuh, R. (2019). Mountain names: Remembering their aboriginal origins. *Long Trail News, 79*(3), 14–15. https://gmcmontpelier.org/Archive_Publications/LTN_Archives/LTN_YYYY_NN/2019_03_Fall.pdf

Hood, G. (2016, August 4). One year after a toxic river spill, no clear plan to clean up Western mines. *National Public Radio.* https://www.npr.org/2016/08/04/488579040/one-year-after-a-toxic-river-spill-no-clear-plan-to-clean-up-western-mines

Hoy, W. G. (2013). *Do funerals matter? The purposes and practices of death rituals in global perspective.* Routledge.

Hulsey, J., & Trusty, A. (n.d.). *It's stilleven, nature morte, dead nature, or still life.* The Artist Life. https://www.artistsnetwork.com/artist-life/its-stilleven-nature-morte-dead-nature-or-still-life/

Hunter-Doniger, T. (2021). Seeing the forest through the trees: At the intersection of forest kindergartens and art-based environmental education. *Journal of Adventure Education and Outdoor Learning, 21*(3), 217–229. https://doi.org/10.1080/14729679.2020.1771388

Hurston, Z. N. (1998). *Their eyes were watching God* [1st Perennial Classics ed.]. Perennial Classics. (Original work published 1937)

Illeris, H. (2012). Interrogations: Art, art education and environmental sustainability. *International Journal of Education through Art, 8*(3), 221–237. https://doi.org/10.1386/eta.8.3.221_1

Imagining Climate. (n.d.). *Inose/field trip* [Sound walk].University of Guelph: Guelph Institute for Environmental Research. https://sites.uoguelph.ca/gier/field-trip/

Infrastructure. (n.d.). ARTE fuktional. http://artefunktional.com/portfolio/infrastructure/

Inwood, H. (2008). Mapping eco-art education. *Canadian Review of Art Education, 35*, 57–73.

Irwin, R. (2006). Walking to create an aesthetic and spiritual currere. *Visual Arts Research, 35*(1), 75–82. https://www.jstor.org/stable/20715404

jagodzinski, j. j. (1987). Toward an ecological aesthetic: Notes on a "green" frame of mind. In D. Blandy & K. G. Congdon (Eds.), *Art in a democracy* (pp. 138–163). Teachers College Press.

Jameson, F. (1994). *The seeds of time*. Columbia University Press.

Jedlicka, W., Faludi, J., Markiewicz, P., Frick, T., & McCahill, M. (2018). Applied sustainability. In R. Engenhoefer (Ed.), *Routledge handbook of sustainable design* (pp. 40–54). Routledge.

Jeremijenko, N. (2011). *The Environmental Health Clinic (xClinic) Farmacy* [Public art]. New York, NY. In S. Pratt. (n.d.). xClinic Farmacy. *Curating cities: A database of eco public art.* http://eco-publicart.org/xclinic-farmacy/

Jeremijenko, N. (2014). Natalie Jeremijenko: The art of the eco-mindshift. *TED.* https://www.ted.com/talks/natalie_jeremijenko_the_art_of_the_eco_mindshift/transcript?language=en

Jeremijenko, N., & x-Design Environmental Health Clinic (n.d.). *No park* [Installation].

Johanson, P. (1999–2009). *Ellis Creek Water recycling facility/wildlife sanctuary* [Ecological-restoration project]. Petaluma, California. https://patriciajohanson.com/projects/ellis-creek.html

Johnson, M. (2007). *The meaning of the body: Aesthetics of human understanding.* The University of Chicago Press.

Jokela, T. (2008). Collaborative project-based studies in art teacher education: An environmental perspective. In G. Coutts & T. Jokela (Eds.), *Art, community and environment: Educational perspectives* (pp. 217–240). Intellect.

Jones, H. P., Jones, P. C., Barbier, E. B., Blackburn, R. C., Rey Benayas, J. M., Holl, K. D., McCrackin, M., Meli, P., Montoya, D., & Mateos, D. M. (2018). Restoration and repair of Earth's damaged ecosystems. *Proceedings of the Royal Society B: Biological Sciences, 285* (1873). https://doi.org/10.1098/rspb.2017.2577

Joyce, E. (2015, April). Glimpses of a pastoral dystopia. *Hyperallergic.* https://hyperallergic.com/190675/glimpses-of-a-pastoral-dystopia/

Joyce, R. (2020). *Walker Art Center commissions new artwork in the form of an urban farm* [Press release]. Walker. https://walkerart.org/press-releases/2020/walker-art-center-commissions-new-artwork-in-the-form-of-an-urban-farm

Justseeds. (n.d.). *I am the change: Chip Thomas.* https://justseeds.org/product/i-am-the-change/

Kade L. Twist. (n.d.). Cultivar. https://cultivar.earth/kade-l-twist-0

Kahiu, W. (2009). *Pumzi* [Short film]. Focus Features. https://www.youtube.com/watch?v=IlR7l_B86Fc

Kahn, R. (2010). *Critical pedagogy, ecoliteracy, and planetary crisis: The ecopedagogy movement.* Peter Lang.

Kalela, A. (1996). [Description of *Tree mountain—A living time capsule*]. http://www.agnesdenesstudio.com/works4.html

Kalin, N. (2019). Decreating entrepreneurialized art education. *Art Education, 72*(6), 44–45. https://doi.org/10.1080/00043125.2019.1648146

Kallio-Tavin, M. (2020). Art education beyond anthropocentrism: The question of nonhuman animals in contemporary art and its education. *Studies in Art Education, 61*(4), 298–311. https://doi.org/10.1080/00393541.2020.1820832

Kasser, T., & Sheldon, K. M. (2000). Of wealth and death: Materialism, mortality salience, and consumption behavior. *Psychological Science, 11*(4), 348–351. https://doi.org/10.1111/1467-9280.00269/

Keitsch, M. (2012). Sustainable design: A brief appraisal of its main concepts. *Sustainable Development, 20*(3), 180–188. https://doi.org/10.1002/sd.1534

Kelly, C., Mohtadi, S., Cane, M., Seager, M., & Kushnir, Y. (2017). Commentary on the Syria case: Climate as a contributing factor. *Political Geography, 60*, 245–247. https://doi.org/10.1016/j.polgeo.2017.06.013

Kenis, A., & Mathijs, E. (2012). Beyond individual behavior change: The role of power, knowledge, and strategy in tackling climate change. *Environmental Education Research, 18*(1), 45–65. https://doi.org/10.1080/13504622.2011.576315

Kheel, M. (2008). *Nature ethics: An ecofeminist perspective.* Lanham.

Kincheloe, J. L. (2012). Critical pedagogy in the twenty-first century: Evolution for survival. *Counterpoints, 422*, 147–183. https://www.jstor.org/stable/42981758

Kings, A. (2017). Intersectionality and the changing face of ecofeminism. *Ethics and the Environment*, 22(1), 63–87. https://doi.org/10.2979/ethicsenviro.22.1.04

Kirksey, S. E., Shapiro, N., & Brodine, M. (2013). Hope in blasted landscapes. *Social Science Information, 52*(2), 228–256. https://doi.org/10.1177/0539018413479468

Kisiel, E. (2011). *At rest* [Photographic series]. http://www.emmakisiel.com/at-rest

Kisiel, E. (2012). *Featured artist: Emma Kisiel/At rest.* F-Stop. https://www.fstopmagazine.com/pastissues/53/kisiel.html

Klein, S. R. (2014). Making sense of data in the changing landscape of visual art education. *Visual Arts Research, 40*(2), 25–33. https://doi.org/10.5406/visuartsrese.40.2.0025

Klosterwill, K. (2019). On displacement: Revealing hidden ways of being through site-specific art. *Environmental Humanities, 11*(2), 324–350. https://doi.org/10.1215/22011919-7754490

Kober, G. (2013). For they do not agree in nature: Spinoza and deep ecology. *Ethics and the Environment, 18*(1), 43–65. https://doi.org/10.2979/ethicsenviro.18.1.43

Konopaki, R., & Neufeld, R. (2013). *Claybank hills* [Woodcut]. http://dev.konopaki.com/wp-content/uploads/2018/08/Walking-Lines-SK.pdf

Korzenik, D. (1990). A developmental history of art education. In D. Soucy & M. A. Stankiewicz (Eds.), *Framing the past: Essays on art education* (pp. 202–212). National Art Education Association.

Kraehe, A. M. (2010). Multicultural art education in an era of standardized testing: Changes in knowledge and skill for art teacher certification in Texas. *Studies in Art Education, 51*(2), 162–175. https://www.jstor.org/stable/40650460

Kraehe, A. M., & Acuff, J. B. (2013). Theoretical considerations for art education research with and about "underserved populations." *Studies in Art Education, 54*(4), 294–309. https://doi.org/10.1080/00393541.2013.11518904

Kuby, A. (2017a). *Sea level 2080 (Captiva Island)* [Site-specific installation]. https://www.adamkuby.com/installations/sea-level-2080-captiva

Kuby, A. (2017b). *Sea level clock #1* [Site-specific installation]. https://www.adamkuby.com/installations/sea-level-clock

Kurtaslan, B. O. (2016). Land art as a contemporary remark on forming the landscape. In R. Efe, I. Curebal, G. Abdalla, & B. Toth (Ed.), *Environmental sustainability and land management* (pp. 396–410). St. Kliment Ohridski University.

Laboratory of Insurrectionary Imagination (2008). *The great rebel raft regatta* [Activist experiment]. https://labo.zone/index.php/the-great-rebel-raft-regatta/?lang=en

Lakin, M. (2019, March). Tennessee flooding: Cleanup recovery efforts continue as rain moves out. *Knoxville News Sentinel.* https://www.knoxnews.com/story/news/local/2019/03/03/tennessee-flooding-cleanup-recovery-work-drags-rain-moves-out/3016851002/

Lankford, E. L. (1997). Ecological stewardship in art education. *Art Education, 50*(6), 47–63. https://doi.org/10.1080/00043125.1997.11652184

LaTocha, A. (2021). *In the wake of . . .* [Installation]. https://athenalatocha.com/section/508022-In-the-Wake-of-2021.html

Lawton, P. H. (2019). At the crossroads of intersecting ideologies: Community-based art education community engagement and social practice art. *Studies in Art Education,* 60(3), 203–218. https://doi.org/10.1080/00393541.2019.1639486

Leavenworth, M. L., & Manni, A. (2021). Climate fiction and young learners' thoughts—a dialogue between literature and education. *Environmental Education Research,* 27(5), 727–742. https://doi.org/10.1080/13504622.2020.1856345

Le Guin, U. K. (1975). *The dispossessed.* Avon.

Le Guin, U. K. (1997). *Dancing at the edge of the world: Thoughts on words, women, places.* Grove Press. (Original work published 1989)

Leis, H. (2012). *Beet mold* [Photograph]. http://heikkileis.com/photos-1/afterlife

Leis, H. (2016). *Afterlife* [Photographic series]. http://heikkileis.com/photos-1/afterlife/

Leopold, A. (1966). *A sand county almanac with other essays on conservation from 'round river'.* Oxford University Press. (Original work published 1949)

Levy, M. (n.d.-a). *Neo fruits* [Artificially designed fruits]. https://meydanish.wixsite.com/portpoliome/project

Levy, M. (n.d.-b). Project. *Meydanish.* https://meydanish.wixsite.com/portpoliome/project

Lewis, S., & James, K. (1995). Whose voice sets the agenda for environmental education? Misconceptions inhibiting racial and cultural diversity. *Journal of Environmental Education,* 26(3), 5. https://doi.org/10.1080/00958964.1995.9941440

Li, C., & Monroe, M. C. (2018). Development and validation of the Climate Change Hope Scale for high school students. *Environment and Behavior, 50*(4), 454–479. https://doi.org/10.1177/0013916517708325

Li, H. (2007). Ecofeminism as a pedagogical project: Women, nature, and education. *Educational Theory,* 57(3), 351–368. https://doi.org/10.1111/j.1741-5446.2007.00262.x

Liao, C. (2016). From interdisciplinary to transdisciplinary: An arts-integrated approach to STEAM education. *Art Education,* 69(6), 44–49. https://doi.org/10.1080/00043125.2016.1224873

Loffeld, R. (n.d.). #6 exotique erotic_interview. *The Green Gallery*. Retrieved on June 1, 2020 from https://www.thegreengallery.com/en/issue-6/interview-azuma-makoto/

Lucas, G. (Director). (1977). *Star wars: A new hope* [Film]. Twentieth Century Fox.

Luzinterruptus. (2019a, December). *Death by plastic*. https://www.luzinterruptus.com/?s=death+by+plastic

Luzinterruptus. (2019b). *Death by plastic* [Guerrilla art installation]. https://www.luzinterruptus.com/?s=death+by+plastic

Maffi, L., & Woodley, E. (2010). *Biocultural diversity conservation: A global sourcebook*. Earthscan.

Makoto, A. (2015). *Box flowers* [Installation]. https://lostinfabrics.com/flower-box-by-makoto-azuma/

Malpas, W. (2007). *Land art in the U.K.* Crescent Moon.

Mandel, N., & Heine, S. J. (1999). Terror management and marketing: He who dies with the most toys wins. *Advances in Consumer Research, 26*, 527–532.

Mann, C. C. (2011). *1493: Uncovering the new world Christopher Columbus created*. Vintage.

Manoli, C. C., Johnson, B., & Dunlap, R. E. (2007). Assessing children's environmental worldviews: Modifying and validating the new ecological paradigm scale for use with children. *Journal of Environmental Education, 38*(4), 3–13. https://doi.org/10.3200/JOEE.38.4.3-13

Marino, L., & Mountain, M. (2015). Denial of death and the relationship between humans and other animals. *Anthrozoos, 28*(1), 5–21. https://doi.org/10.2752/089279315X14129350721777

Marsh, D. (2014). *Nababeep South Mine—302,500 tonnes of copper* [Digitally altered photograph]. http://dillonmarsh.com/copper03.html

Marshall, J., & Donahue, D. (2014). Art-centered research and integrated learning. In J. Marshall & D. M. Donahue (Eds.), *Art-centered learning across the curriculum: Integrating contemporary art in the secondary school classroom* (pp. 16–34), Teachers College Press.

Martínez, C. (n.d.). Crístobal Martínez: Artist biography. *Arizona Commission on the Arts*. https://azarts.gov/ardg/cristobal-martinez/

Martusewicz, R. A., Edmundson, J., & Lupinacci, J. (2021). *Ecojustice education: Toward diverse, democratic, and sustainable communities* (3rd ed.). Routledge.

Masini, E. (2006). Rethinking future studies. *Futures, 38*(10), 1158–1168. https://doi.org/10.1016/j.futures.2006.02.004

Matsuura, T. (n.d.). *Micro art: "Withered plant."* http://ensl.jp/tomoyamatsuura/micro/withered.html/

Matsuura, T. (2015). *Withered plant* [Photograph]. http://ensl.jp/tomoyamatsuura/micro/withered.html/

Mayer, F. S., & Frantz, C. M. (2004). The connectedness to nature scale: A measure of individuals' feeling in community with nature. *Journal of Environmental Psychology, 24*(4), 503–515.

McBrien, J. (2016). Accumulating extinction: Planetary catastrophism in the Necrocene. In J. Moore (Ed.), *Anthropocene or Capitalocene: Nature, history, and the crisis of capitalism* (pp. 116–137). PM Press.

McCarthy, C. (2006). *The road*. Alfred A. Knopf.

McCaw, C., & Smith, V. (2021). Sounding walks: Evoking empathy through social, sound and walking practices. *Performance of the Real, 2*. https://doi.org/10.21428/b54437e2.eca2de82

McDermott, A. (2016, December). In wildfire-riddled Tennessee, climate change is a hot topic. *Grist*. https://grist.org/article/in-wildfire-riddled-tennessee-climate-change-is-a-hot-topic/

McDonald, G. W., & Patterson, M. G. (2007). Bridging the divide in urban sustainability: From human exemptionalism to the new ecological paradigm. *Urban Ecosystems, 10*, 169–192. https://doi.org/10.1007/s11252-006-0017-0

McFall-Johnsen, M., & Woodward, A. (2019, August). 40% of US honeybee colonies disappeared last year. This is what the world would look like without any bees at all. *Business Insider*. https://www.businessinsider.com/world-without-bees-food-less-nutritious-more-expensive-2019-8#human-hands-and-technology-can-pollinate-crops-but-its-pricey-19

McGown, T. (2016). *Capitalism and desire: The psychic cost of free markets*. Columbia University Press.

McNeil, J. D. (2014). *Contemporary curriculum: In thought and action* (8th ed.). Wiley.

Micro Galleries. (2020, February). *Disrupting climate disruption* [Online video]. https://www.youtube.com/watch?v=pMxXvBszxNs

Miéville, C. (2002). *The scar*. Macmillan.

Mikash, L. (2009). *Nature, culture, spirituality: Land art as an embodiment of sacred space* (Publication No.1464521). [Master's thesis, University of Colorado]. ProQuest.

Milbrandt, M. (1998). Postmodernism in art education: Content for life. *Art Education, 51*(6), 47–54. https://doi.org/10.2307/3193752

Miller, G. (Director). (2015). *Mad Max: Fury road* [Film]. Warner Brothers.

Misiaszek, G. W. (2016). Ecopedagogy as an element of citizenship education: The dialectic of global/local spheres of citizenship and critical environmental pedagogies. *International Review of Education, 62*(5), 587–607. https://doi.org/10.1007/s11159-016-9587-0

Misiaszek, G. W. (2020). Ecopedagogy: Teaching critical literacies of "development," "sustainability," and "sustainable development." *Teaching in Higher Education, 25*(5), 615–632. https://doi.org/10.1080/13562517.2019.1586668

Misiaszek, G. W. (2021). Editorial: De-distancing "us" from the rest of Earth: Ecopedagogical analysis and approaches. *International Studies in Sociology of Education, 30*(1–2), 1–12. https://doi.org/10.1080/09620214.2021.1880333

Mitter, S. (2021, November 24). Her art reads the land in deep time. *New York Times*. https://www.nytimes.com/2021/11/24/arts/design/athena-latocha-bric-sculpture-native-american.html

Miyazaki, H. (Director). (1986). *Castle in the sky* [Film]. Toei Company.

Molina-Motos, D. (2019). Ecophilosophical principles for an ecocentric environmental education. *Education Sciences, 9*(37), 15. https://doi.org/10.3390/educsci9010037

Moore, J. W. (2017) The Capitalocene, Part I: On the nature and origins of our ecological crisis. *The Journal of Peasant Studies, 44*(3), 594–630. https://doi.org/10.1080/03066150.2016.1235036

Morales, L. (2015, August 17). Navajo Nation farmers feel the weight of Colorado mine spill. *National Public Radio*. https://www.npr.org/2015/08/17/432600254/navajo-nation-farmers-feel-the-weight-of-colorado-mine-spill

Murdock, E. G. (2020). A history of environmental justice: Foundations, narrative, and perspectives. In B. Coolsaet (Ed.), *Environmental justice: Key issues*. Taylor & Francis.

Nabolagshager, A.S., Makers' Hub, Oslo Living Lab, & Plakathuset Youth. (2019). *Pop-up furniture* [Seating project]. https://placemaking-europe.eu/listing/the-story-behind-the-pop-up-furniture-at-hersleb-high-school-oslo/

Nai, C., & Meyer, V. (2016). The beauty and the morbid: Fungi as source of inspiration in contemporary art. *Fungal Biology and Biotechnology, 3*(10), 5. http://doi.org/10.1186/s40694-016-0028-4/

National Endowment for the Arts. (n.d.). Fargo, ND: The Fargo Project. https://www.arts.gov/impact/creative-placemaking/exploring-our-town/fargo-nd-fargo-project

National Environmental Education Act, 104 U.S.C. § 3325 (1970). https://www.govinfo.gov/app/details/COMPS-814

Negley, E. (2015, November). Boating in a sewage treatment plan? How this artist designs inviting and functional landscapes. *Lancaster Online*. https://lancasteronline.com/

Neperud, R. W. (1978). The what and why of environmental design education. *Art Education, 31*(4), 4–7. https://doi.org/10.2307/3192263

Neperud, R. W. (1995). Texture of community: An environmental design education. In R. W. Neperud (Ed.), *Context, content, and community in art education* (pp. 222–247). Teachers College Press.

Newell-Hanson, A. (2019, September 13). The sculptor making massive moldy fruits from gemstones. *The New York Times*. https://www.nytimes.com/2019/09/13/t-magazine/kathleen-ryan-artist.html/

Nguyen, H. V., Thu Le, M. T., Pham, C. H., & Cox, S. S. (2022). Happiness and pro-environmental consumption behaviors. *Journal of Economics and Development, 14*. https://doi.org/10.1108/JED-07-2021-0116

Nolte, V. (n.d.). Min Jeong Seo: *To live on. Art and Science Journal*. https://www.artandsciencejournal.com/post/45132816609/min-jeong-seo-to-live-on/

Nonino, C. B. (2021, February 26). Wilfred Ukpong: An interview with multidisciplinary artist Wilfred Ukpong on his practice, values and callings. *Photo Vogue*. https://www.vogue.com/article/wilfred-ukpong

Norat, M., Herreria, A. F., & Rodriguez, M. M. (2016). Ecopedagogy: A movement between critical dialogue and complexity: Proposal for a categories system. *Journal of Education for Sustainable Development, 10*(1), 178–195. https://doi.org/10.1177/0973408215625552

Northern Lights. (2011, January). *Art for animals*. http://northern.lights.mn/tag/ai-weiwei/

Nowak, D. J., & Ogren, T. L. (2021). Variations in urban forest allergy potential among cities and land uses. *Urban Forestry & Urban Greening, 63*, 9. https://doi.org/10.1016/j.ufug.2021.127224

Nxumalo, F., & Cedillo, S. (2017). Decolonizing place in early childhood studies: Thinking with Indigenous onto-epistemologies and Black feminist geographies.

Global Studies of Childhood, 7(2), 99–112. https://doi.org/10.1177/2043610617703831

Nxumalo, F., & Tepeyolotl Villanueva, M. (2020). (Re)storying water: Decolonial pedagogies of relational affect with young children. In B. P. Dernikos, N. Lesko, S. D. McCall, & A. D. Niccolini (Eds.), *Mapping the effective turn in education* (pp. 209–228). Routledge.

Oaks, J., & Bibeau, D. L. (1987). Death education: Educating children for living. *The Clearing House, 60*(9), 420–422. https://doi.org/10.1080/00098655.1987.9959393/

O'Brien, M., & McCormick, D. (2014). *Watershed sculpture: Nevada Rivers Project.* https://watershedsculpture.blogspot.com/2014/04/nature-of-art.html

Ojala, M. (2005). Adolescents' worries about environmental risks: Subjective well-being, values, and existential dimensions. *Journal of Youth Studies, 8*(3), 331–347. https://doi.org/10.1080/13676260500261934

Ojala, M. (2012). Hope and climate change: The importance of hope for environmental engagement among young people. *Environmental Education Research, 18*(5), 625–642. https://doi.org/10.1080/13504622.2011.637157

Ojala, M. (2017). Hope and anticipation in education for a sustainable future. *Futures, 94*, 7–84. https://dx.doi.org/10.1016/j.futures.2016.10.004

Ojala, M., Cunsolo, A., Ogunbode, C. A., & Middleton, J. (2021). Anxiety, worry, and grief in a time of environmental and climate crisis: A narrative review. *Annual Review of Environment and Resources, 46*, 35–58. https://doi.org/10.1146/annurev-environ-012220-022716

Olsson, D., Gericke, N., Sass, W., & Boeve-de-Pauw, J. (2020). Self-perceived action competence for sustainability: The theoretical grounding and empirical validation of a novel research instrument. *Environmental Education Research, 26*(5), 742–760. https://doi.org/10.1080/13504622.2020.1736991

O'Neill, M., & Roberts, B. (2020). *Walking methods: Research on the move.* Routledge.

O'Rourke, K. (2016). *Walking as mapping: Artists as cartographers.* MIT Press.

Palmer, M. A., Falk, D. A., & Zedler, J. B. (2006). Ecological theory and restoration ecology. In D. A. Falk, M. A. Palmer, & J. B. Zedler (Eds.), *Foundations of restoration ecology* (pp. 1–13). Island Press.

Panno, A., Theodorou, A., Carrus, G., Imperatori, C., Spano, G., & Sanesi, G. (2020). Nature reappraisers, benefits for the environment: A model linking cognitive reappraisal, the "being away" dimension of restorativeness and eco-friendly behavior. *Frontiers in Psychology, 11*(1986), 10. https://doi.org/10.3389/fpsyg.2020.0198

Panzeca, A. (2014). Naturalism and the Florida setting in *Their eyes were watching God. Excavatio, 24*, 1–10. http://aizen.zolanaturalismassoc.org/excavatio/articles/v24/PanzecaFinalPDF3.pdf

Papanek, V. (2009). *Design for the real world: Human ecology and social change* (2nd ed., completely revised). Academy Chicago. (Original work published 1984)

Parsons, M. J. (2004). Art and integrated curriculum. In E. Eisner & M. Day (Eds.), *Handbook of research and policy in art education* (pp. 775–794). Mahwah, NJ: Lawrence Erlbaum Associates.

Payne, P., Rodrigues, C., de Moura Carvalho, I. C., Freire dos Santos, L. M., Aguayo, C., & Iared, V. G. (2018). Affectivity in environmental education research. *Journal of Environmental Education Research, 13*, 93–114. https://dx.doi.org/10.18675/2177-580X

Payne, P. G., & Wattchow, B. (2008). Slow pedagogy and placing education in post-traditional outdoor education. *Australian Journal of Outdoor Education, 12*(1), 25–38. https://doi.org/10.1007/BF03401021

Payne, P. G., & Wattchow, B. (2009). Phenomenological deconstruction, slow pedagogy, and the corporeal turn in wild environmental/outdoor education. *Canadian Journal of Environmental Education, 14*, 15–32.

Pearce, M. (1996). *Eastgate Harare* [Architecture]. Harare, Zimbabwe. https://www.mickpearce.com/index.html

Pelletier, L. G., Tuson, K. M., Green-Demers, I., Noels, K., & Beaton, A. M. (1998). Why are you doing things for the environment? The Motivation Toward the Environment Scale (MTES). *Journal of Applied Social Psychology, 28*(5), 437–468. https://doi.org/10.1111/j.1559-1816.1998.tb01714.x

Pelto, J. (2021a). *Rising mitigation* [Mixed media data visualization]. https://www.jillpelto.com/mitigation

Pelto, J. (2021b). *Rising mitigation.* https://www.jillpelto.com/mitigation

Perkins, H. E. (2010). Measuring love and care for nature. *Journal of Environmental Psychology, 30*(4), 455–463. https://doi.org/10.1016/j.jenvp.2010.05.004

Permaculture Design Principles. (n.d.). Deep Green Permaculture. https://deepgreenpermaculture.com/permaculture/permaculture-design-principles/

Perry, S. (2009). *Skin deep* [Photographic series]. http://www.rememberinganimals.art/sarah-perry/

Phillips, M. (2016). Developing ecofeminist corporeality: Writing the body as activist poetics. In M. Phillips & N. Rumens (Eds.), *Contemporary perspectives on ecofeminism* (pp. 57–75). Routledge.

Plumer, B. (2019, September 25). The world's oceans are in danger, major climate change report warns. *New York Times.* https://www.nytimes.com/2019/09/25/climate/climate-change-oceans-united-nations.html

Popp, J. (n.d.). *Conservation through Reconciliation Partnership.* https://conservation-reconciliation.ca/knowledge-systems-people/jesse-pop

Postcommodity. (2011). *The night is filled with the harmonics of suburban dreams* [Installation]. Lawrence Art Center, Lawrence, Kansas. http://postcommodity.com/SuburbanDreams.html

Postcommodity. (2012). *Do you remember when?* [Installation]. Arizona State University Art Museum, Tempe, Arizona. (Original work installed 2009)

Postcommodity. (2015). *Pollination* [Installation]. Scottsdale Museum of Contemporary Art, Scottsdale, Arizona. http://postcommodity.com/Pollination.html

Preece, R. J. (2011). Lynne Hull interview: Heart and soul (2009). *Artdesigncafe.* https://www.artdesigncafe.com/lynne-hull-art-interview

Priegert, P. (2012, April 5). 20 artists featured at print triennial. *The Daily Courier.* https://www.kelownadailycourier.ca/entertainment/article_9fad71ba-e5cf-5ec4-ae3b-4fe1f786a280.html

Pujol, E. (2018). *Walking art practice: Reflections of socially engaged paths.* Triarchy.

Rajme, O. D., (2020). T'uy't'tanat-Cease Wyss: Semi-public 半公開, Vancouver, ongoing since July 6, 2019. Reviews. *Canadian Art*. https://canadianart.ca/reviews/tuyttanat-cease-wyss/

Randazzo, G., & Lajevic, L. (2013). Cleaning our world: Through reverse graffiti. *Art Education, 66*(5), 39–45. https://doi.org/10.1080/00043125.2013.11519239

Reich, C. (2019). The story behind the pop-up furniture at Hersleb high school, Oslo. *Placemaking Europe*. https://placemaking-europe.eu/listing/the-story-behind-the-pop-up-furniture-at-hersleb-high-school-oslo/

Reid, A., Payne, P. G., & Cutter-Mackenzie, A. (2010). Openings for researching environment and place in children's literature: Ecologies, potentials, realities and challenges. *Environmental Education Research, 16*(3–4), 429–461. https://doi.org/10.1080/13504622.2010.488939

Reyes-García, V., Fernández-Llamazares, A., McElwee, P., Molnár, Z., Öllerer, K., Wilson, S. J., & Brondizio, E. S. (2019). The contributions of Indigenous Peoples and local communities to ecological restoration. *The Journal of the Society of Ecological Restoration, 27*(1), 3–8. https://doi.org/10.1111/rec.12894

Rhea, Z. (2018). Toward an Indigenist, Gaian pedagogy of food: Deimperializing foodscapes in the classroom. *The Journal of Environmental Education, 49*(2), 103–116. https://doi.org/10.1080/00958964.2017.1417220

Rico, A. R. (2017). Gendered ecologies and Black feminist futures in Wanuri Kahiu's *Pumzi*, Wangechi Mutu's *The end of eating everything*, and Ibi Zoboi's "The farming of gods." *Wagadu: A Journal of Transnational Women's and Gender Studies*, 18, 81–99. https://link.gale.com/apps/doc/A600665858/AONE?u=anon~7909c36d&sid=googleScholar&xid=97be97ff

Ricou, J. (n.d.). *Other selves, exploring the human microbiome*. https://www.joanaricou.com/microbiomeprocess

Ricou, J. (2013). *Other self portraits (bellybutton portraits)* [Portrait]. https://www.joanaricou.com/bellybutton-portraits/

Riley, S. (2020, February 6). Knoxville flooding: Look back to how bad things were in 2019. *Knoxville News Sentinel*. https://www.knoxnews.com/story/weather/2020/02/06/knoxville-flooding-look-back-how-bad-things-were-february-2019/4677255002/

Ritchie, J. (2013). Indigenous onto-epistemologies and pedagogies of care and affect in Aotearoa. *Global Studies, 3*(4). https://doi.org/10.2304/gsch.2013.3.4.395

Robinson, K. S. (2013). *Pacific edge: Three Californias* [ebook]. Tom Doherty Associates. (Original work published in 1990)

Robottom, I. (1991). Technocratic environmental education: A critique and some alternatives. *The Journal of Experiential Education, 14*(1), 20–26. https://journals.sagepub.com/doi/pdf/10.1177/105382599101400103

Rockman, A. (2000). *The farm* [Painting]. https://alexisrockman.net/wonderful-world/

Rockman, A. (2000–2012). *Wonderful world* [Painting series]. https://alexisrockman.net/wonderful-world/

Rockman, A. (2001–2004). *Sea world* [Painting]. https://alexisrockman.net/wonderful-world/

Rockman, A. (2004). *Pet store* [Painting]. https://alexisrockman.net/wonderful-world/

Rockman, A. (2015). *Watershed* [Painting]. https://alexisrockman.net/great-lakes/

Rockman, A. (2015–2017). *The Great Lakes cycle* [Painting series]. https://alexisrockman.net/great-lakes/

Rockman, A. (2017a). *Forces of change* [Painting]. https://alexisrockman.net/great-lakes/

Rockman, A. (2017b). *Spheres of influence* [Painting]. https://alexisrockman.net/great-lakes/

Román-Palacios, C., & Wiens, J. J. (2020). Recent responses to climate change reveal the drivers of species extinction and survival. *PNAS, 117*(8), 4211–4217. www.pnas.org/cgi/doi/10.1073/pnas.1913007117

Rome, A. (2003). "Give Earth a chance": The environmental movement and the sixties. *The Journal of American History, 90*(2), 525–554. https://doi.org/10.2307/3659443

Ron Finley Project. (2022a). *About.* https://ronfinley.com/pages/about

Ron Finley Project. (2022b). *Home.* https://ronfinley.com/

Rosenstock, J. (2016). *Deconstructed food miles smoothie [Data performance].* Data Cuisine. http://data-cuisine.net/data-dishes/deconstructed-food-miles-smoothie

Rousell, D., Cutter-Mackenzie, A., & Foster, J. (2017). Children of an Earth to come: Speculative fiction, geophilosophy and climate change education research. *Educational Studies, 53*(6), 654–669. https://doi.org/10.1080/00131946.2017.1369086

Ryan, K. (2019). *Bad lemon (creep)* [Sculpture]. https://www.thisiscolossal.com/2019/10/kathleen-ryan-moldy-fruit/

Salazar, G., Kunkle, K., & Monroe, M. C. (2020). *Practitioner guide to assessing connection to nature.* North American Association for Environmental Education. https://naaee.org/eepro/publication/practitioner-guide-assessing-connection

Schaffer, A. (2008, August 12). Prescriptions for health, the environmental kind. *New York Times.* https://www.nytimes.com/2008/08/12/health/12clin.html

Schmelzer, P. (2017, March 9). Aesthetic portals: A postcommodity primer. *Walker.* https://walkerart.org/magazine/aesthetic-portals-a-postcommodity-primer

Schneller, A. J., Harrison, L. M., & Adelman, J. (2021). Outcomes of art-based environmental education in the Hudson River Watershed. *Applied Environmental Education and Communication, 20*(1), 19–33. http://dx.doi.org/10.1080/1533015X.2019.1617805

Schultz, P. W. (2002). Inclusion with nature: The psychology of human-nature relations. In P. Schmuck, W. P. Schultz, & T. L. Milfont (Eds.), *Psychology of sustainable development* (pp. 61–78). Kluwer Academic.

Scott, R. (Director). (1982). *Blade runner* [Film]. Warner Brothers.

Scrivens, R. (2021). A "new" walking pilgrimage: Performance and meaning on the North Wales Pilgrim's Way. *Landscape Research, 46*(1), 64–76. https://doi.org/10.1080/01426397.2020.1829574

Searle, A. (2004, April 27). Tomorrow's world. *The Guardian.* https://www.theguardian.com/culture/2004/apr/27/1

Semi-Public. (n.d.). *T'uy't'tanat-Cease Wyss*. https://semi-public.com/

Semiconductor. (2014). *Cosmos* [Public sculpture]. https://semiconductorfilms.com/art/cosmos/

Seo, M. J. (2005). *To live on* [Installation]. http://seo-minjeong.de/to-live-on.html/

Sheldrake, M. (2020). *Entangled life: How fungi make our worlds, change our minds, and shape our futures* [ebook]. Random House Publishing.

Slater, E. (2016). Patricia Johanson: The layered landscape, discovered and recovered. *Woman's Art Journal, 37*(2), 3–11. https://www.jstor.org/stable/26430778

Smith, D. L. (2011). Material culture and issues-based art education. *International Journal of Arts Education, 9*(2), 92–100. www.ijea.org

Smith, G. A. (2002). Going local. *Educational Leadership, 60*(1), 30–33.

Smith, G. A. (2007). Place-based education: Breaking through the constraining regularities of public school. *Environmental Education Research, 13*(2), 189–207. https://doi.org/10.1080/13504620701285180

Smith, G. A., & Sobel, D. (2014). *Place- and community-based education in schools.* Taylor & Francis.

Smith, R. A. (1970). On the third domain: Spaceship earth and aesthetic education. *Journal of Aesthetic Education, 4*(4), 5–8. https://www.jstor.org/stable/3331282

Smith, R. A., & Smith, C. M. (1970). Aesthetics and environmental education. *Journal of Aesthetic Education, 4*(4), 125–140. https://doi.org/10.2307/3331291

Smithson, R. (1970). *Spiral jetty* [Land artwork]. Great Salt Lake, Utah. https://holtsmithsonfoundation.org/spiral-jetty

Snell, B., Braun, S., & McDonald, A. (2016). Unequal exposure [Culinary eco-visualization]. *Data Cuisine.* http://data-cuisine.net/data-dishes/inequal-exposure

Snyder, C. R., Rand, K. L., King, E. A., Feldman, D. B., & Woodward, J. T. (2002). *Journal of Clinical Psychology, 58*(9), 1003–1022. https://doi.org/10.1002/jclp.10096

Sobel, D. (2008). *Childhood and nature: Design principles for educators.* Stenhouse.

Society for Ecological Restoration. (2020). *What is ecological restoration?* https://www.ser-rrc.org/what-is-ecological-restoration/

Sonfist, A. (1965). *Time landscape* [Land artwork]. https://www.publicartfund.org/exhibitions/view/time-landscape/

Sparks, A. C., Ehret, P. J., & Brick, C. (2022). Measuring pro-environmental orientation: Testing and building scales. *Journal of Environmental Psychology, 81.* https://doi.org/10.1016/j.envp.2022.101780

Springgay, S., & Truman, S. E. (2019). Critical walking methodologies and oblique agitations of place. *Qualitative Inquiry, 28*(2), 171–176. https://doi.org/10.1177/10778004211042355

Staples, A. F., Larson, L. R., Worsley, T., Green, G. T., & Carroll, J. P. (2019). Effects of an art-based environmental education camp program on the environmental attitudes and awareness of diverse youth. *The Journal of Environmental Education, 50*(3), 208–222. https://doi.org/10.1080/00958964.2019.1629382

Stecyk, C. R. (n.d.). *Remembering animals: Rituals, artifacts, and narratives.* http://www.rememberinganimals.art/craig-stecyk/

Stecyk, C. R. (1983). *Road rash* [Mixed media]. http://www.rememberinganimals.art/craig-stecyk/

Stephenson, N. (1992). *Snow crash*. Bantom Books.

Stern, P. C. (2012). Fear and hope in climate messages. *Nature Climate Change, 2*, 572–573. https://doi.org/10.1038/nclimate1610

Stevenson, R. B. (2007). Schooling and environmental education: Contradictions in purpose and practice. *Environmental Education Research, 13*(2), 139–153. https://dx.doi.org/10.1080/13504620701295726

Steves, A., & Silver, R. (2018). Sustainable design for scale. In R. Egenhoefer (Ed.), *Routledge handbook of sustainable design* (pp. 55–72). Routledge.

Stibbe, A. (2010). Ecolinguistics and globalization. In N. Coupland (Ed.), *The handbook of language and globalization* (pp. 406–425). John Wiley & Sons.

Suggestions From Kamloops. (2014). *Kamloops Art Gallery*. https://kag.bc.ca/all-exhibitions/suggestions-from-kamloops

Sulaeman, D., & Westhoff, T. (2020, February). The causes and effects of soil erosion, and how to prevent it. *World Institute Resources*. https://www.wri.org/insights/causes-and-effects-soil-erosion-and-how-prevent-it

Sundberg, J. (2014). Decolonizing posthumanist geographies. *Cultural Geographies, 21*(1), 33–47. http://doi.org/10.1177/1474474013486067

Suvin, D. (1979). *Metamorphoses of science fiction: On the poetics and history of a literary genre*. Yale University Press.

Tavin, K. (2003). Wrestling with angels, searching for ghosts: Toward a critical pedagogy of visual culture. *Studies in Art Education, 44*(3), 197–213. https://doi.org/10.1080/00393541.2003.11651739

The Tempestry Project. (n.d.). *The tempestry project*. https://www.tempestryproject.com/about/

Thomas, C. (2015). *I am the change* [Screen print]. https://justseeds.org/product/i-am-the-change/

Thomas, E. (2018). *Petri dish no. 36* [Textile art]. https://www.elinthomas.com/

Thomson, R. (1978). The art teacher and environmental education: A Scottish viewpoint. *Art Education, 31*(4), 19–21. https://doi.org/10.2307/3192267

Todorov, T. (1975). *The fantastic: A structural approach to a literary genre*. Cornell University Press.

Tolkien, J. R. (1995). *The fellowship of the ring* (Quality Paperback Book Club ed.). Quality Paperback Book Club. (Original work published 1954)

Topaz, C. M., Klingenberg, B., Turek, D., Heggeseth, B., Harris, P. E., Blackwood, J. C., Chavoya, C. O., Nelson, S., & Murphy, K. M. (2019). Diversity of artists in major U.S. museums. *PLoS One, 14*(3), e0212852. https://doi.org/10.1371/journal.pone.0212852

Tran, N. (2021, November 29). As Bradford pears remain a nuisance in South Carolina, methods of attack range from bounties to bans. *USA Today*. https://www.usatoday.com/story/news/nation/2021/11/29/bradford-pear-south-carolina-sets-2024-ban-bounties-tree/8793351002/

Trott, C. D. (2020). Children's constructive climate change engagement: Empowering awareness, agency, and action. *Environmental Education Research, 26*(4), 532–554. https://doi.org/10.1080/13504622.2019.1675594

Tsang, J. (2019, November). This gorgeous art was made with a surprising substance: Live bacteria. *National Geographic*. https://www.nationalgeographic

.com/science/2019/11/agar-art-contest-winners-create-gorgeous-art-from-live-bacteria/

Tsevreni, I. (2011). Towards an environmental education without scientific knowledge: An attempt to create an action model based on children's experiences, emotions and perceptions about their environment. *Environmental Education Research, 17*(1), 53–67. https://doi.org/10.1080/13504621003637029

Tuck, E., McKenzie, M., & McCoy, K. (2014). Land education: Indigenous, post-colonial, and decolonizing perspectives on place and environmental education research. *Environmental Education Research, 20*(1), 1–23. https://doi.org/10.1080/13504622.2013.877708

Ukpong, W. (n.d.). *BC1-ND-FC: Alas, my thirst lumbers to the sea for our saline zone is barren with crude* #2 [Photograph]. http://lenscratch.com/2022/05/wilfred-ukpong/

Ukpong, W. (2010–20). *Blazing century 1* [Art project]. https://www.blazingcentury.net/about

Ukpong, W. (2010–ongoing). *Blazing century* [Ten-part art project series]. https://www.blazingcentury.net/about

Ukpong, W. (2017). *BC1: Mediating Object #1 Dream Chasers (Boys) on a Time Capsule* [Photograph]. https://www.blazingcentury.net/contact

United Nations Permanent Forum on Indigenous Issues. (2006). *Indigenous peoples, Indigenous voices: Factsheet.* https://www.un.org/esa/socdev/unpfii/documents/5session_factsheet1.pdf

United States General Services Administration. (n.d.). *Sustainable design.* https://www.gsa.gov/real-estate/design-construction/design-excellence/sustainability/sustainable-design

Vagner, K. (2015, March). Natural art world: Two artists build sculptures that double as conservation projects—including one on the Truckee River. *Reno News & Review.* https://www.newsreview.com/reno/content/natural-art-world/16598912/

Vail, K. E., Juhl, J., Arndt, J., Vess, M., Routledge, C., & Rutjens, B. T. (2012). When death is good for life: Considering the positive trajectories of terror management. *Personality and Social Psychology Review, 16*(4), 303–329. https://doi.org/10.1177/1088868312440046

van Andel, J., & Grootjans, A. P. (2006). In J. van Andel & J. Aronson (Eds.), *Restoration ecology: The new frontier* (pp. 16–28). Blackwell.

van Boeckel, J. (2015). At the heart of art and earth: An exploration of practices in arts-based environmental education. *Environmental Education Research, 21*(5), 801–802. https://doi.org/10.1080/13504622.2014.959474

van den Bogerd, N., Dijkstra, S. C., Tanja-Dijkstra, K., de Boer, M., Seidell, J. C., Koole, S. L., & Maas, J. (2020). Greening the classroom: Three field experiments on the effects of indoor nature on students' attention, well-being, and perceived environmental quality. *Building and Environment, 171*, 10. https://doi.org/10.1016/j.builenv.2020.106675

van Dooren, T., Kirksey, E., & Munster, U. (2016). Multispecies studies: Cultivating arts of attentiveness. *Environmental Humanities, 8*(1), 1–23. https://doi.org/10.1215/22011919-3527695

Vásquez-Fernández, A. M., & pii tai poo taa, C. A. (2020). Resurgence of relationality: Reflections on decolonizing and indigenizing "sustainable development." *Current Opinion in Environmental Sustainability, 43*, 65–70. https://doi.org/10.1016/j.cosust.2020.03.005

Vatovec, C., & Ferrer, H. (2019). Sustainable well-being challenge: A student-centered pedagogical tool linking human well-being to ecological flourishing. *Sustainability*, 11(24), 7178–. https://doi.org/10.3390/su11247178

Vaughn, K. J., Porensky, L. M., Wilkerson, M. L., Balachowski, J., Peffer, E., Riginos, C., & Young, T. P. (2010). Restoration ecology. *Nature Education Knowledge, 3*(10), 66. https://www.nature.com/scitable/knowledge/library/restoration-ecology-13339059/

Vierling, R. J. (2003). Close encounters of the fourth kind: The art of Lynne Hull. *Land Views.* https://www.landviews.org/la2003/encounters-rjv.html

Voon, C. (2017, March 14). Animal rights activists protest Damien Hirst show in Venice with 88 pounds of dung [Updated]. *Hyperallergic.* https://hyperallergic.com/365073/animal-rights-activists-protest-damien-hirst-show-in-venice-with-88-pounds-of-dung/

Voon, C. (2018, March 12). Alexis Rockman paints the past and possible futures of the Great Lakes. *Hyperallergic.* https://hyperallergic.com/430294/alexis-rockman-great-lakes-grand-rapids-art-museum-review/

Wachira, J. (2020). Wangari Maathai's environmental Afrofuturist imaginary in Wanuri Kahiu's Pumzi. *Critical Studies in Media Communication*, *37*(4), 324–336. https://doi.org/10.1080/15295036.2020.1820543

Walker Art Center. (2013, August). *Domestic integrities for Fritz Haeg.* https://bodycartography.org/portfolio/4920/

Walker, M. (2019). The mountains through a different cultural lens: An Abenaki perspective. *Long Trail News, 79*(3), 14–15. https://gmcmontpelier.org/Archive_Publications/LTN_Archives/LTN_YYYY_NN/2019_03_Fall.pdf

Wang, L. (2020, January 21). Luzinterruptus turns plastic waste into "Death by Plastic" eco-art for COP25. *Inhabitat.* https://inhabitat.com/luzinterruptus-turns-plastic-waste-into-death-by-plastic-eco-art-for-cop25/

Warnke, A. (2018, February 27). *Playing with death: The morbid obsessions of contemporary Polish artists.* Culture.pl. https://culture.pl/en/article/playing-with-death-the-morbid-obsessions-of-contemporary-polish-artists/

Wasilewski, A. (2008). *Pin-ups fruits* [Oil on canvas]. http://fotofestiwal.com/2010/andrzej-wasilewski-2/

Water Technology. (n.d.). *Ellis Creek Water Recycling Facility.* https://www.water-technology.net/projects/ellis-creek/

Watson, M. (2015) 'Centring the Indigenous': Postcommodity's trans-Indigenous relational art. *Third Text, 29*(3), 141–154. https://doi.org/10.1080/09528822.2015.1076209

Weber, J. (2021). *Prototype for poetry vs rhetoric (deep roots)* [Urban farm and sculptural installation]. http://jordanjweber.com/

Weber, J. (2022). Hoops and pollinators. *New Suns.* https://newsuns.net/jordan-weber-hoops-and-pollinators/

Weintraub, L. (2012). *To life! Eco art in pursuit of a sustainable planet.* University of California Press.

Weintraub, L. (2019). *What's next? Eco materialism & contemporary art.* Intellect.

Weiwei, A. (2010). *Owl house* [Sculptural installation]. San Francisco, California. https://www.for-site.org/project/presidio-habitats-ai-weiwei-western-screech-owl-habitats/

What Is Placemaking? (2007). Project for Public Spaces. https://www.pps.org/article/what-is-placemaking

Whitmarsh, L. (2011). Scepticism and uncertainty about climate change: Dimensions, determinants and change over time. *Global Environmental Change, 21*, 690–700. https://doi.org/10.1016/j.gloenvcha.2011.01.016

Whittaker, R. (2016, August). Restoration: A conversation with Daniel McCormick and Mary O'Brien. *Works & Conversations.* https://www.conversations.org/story.php?sid=481

Whyte, K. P. (2013). On the role of traditional ecological knowledge as a collaborative concept: A philosophical study. *Ecological Processes, 2*(7), 12. http://www.ecologicalprocesses.com/content/2/1/7

Wilson, E. O. (2005). Forward from the scientific side. In J. Gottschall & D. S. Wilson (Eds.), *The literary animal: Evolution and the nature of narrative (rethinking theory)* (pp. vii-xi). Northwestern University Press.

Wilson, S. (2015). *One a day: Day 276* [Installation]. In *One a day: An ephemeral art adventure.* http://shonawilson.com/files/8815/2213/0966/One_a_Day_Book.pdf

Wolfe, C. (2018). Posthumanism. In R. Braidotti & M. Hlavajova (Eds.), *Posthuman glossary* (pp. 356–359). Bloomsbury.

Wunderling, N., Donges, J. F., Kurths, J., & Winkelmann, R. (2021). Interacting tipping elements increase risk of climate domino effects under global warming. *Earth System Dynamics, 12*, 601–619. https://doi.org/10.5194/esd-12-601-2021

Wyss, T. C. (2019–ongoing). *x̱a"s she"áý New Growth 《新生林》* [Permaculture community space]. https://semi-public.com/

Wyss, T. C. (2022). About *T'uy't'tanat Cease Wyss.* https://tuyttanatceasewyss.ca/

Xiao, J. J., & Li, J. (2011). Sustainable consumption and life satisfaction. *Social Indicators Research, 104*, 323–329. https://doi.org/10.1007/s11205-010-9746-9

XTU Architects. (n.d.-a). *Flohara* [Installation integrating housing]. https://www.xtuarchitects.com/xtu-nos-utopies#/flohara/

XTU Architects. (n.d.-b). *Rigs city* [City concept]. https://www.xtuarchitects.com/xtu-nos-utopies#/rig-city/

XTU Architects. (2019). *X cloud* [Installation]. https://www.xtuarchitects.com/x_cloud

XTU Architects & Myers, L. (Eds.). (2020). XTU imagines living in the clouds to escape polluted air and an uninhabitable earth. *Design Boom.* https://www.designboom.com/architecture/xtu-architects-living-in-the-clouds-to-escape-uninhabitable-earth-01-29-2020/

Xu, Z., Shan, W., Guo, Y., Zhang, C., & Qiu, L. (2022). Swamp wetlands in degraded permafrost areas release large amounts of methane and may promote wildfires through friction electrification. *Sustainability, 14*(15), 28. https://doi.org/10.3390/su14159193

YBCA. (n.d.). *Public art: We are the asteroid III.* https://ybca.org/event/we-are-the-asteroid-iii/

Zhou, X., & Kim, J. (2013). Social disparities in tree canopy and park accessibility: A case study of six cities in Illinois using GIS and remote sensing. *Urban Forestry & Urban Greening, 12*(1), 88–97. https://doi.org/10.1016/j.ufug.2012.11.004

Author Index

Subject Index

About the Author and Contributors

Joy G. Bertling is assistant professor of art education at the University of Tennessee. Her research engages with critical place-based art education and other arts-based forms of environmental education, such as ecopedagogy. She has published articles in various peer-reviewed journals including *Art Education, Studies in Art Education,* and *Environmental Education Research.* She is founder and chair of the National Art Education Association's Ecology and Environment Interest Group. Additionally, she chairs the American Educational Research Association's Arts and Learning Special Interest Group. Awarded a U.S. Department of Education Assistance for Arts Education Grant in 2021, she manages *The Data Visualization Project*, a STEAM project inspiring and supporting Grade 4–8 students' socially and ecologically oriented data visualizations across arts and STEM learning contexts.

Lauren Farkas is an artist and middle school art educator in Knoxville, Tennessee. She earned a BFA in drawing and painting and a MA in art education at the University of Tennessee Knoxville. She is an artist enlivened by the intersections of fine art, botany, sustainability, and community education. Focused on unearthing the whole story of a material, tool, or work, Lauren uses craft to provide access points to place-based conversations. Recent explorations include plant-based papermaking and collaging parts of invasive plant species into decomposing artworks.

Jonathan Purtill is an artist, educator, and curator from Las Vegas who lives and works in Knoxville, Tennessee. His work explores the gothic sublime, speculative fiction, and the subcultural iconography of punk and extreme metal. He teaches art to kindergarten–4th grade students at Glenwood Elementary in Oak Ridge, Tennessee. This is his first published work.